The
Sorrow
of the Lonely
and the Burning of
the Dancers

Edward L. Schieffelin

The
Sorrow
of the Lonely
and the Burning of
the Dancers

St. Martin's Press · New York

Library of Congress Catalog Card Number: 75–10999
Copyright © 1976 by St. Martin's Press, Inc.
All Rights Reserved.
Manufactured in the United States of America.
09876
fedcba
For information, write: St. Martin's Press, Inc.,
175 Fifth Avenue, New York, N. Y. 10010

Acknowledgments

In both the field research and the writing of this book, I owe a great deal to many people. I did the research from 1966 to 1968 on funds provided by a grant and predoctoral fellowship from the National Institute of Health (NIH grant number 1 RO4 MH 2532–01 and accompanying fellowship number 1–FL–MH–31, 120–01). My field work in Bosavi was greatly facilitated by the generosity of Murray Rule, of the Unevangelized Field Mission, who kindly gave me a copy of his unpublished study of the Kaluli language. Without this avenue into the verb system, my field work in the monolingual situation would have been much more difficult. I also wish to thank Ivor Manton of Mt. Hagen for his hospitality, generosity, and good company at the times when I needed them most.

The excitement and trials of the second year in the tropical forest were shared by my wife, Bambi, who came to live in Bosavi within two weeks of our marriage. Few people could have managed such a novel and difficult situation. Bambi was magnificent, providing encouragement, support, and love in extremely unfamiliar and primitive conditions and contributing fruitful insights to the work.

In many ways, the writing of this book was more arduous than the field research itself. The final form of the analysis is my own, but I am indebted to many others who have contributed substantially to its development. The writings of Claude Lévi-Strauss and Gregory Bateson have each in their own way influenced my thinking more deeply than I could possibly acknowledge by citation. The basic outline of the argument began to take form during long conversations with Victor Turner and Gene Gendlin at the University of Chicago. Terry Turner, Victor Turner, Milton Singer, Roy Wagner, and Barbara Price offered useful comments and criticism of the various drafts of the work. Tom Ernst and Ray Kelly provided perspective on neighboring groups around Bosavi on the Papuan Plateau, and Steven Feld helped clarify the nature of the music of Gisaro songs.

Through the long seige at the typewriter, Bambi put in countless hours while simultaneously commencing her own graduate career in anthropology. She then delayed her field research so that I could bring this book to completion. I also owe an enormous debt to Jim and Susan Matisoff and their daughters, Nadya and Alexandra, who shared their home and their lives with us for a year. Both Jim and Susan generously gave their time to read and help revise the manuscript, and then Jim proofread the galleys after I had returned to the field in New Guinea.

Finally, I owe the genesis of this book to the Kaluli people of Mt. Bosavi, whom it is about. It is to my many friends, including Selibi, Wanalugo, Sialo, Jibi, Hɔwæ, Kiliyæ, Dalabiæ, Agali, Ayaka, and especially Gigio, that this work is dedicated. If I can successfully convey something of the significance and substance of their lives, it will be to pass on only a small part of what they have passed on to me.

EDWARD L. SCHIEFFELIN

Contents

Kaluli Pronunciation

a   as *a* in f*a*ther
e   as *e* in b*e*t
o   as *oa* in b*oa*t
ɔ   as *ou* in *ou*ght
i   as *i* in mach*i*ne
u   as *u* in fl*u*te
æ   as *a* in h*a*t
š   as *sh* in *sh*oe
ɨ   as *i* in s*i*ster

The
Sorrow
of the Lonely
and the Burning of
the Dancers

Introduction

This book is a cultural ethnography. The discussion focuses on the significance of a single ceremony known as Gisaro, which is performed by the Kaluli people of Papua New Guinea. My intention is to use Gisaro as a lens through which to view some of the fundamental issues of Kaluli life and society.

The basic theme that underlies both the ceremony and Kaluli society is reciprocity. In Papua New Guinea, concern with formal reciprocity in food, wealth, and/or women is basic to the functioning of most social relationships. Most treatments of New Guinea societies have tended to deal with reciprocity in one of four ways. The traditional approach in social anthropology concentrates on the structure of social relationship and views reciprocity in its function of defining, maintaining, and carrying forward these relationships. Another approach draws its inspiration from Lévi-Strauss's *Elementary Structures of Kinship* and sees the social system as deriving its structure through reciprocity in women and prestations in the marriage system. Analyses that take an economic perspective focus on the distribution of food and wealth through trade and exchange and on the ways that this distribution is affected by, and in turn affects, social and political relationships. Finally, the cultural ecologists regard the social system, population structure, subsistence practices, production and reciprocity of food and wealth as parts of a total ecological system.

1

The picture of the New Guinea individual that tends to emerge is that of a tough, practical, hard-working manipulator caught up in an endless game of obligations, exchanges, debts, and credits, which he tries to play to his own or his group's advantage. For those people who lives are pervaded by it, however, reciprocity and practical activity—the exchange of gifts, hospitality, assistance in garden labor—are more than simply the rational, end-seeking activity of practical men. They are means of expressing personal fellowship and ways of expressing affection. At the level of a person's perception of his own life, reciprocity is involved with considerations of personal sentiment, ambition, grievance, obligation, and manliness. Reciprocity is also bound up with cultural values pertaining to balance and proportion in human relationships and consequently becomes implicated in matters as far afield as sexual desire, moral philosophy, medicine, and theater.

In this book, I shall explore this aspect of reciprocity from a cultural point of view. Cultural analysis refers primarily to the symbolic dimension of human experience and the systems of symbols out of which it is constituted. Although reciprocity, on one level, creates and maintains social and political relationships, I am more concerned with the systems of symbolic action and cultural value that it embodies, through which its social functions may be accomplished.

Symbols are usually conceived as "meaning" or "standing for" something else. At the same time, they exist in various logico-meaningful relationships with other symbols in a larger system. A traditional view holds that meanings are primarily stored in symbols and brought out for use when they are required. Though symbols undoubtedly have this storage capacity, I would like to emphasize their more creative aspect. Symbols do not just "stand for" something else. They constantly and actively "bring things into meaning." This happens because symbolic activity brings objects and concepts into new and different kinds of relationships in a larger system of meaning, formulating and organizing them in new ways according to a few simple procedures. This "rendering into meaning" is the symbolic process by which human consciousness continually works reality into intelligible forms.

As a practical matter for ethnography, we are interested in

examining the way meanings develop over a series of events to which they give form. I deal with this issue primarily by examining sequences of events that I call "cultural scenarios." A cultural scenario is a series of events embodying a typical sequence of phases or episodes, which between its commencement and resolution effects a certain amount of social progress or change in the situation to which it pertains. The concept of cultural scenario differs from that of a ritual (which may, however, express or dramatize a cultural scenario) in that the cultural scenario is embodied in everyday, informal courses of action. It is empirically recognizable in the general procedure by which a people repeatedly approach and interpret diverse situations and carry them to similar types of resolution. The situations themselves need not be similar; it is the similar manner in which they are interpreted, carried forward, and resolved that is important.

The structure of the cultural scenario must be not only analytically visible to the observer but also in some way present in the awareness of the participants. This is sometimes a difficult matter to specify. In general, a people may be said to be aware of a cultural scenario when they feel that a given situation admits of a certain kind of resolution and implicitly direct their actions and expectations toward attaining that resolution. The implication is that people orient themselves and interpret events in terms of the culturally familiar implications of a larger, well-known course of action.

A cultural scenario, as a typical event sequence, has a structure of its own that may be dealt with apart from the social organization of the society in which it takes place. On the other hand, however, many of the normative principles of the society may pertain to behavior in particular cultural scenarios, and the organization of the society may be to a large degree maintained by the processes entailed in them. This would more or less be the case for those scenarios related to exchange and reciprocity in New Guinea societies.

The thrust of this book is basically processual. I am interested in the theme of reciprocity less for what it contributes to the structure and coherence of the social organization than for what it implies about the way Kaluli approach and conceive situations and understand their lives. The discussion is organized as follows.

A short summary of the history and the present situation of the Kaluli people is furnished in the second half of the introduction. Chapter 1 describes the Gisaro ceremony briefly, then outlines the occasions of social reciprocity that it celebrates and considers the problem of what reciprocity means for the Kaluli in relation not only to their social organization but also to their cultural experience.

The songs that are sung in the Gisaro ceremony refer to places on Kaluli lands. Chapter 2 stresses the importance of locale, outlining the relation of Kaluli society to its context in the tropical forest. Residential units and descent groups are conceptualized in terms of how the Kaluli identify themselves with their lands and are distributed according to the contingencies of subsistence and defense. To the Kaluli, subsistence represents more than merely getting enough to eat. Chapter 3 shows that the symbolism and management of food are basic to the way they conceptualize social relationships and develop them concretely in daily life.

Kaluli society is organized less in terms of corporate descent groups and resident communities than in terms of a multitude of overlapping networks of social ties between individuals that are maintained through reciprocal gifts of food. Chapter 4 discusses how various types of action groups are recruited and organized to perform cooperative tasks. It emerges that a great many social transactions are set up and staged as oppositions between such action groups. These oppositions are fundamental to Kaluli cosmology, as Chapter 5 demonstrates. A notion that oppositions are formed and resolved through reciprocity underlies Kaluli methods of curing illness, settling disputes, and furthering social relationships. The formation and resolution of oppositions makes up one of the most important cultural scenarios that animate Kaluli society.

In Chapter 6, the focus shifts to cultural themes in Kaluli personality and style. A strong sense of personal autonomy and a volatile temperament contrast paradoxically with a person's strong sense of obligation to others and his dependence on their assistance to achieve his ends. Chapter 7 discusses how anger and volatility are understood and modulated in ordinary behavior through the forms of opposition and reciprocity. The cultural scenario of opposition provides a sense of proportion and a course of action that shapes all levels of personal interaction. As a result, it is deeply bound up with the Kaluli sense of causality and time.

Kaluli modes of perceiving and responding to situations both reflect and provide their sense of the quality of their lives. Chapter 8 deals with Kaluli nostalgia and sentimentality, their love of exuberant company, and their fear of death as abandonment. In the end, they do not formulate any overall characterization of their view of life. Rather, they evoke it in images and action in their ceremonies.

Chapter 9 outlines the way Gisaro ceremonies are prepared and the events leading up to their performance. Then, in Chapter 10, the Gisaro ceremony is described in depth. The final chapter analyzes the Gisaro in relation to the opposition scenario and social organization and brings out the cosmological significance of the ceremony by reference to the invisible world of spirits. Gisaro emerges as a means by which the Kaluli consider and express the tragic side of their lives and at the same time attempt to overcome it.

The Papuan Plateau

The Kaluli people live in the tropical forest of the Great Papuan Plateau on the island of New Guinea.

The Papuan Plateau stretches from the Kikori River (or Hegigio, as it is called locally) westward toward the Strickland River. The area with which we are concerned (see Map I.1) is bordered to the north by the escarpment of the Karius Range, which forms the edge of the New Guinea Highlands. To the south, the region is bordered by the collapsed cone of an extinct volcano, Mt. Bosavi. This region, which covers roughly 525 square miles,[1] is sparsely populated by about 2,100 people (1966 government census), who speak at least five different languages.

Because of their small numbers and awkward geographical location in relation to administration centers, the people of this

[1] Between the Sioa and Hegigio rivers.

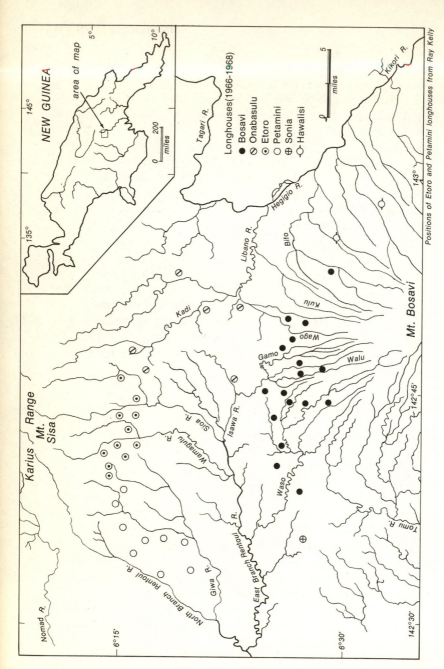

MAP I.1   Distribution of Longhouses on Papuan Plateau North of Mt. Bosavi, 1968

portion of the plateau are governed from the highlands. They make up three census divisions of the Tari subdistrict of the Southern Highlands District, which has its headquarters in Mendi, sixty miles away. Since 1964, they have been under the immediate jurisdiction of the government officer at Komo patrol post. Komo is situated on the northern side of the Karius Range among people related to the Huli (Glasse, 1968), about three days' trek over forest trails from the longhouse at Sululib where my field work was based. This was the nearest European station during the time I was there.

Besides me and my wife, there were few outsiders on the plateau during my field work. In 1964, the Unevangelized Fields Mission (UFM)[2] had built a small airstrip at Wayue near the communal longhouse of clan Didesa. Mission stations were opened there and at Waragu village and operated by Gogodaila pastors from the south coast. In December 1966, a government medical post was opened at Bono village and staffed intermittently by Papuan medical orderlies.

The Kaluli people with whom we stayed are one of a number of local groups who characterize themselves collectively as Bosavi *kalu*, or "men of Bosavi," as distinct from the Onabasulu and Etoro groups nearby to the north and west. The Bosavi *kalu* live in about twenty isolated longhouses (Map I.2) around the base of the northern flanks of Mt. Bosavi. They make up the largest single language group and more than half of the population north of the mountain, numbering about 1,200 in 1966. Most of their longhouses are located between the altitudes of 900 and 1,100 meters on land drained by the Isawa and Bifo rivers. The northern edge of this drainage provides their boundary and may be located roughly by a line arching westward from the Hegigio River via the Bifo and Kulu and then along the Isawa where it turns toward the Strickland.

North of this line live the much less numerous Onabasulu people (population 440, Waragu census division; Ernst, 1972), who speak a different language. Northwest of the Onabasulu people and west of the Sioa River is another language group known

2 Now the Asia Pacific Christian Mission (APCM).

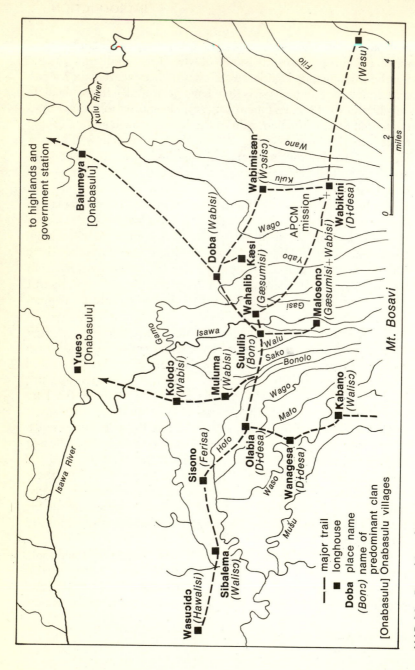

MAP I.2 Bosavi Longhouses

to Bosavis as the Yɔli people (that is, the Etoro, population 386; Kelly, 1973), who were traditional enemies to the Bosavi. On the west, beyond the Bosavi longhouse of Amine, live the speakers of the Sonia language (longhouses of Banisa and Hasif) including, apparently, a few groups that had not yet been contacted by the government (in 1968). On the east, across the Mungasu River, are the Hawalisi people, also speakers of a different language, whose longhouses are distributed around to the south side of the mountain.

The Bosavi People

The Bosavi people distinguish four different groups among themselves, on the basis of what they claimed to be linguistic and ethnic differences. The group among whom we spent most of our time called themselves Kaluli *kalu,* or Kaluli men. The name is possibly derived from a conjunction of the word *kalu,* which means "man" or "men," and the suffix *-li,* which connotes validation: "actual" or "real"; thus it might be approximately glossed as "the real men." The Kaluli group occupies the region between the Sako and Wanu rivers north of the mountain, as distinct from the Orogo people to the east as far as the longhouse of Wasu, and the Walulu and Wisæsi people to the west. In all but a few linguistic details, the Orogo, Kaluli, and Walulu people appear to be essentially the same. Although I speak primarily of the Kaluli group throughout this ethnography, what I say may be taken to apply to these other two groups as well.

The origin of the Bosavi people is obscure. Despite their close geographical proximity to the heavily populated highlands and fairly extensive trading contact with the Huli people north of the Karius Range, they are neither physically nor culturally very similar to highlands groups. The Bosavi are rather part of the broadly lowland Papuan series of cultures that range from the Daribi of Mt. Karimui (Wagner, 1967) through the inhabitants of the Lake Kutubu area (Williams, 1940) westward to the Strickland River and south to the coast.

According to the Bosavi people, they have always inhabited the plateau, and their mythology and traditions do not point to

Longhouse at Didesa seen from the air. The small outbuildings house government patrols that come through once a year. New growth from the original garden is visible behind the longhouse; the present gardens are out of sight.

an origin elsewhere. There is some evidence to suggest that they may have originated on the plateau somewhat to the west of their present location.

Contact through trade with peoples to the east, in the Lake Kutubu area, has been sporadic and comparatively recent. Most Bosavi trading relations in the easterly direction are oriented, not to peoples across the Kikori, but to those around to the south of the mountain along the Turama River and perhaps also the Awarra (Bamu) River, in an area the Kaluli call Tulomisi (Tulom country). Cultural influences from this direction—east and south —do not seem to run deep. The Bosavi people do not possess a variant of the extremely important myth of Sido, or Souw, which is widespread to the east. Roy Wagner (1972) has traced this myth from the people of the Papuan Gulf, up the Kikori River, through the Lake Kutubu region, all the way to Mt. Karimui, where it is a fundamental expression of local cultural orientation.

On the other hand, Bosavis borrow freely from the mythology and folklore of the Onabasulu people to the north. Bosavi social organization, witchcraft beliefs, and notions of the spirit world share many similarities with these northern neighbors (Ernst, 1970). Moreover, the mythological origins of their major ceremonies are located traditionally among the Sonia people to the west.

At the same time, despite some recent work (Wurm, 1971; Franklin, 1968), the linguistic picture of the region remains murky, and at present it is unclear whether the Kaluli language is more closely related to Onabasulu and Etoro to the north or to Faso to the east, or whether it differs from all of them at a significant level (Kelly, 1973).

The movements of various Bosavi (Kaluli) groups that are remembered as having taken place over the last three or four generations were mostly from west to east. They are usually characterized as having been moves away from established populations into virgin territory—or into an area abandoned by another group that was itself moving eastward. The motivation for moving is usually said to have been the search for richer food resources, flight from sickness, or, in one case, escape from raiding.

What larger historical conditions these movements represent

is not clear. Some pressures for movement may have originated from the expansion of the fierce Biame people to the west. Both Bosavi tradition and the reports of early government patrols describe the most vigorous traditional warfare (*giš*) as having been carried on with the Bosavi's traditional enemies to the north-west, the Wasamo (a Biame group) and the Yɔli (Etoro) peoples. However this may be, the population of the plateau was at one time considerably greater than it is today and apparently was still expanding eastward as late as the 1930s.

Between groups not traditionally at war, considerable trading was carried on. This was facilitated among the Bosavis by the fact that adjacent longhouse groups were generally intermarried. One could trace a chain of marital alliances from house to house and group to group, from the Hawalisi people on the east of the mountain through the Bosavis to the Sonia-speaking groups on the west, and from the "Aibalisɔ" people of Kokonesi longhouse on the southwest through the Bosavis to the Onabasulu people to the north. These marriages between house groups provide the principal relationships by which hospitality could be guaranteed and conflicts or disputes resolved. Longhouses without marriage or other relational ties, or without intervening houses with whom they were mutually related, existed in a state of nonrelationship or, as between Bosavi and Etoro groups, permanent hostility.

The Bosavi people clearly distinguished between retributive raids on nearby house groups, which could be expected eventually to result in a settlement (*kalu sandan, sei sandan*) and a perma-nent or traditional situation of fighting back and forth in an end-less series of raids (*giš*). In the first case, fighting usually took the form of an ambush or sudden forced entrance of a longhouse at dawn to murder a particular individual against whom the attackers had a serious grievance. Once the man was dead, the resulting furor could be settled by payment of compensation mediated through the relational ties between the longhouse groups. Before the arrival of the Australian government in the 1950s, there may have been as many as two or three such raids between Bosavi house groups every year.

The second kind of fighting, *giš*, may more legitimately be called warfare. It was directed indiscriminately against members of an enemy group in return for the murder of someone in one's own group. Since there were no ties of relationship, there was no way to adjudicate such fighting. Tension remained between such enemy groups, and intermittent raiding continued from generation to generation.

Thus the Onabasulu, and some of their Kaluli relatives at Wabimisæn, were in a state of *giš* with the Namabolo and Hawalisi people by the side of the Hegigio east of Wasu. Similarly, the people of Bænisa, Amine, Wasuɔidɔ, and Sibalema fought *giš* with Waˆsamo and the various southern branches of the Yɔli people.[3] In the worst of this kind of fighting, a large party would creep up on an enemy's house at night and set the thatch on fire. The occupants were then shot or clubbed to the last man as they fled the conflagration. This sort of drastic action fortunately was infrequent, but in the 1940s at least one Bosavi group northwest of Kolodɔ was exterminated in this way by Yɔli people from Koborasado and Sarodo.

In the midst of this somewhat precarious situation, the Bosavi people maintained continuous relations of trade with their friendlier neighbors. There were several significant trade routes into the Bosavi area. From the west, in the direction of the Sonia people, came strings of dogs' teeth and hornbill beaks. These, together with netted string bags and black-palm bows manufactured locally and tree oil traded in from the southeast, were in turn traded on to Huli people from the highlands beyond the Karius Range. Before government stations were opened at Tari in the early 1950s and Komo in 1964, the Huli used to make frequent trading trips bringing tobacco, home-processed vegetable salt (*aibi*), and netted pubic aprons down to the plateau to exchange for these things. Curiously, red bird of paradise (*raggiana*) feathers, though easily obtainable in the Bosavi area, appear never to have been an important trade item.

The most important trade routes were those around the east

---

3 Sialo of Bonɔ told me that when he was a boy he traveled with his father to visit relatives at Bænisa and saw there a line of skulls of Wasamo enemies that stretched the length of the longhouse. When I said that it must have been an impressive sight, he remarked philosophically that there was undoubtedly a line of Bænisa skulls just as long at Wasamo.

to the south of the mountain, along the Turama River. This was the area of Tulomisi where the farthest Kaluli trading expeditions went. Beyond it somewhere to the south lay the mysterious place of Helebe, later associated with the origin of the earliest government patrols. Up these routes came cowrie and occasional small pearl shells from the coast, which were used as bridewealth. Drums and other miscellaneous items came as well. Early in this century, Seli of Bonɔ's father introduced from Tulomisi the plant called *helebe bin* (*Bixaceae, Bixa orellana*). The blood-red juice of the seed pod replaced the reddish ocher (*bin*) that had been used previously as body and face paint. Later, glass beads, mirrors, and a few ax heads appeared. These objects began to trickle into Bosavi in the early 1930s and despite their small quantity rapidly assumed great importance both in the domestic economy and as items of bridewealth. Kaluli men would make long trips south of the mountain to trade dogs' teeth, net bags, and tobacco for them.

European Contact and Development of the Plateau

About this time a series of historical circumstances began to take shape that radically affected the people of the plateau and culminated in the particular historical situation in which I found them in 1966.

In 1935 the first European visitors, Jack Hides and Jim O'Malley, reached the plateau and passed through Onabasulu country. The following year, Ivan Champion and C. I. J. Adamson moved through the Bosavi area on their famous Bamu-Purari patrol. Within a year, the government station at Lake Kutubu across the Kikori, thirty-five miles away, was opened in preparation for the systematic exploration of the highlands. This facilitated a flow of axes, beads, mirrors, and pearl shells into the Bosavi area from the east such as had never been available previously from the trade routes to the south. World War II, however, prevented further exploratory penetration into the plateau area by the Australian administration until seventeen years later.

In the interim, during the late 1940s, a series of epidemics of measles and influenza swept over the plateau with disastrous results for the local population. The Etoro and Onabasulu peoples suffered most heavily, losing in some places 30 percent of the population and in other places as much as 70 percent (Kelly, 1973; Ernst, 1970). Remnant groups gathered together in new longhouses, leaving previously occupied stretches of forest land uninhabited. (The disorganization of social structure and re-arrangement of population among these people is documented by Kelly and Ernst in their unpublished doctoral dissertations.) My own census material indicates that the Bosavi people suffered much less severely than the northern groups—probably losing no more than about 25 percent of their population and leaving no previously inhabited areas completely unoccupied.

The psychological effect of this dreadful plague on the people of the plateau is difficult to assess. Given the cultural importance of a concern with curing illness, with witchcraft, and with death, it looms in some respects larger than any of the other important changes in Kaluli life that have accompanied increasing contact with European civilization. It very likely enhanced the sense of fatality that grips Bosavi people in their gloomier moments: the feeling that they are a dying people. Unfortunately, their intuition is correct. Despite vigorous inoculation efforts by the present administration, the population continues to drop slowly because of a high infant mortality rate and continued epidemics of flu that come down every year from the highlands.

In 1953 the second administration patrol, led by C. D. Wren, came onto the plateau from Lake Kutubu escorting a team of petroleum geologists. Five years later, in 1958, the initial census was taken by a patrol led by D. N. Butler. By this time significant changes had taken place in other spheres of Bosavi life. In the 1930s the primary forest cutting tool was the stone adz; bride-wealth consisted of stone adz blades, cowrie shell necklaces (*fu*; the word for bridewealth, *fudɔ*, comes from this item), headbands of dogs' teeth, pig tusks, and netted string bags. As axes began to come in, they rapidly replaced stone adz blades as forest tools and bridewealth items. Even with few axes available, whenever a garden needed to be cleared, all the axes in the area would be called in for the job along the relationship networks between longhouses.

The stone adz also yielded to the ax as a bridewealth item,

dropping out by the late 1940s though it continued to be used as a domestic tool in the 1950s. The increasing availability of valued cowrie shells, pearl shells, glass beads, and the appearance of bush-knives on the trade route rendered net bags, dogs' teeth, and pig tusks obsolete. By the late fifties, only the cowrie shell necklace remained of the traditional bridewealth items, and the rest of the inventory consisted of axes, pearl shells, bushknives, glass beads, and beaded chest bands (*soma alu*).

Increasing administration contact with the people of the plateau resulted in the cessation of warfare and cannibalism and promoted an increase in the frequency of visiting between friendly long houses. Retributive raiding was ended in 1960. At that time an Onabasulu man accused of causing a death by witchcraft was killed and eaten by the aggrieved clan group and its allies. When an administrative patrol arrived, about six months later, the offenders were forced to flee into the forest where they lived under considerable hardship for several weeks until the patrol left the area. Fighting was abandoned after that. *Giš* between the Bosavis and their traditional enemies to the northwest had subsided by 1966 into an uneasy state of suspension.

However, until the arrival of the missionaries, the people of Bosavi never fully acknowledged the passing of their traditional autonomy or accepted the inevitability of Australian guidance for the future. Up to that time, the arduous and irregular government patrols into the area tended to meet with an uncertain reception. Rumors of government disapproval of killing and fighting had made the people uneasy. They would appear curious and friendly one day and vanish into the forest the next. Those groups that were temporarily on hostile terms would hurriedly patch things up whenever they heard that a government patrol was entering the area, for fear they would all be taken away. In 1964, when the UFM missionaries[4] arrived in the Bosavi area to build an airstrip for a mission station, most of the unmarried men of the local longhouse communities were in seclusion at two secret

---

[4] A single attempt by a Papuan pastor to set up a Seventh Day Adventist mission among the Onabasulu in 1964 quickly failed when the people found out that the Adventists forbade the eating of pork. They thought the pastor was crazy, and he was obliged to leave.

ceremonial hunting lodges (*bau aa*). The missionaries sent out a demand for labor to build the airstrip. The Kaluli, caught between building the strip and keeping their youths in seclusion, decided to terminate the lodges and build the strip. The missionaries never knew about the lodges, but in most men's minds that was the end of the old way. The Kaluli told me that another *bau aa*, the highest point in their ceremonial life, will never be built at Bosavi.

Two years after this, in October 1966, I arrived at Bosavi to live among and learn about the people. In all, I spent almost two years with the Kaluli—between October 1966 and December 1968. The first year was spent alone; for the second I was joined by my wife, Bambi. Most of the time our major base was a small house of sago slats opposite the longhouse of clan Bonɔ at Sululib. Every two or three months we made two-week visits to other longhouses for further information. Throughout this book I refer to the Bosavi people—in particular, the Kaluli—in the present. This is not a timeless present but a historical one relating to the conditions under which I found them when I was with them, from 1966 to 1968.

Chapter 1

Ceremonies and Reciprocity

The first Europeans to visit the region of the Great Papuan Plateau, Jack Hides and Jim O'Malley, led a patrol from the Strickland River to the Purari River in 1934 and 1935.[1] Traveling northward up the Strickland, they turned east and approached the Bosavi region along the Rentoul (Isawa) River. Five miles below the confluence of the northern and eastern branches of the Rentoul, they left their canoes and continued eastward on foot through the forest along the south side of the river. After traveling for several days without seeing a single person or sign of habitation, they camped on a ridge opposite the confluence of the Rentoul and the Sioa rivers in plain view of three longhouses that were situated across the river about half a mile away on the other side of the valley. The native people were visible, but they seemed to take no notice of the tents of the European patrol.

After nightfall, however, lights—apparently torches—appeared in the distance near the houses. According to Hides:

The lights moved forward and backward as though in lines. . . . We watched them interestedly for some time: then suddenly

---

[1] Their route has been traced in detail by Kelly (1973). They were moving through the country of the Sonia people toward the Bosavi area. This was an uninhabited no man's land between Petameni, Etoro, and Onabasulu groups to the north and Sonia and Bosavi groups to the south, which were in a permanent state of hostility toward each other.

from across the valley, there came to our ears the sound of beautiful music. At first the sounds resembled the sounds of the deep baying of hounds: but gradually it rose and rose in volume in delightful harmony. Then it slowly died away as though on the bass notes of some organ.

I knew now why these people had not shown any outward sign of their discovery [of the patrol]. They had seen us all right, and probably their scouts had watched us from close quarters: but they were afraid. This singing and dancing was a call to strength, something to steel them against the strange and unearthly invaders.

We sat there that evening until a late hour listening to this glorious burst of song. . . . (Hides, 1936, p. 49)

The longhouses Hides saw were evidently Etoro and Onabasulu border villages, since the Sioa forms the boundary between these two groups at this point. According to Kelly (1973), the singing was very likely part of a seance to consult the spirits who aid these people in war. In any case, the next morning, Hides was threatened by a large party of natives who had crossed the river during the night. He avoided them, but, in the days that followed, as he headed north along the east bank of the Sioa through Onabasulu country, the natives he encountered refused all friendly overtures. Hides was forced to fire on some who ambushed him, killing three.[2] Eventually the patrol passed out of the area over the rim of the Karius Range.

Rumors of these events spread south and east across the plateau from the Onabasulu people to Bosavi, mixed with anxious speculation as to what they meant. An ax traded into the Kaluli at this time from the direction of Lake Kutubu caused much consternation among their northern neighbors. The Onabasulu perceived that chips made by the tool were the same as those left behind by the recent fearsome visitors to their country and feared it meant that they would return. About a year later, in March 1936, Ivan Champion and Richard Archbold flew over the northern foothills of Mt. Bosavi to reconnoiter for the forthcoming Bamu-Purari

[2] Hides reports firing four times but found only one body. According to Onabasulu sources, three men were killed, two Etoro and one Onabasulu (Ernst, 1970).

patrol. The people's response to this event was remembered by Wanalugo of clan Bonɔ.

> When we [the people of clan Bonɔ] were staying at a place called Tumosawel, we heard a sound—woo-oo-oo. We thought it was coming along the ground, but we could not tell where it was coming from. It got louder and louder until finally they yelled "Edowomal" and everyone fled out of the house into the bush. When it passed, they thought that whatever it was had been coming along the ground and they searched around to see what it was but they couldn't find it. Then word came through from [clan] Wasu [to the east]. "It didn't come along the ground. It came in the sky. We saw it." People asked themselves, "Does this mean that we are all going to die?" and so they decided to dance. They went up to the longhouse at Galamisen and danced. They told [clan] Wabisi at Muluma that they were going to dance there and to prepare food. When the food was prepared, they went there, a great many people, and danced. Many beautiful girls joined the dance [Heyalo, in which men and women both participate] and many people cried. (Field notes)

Nearly all the longhouse communities held ceremonial dances. Some feared that a great mythological fire was going to come and consume the world in flames. When the Bamu-Purari patrol came through the area several months later, many people fled their longhouses and camped hidden in the forest.[3]

These accounts of events in the past give us only a glimpse at a distance of an obscure people trying to come to terms with a situation they feared and did not understand.

When approached with the unknown, the Etoro and Onabasulu sang with their spirits, who advised them to show force. The Bosavis responded with ceremonial dancing and later fled into the forest. To a Westerner, this sort of response was exotic. The ceremonies the people performed in the midst of their anxiety were ones they otherwise usually performed on festive social occasions, such as marriages or food distributions—times when

---

[3] Some Kaluli did contact the patrol, however. Amid the general consternation, a man named Matayame, who could dream wealth, dreamed he would receive an ax if he approached the patrol. He did so the next day and received the ax as he had predicted. However, he cautiously waited until he had first seen that Huli men, who were visiting Bosavi on a trading expedition from the highlands, approached Champion without suffering harm.

new relationships are formed between people or when old ones are reaffirmed.

The Gisaro Ceremony

The most elaborate and characteristic ceremony of this type in Bosavi is called Gisaro. Like all Kaluli ceremonies, Gisaro takes place at night in the longhouse. It is performed by the guests at a formal social occasion for the benefit of their hosts and lasts until dawn. The first Gisaro I saw was held to celebrate the gathering of pigs for a forthcoming pork distribution. Preparations at the host longhouse at Wasu took two days. The Wasu people cooked large quantities of pandanus, a tropical fruit, and painted and decked themselves in their shell and feather ornaments.

The guests had been preparing for the ceremony for more than two weeks. They arrived at midday on the appointed day in a dramatic procession out of the forest accompanied by drums. They were entertained for the afternoon in the yard outside the long-house. In the evening, the hosts went inside to wait for the performance to begin.

The dark interior of the longhouse was packed with spectators sitting on the sleeping platforms behind the row of houseposts that lined each side of the central hall. Light was provided by five or six resin-burning torches held by young men at the sidelines. Everyone was turned expectantly toward the front doorway for the dancers and chorus to enter.

A group of about twenty-five men came in, their faces downcast. They moved in a body quietly up the hall to the middle of the house. There they drew apart to reveal the resplendent figures of the four Gisaro dancers in their midst. After a moment, all whispered "shhhh" and sat down, leaving one dancer standing alone.

His body was painted in red ocher with black markings, his head crowned with feathery black cassowary plumes tipped with white cockatoo feathers. His chest was hung with shell necklaces; his wrists, arms, and legs decorated with bracelets and bands. His whole figure was outlined against waving streamers of stripped yellow palm leaf, which shot up to shoulder height from behind

Gisaro dancer at Wasu

his belt and fell away to his feet: "break like a waterfall," as the Kaluli say. The dancer was slowly bouncing up and down in place, his eyes downcast, his manner withdrawn. A rattle suspended from his hand was clashing softly on the floor in time with his motion. As the house became quieter, his voice became audible, singing softly in a minor key.

The ceremony had a simple form. Throughout the night, one by one the four dancers took turns dancing in place or moving up and down the small space in the middle of the hall, singing songs in company with the choruses seated at each end. The songs concerned familiar places in the surrounding countryside known to most of those who were present. As dancer followed dancer, the songs began to refer to specific places on the host's clan lands and recalled to the listeners former houses and gardens and close relatives, now dead, who lived there.

One dancer sang a song that alluded to the dead son of a senior man of the host clan. The youth had died at a small house near a creek called Abo, and his soul was believed to have gone to the treetops in the form of a bird. The dancer sang:

> There is a Kalo bird calling by the Abo waterfall, juu-juu-juu.
> Do I hear my son's voice near the Abo spring?
> Perched, singing in a *dona* tree, is that bird my son?

The senior man, who was sitting with the crowd at the sidelines, brooding and withdrawn, suddenly became overcome with grief and burst into loud wails of anguish. Enraged, he jumped up, grabbed a torch from a bystander and jammed the burning end forcefully into the dancer's bare shoulder. With a tremendous noise, all the youths and young men of the host community jumped into the dancing space, stamping and yelling and brandishing axes. The dancer was momentarily lost in a frightening pandemonium of shadowy figures, torches, and showers of sparks. Showing no sign of pain, he moved slowly across the dancing space; the chorus burst into song. The senior man broke away from the crowd and ran out the back door of the house to wail on the veranda. This scene was repeated over and over from dancer to dancer during the course of the night.

Finally, at dawn, when the first birds began to sing, the dancers, the chorus, and the rest of the visitors suddenly rose to their feet with a shout, "Buuwɔɔɔ!" breaking the spell of their performance and bringing it abruptly to an end. The dancers, whose shoulders were quite badly burned, then paid compensation to those they had made weep, and all the visitors trooped out of the house to go home. Since many people wept, the ceremony was felt to have been a good one. Some of the visitors left wailing out of sympathy with their grief-stricken relatives among the hosts. The rest were exhilarated, and hosts and visitors shouted to each other that they would surely live long.

For several days afterward, the performance loomed large as a topic of conversation. Men remarked on how well so-and-so had danced, how much they themselves had cried, and what they had received in compensation (or complained that they had not received enough). Young people and children sang the songs and played at dancing in off moments, while others responded with mock crying and mimed the plunging of the torch.

The Kaluli regard Gisaro with enthusiasm and affection. They find it exciting, beautiful, and deeply moving. The dancer in full regalia is a figure of splendor and pathos. This is not because of the ordeal of burning he must face; rather, it is the very beauty and sadness that he projects that causes people to burn him. From the Kaluli point of view, the main object of Gisaro is not the burning of the dancers. On the contrary, the point is for the dancers to make the hosts burst into tears. The hosts then burn the dancers in angry revenge for the suffering they have been made to feel. To the dancer and the chorus, this reflects rather well on their songs. Moreover, a well-decorated and graceful dancer may project such magnificence as to cause a girl among the hosts to lose her heart and elope by following him home after the performance— a significant social coup for the visitors.

The dancers are always volunteers. When it is decided to perform Gisaro, several men immediately step forward. For ceremonies involving less severe ordeal, I have seen boys of ten or twelve proudly and excitedly announce that they were going to participate.

Gisaro is the most widely known ceremony among the people

of the plateau and seems to be historically the oldest. The Kaluli and their neighbors also perform five other kinds of ceremonies,[4] which differ in the number of dancers, the nature of the songs, the appearance of the regalia. However, most of them have the same basic themes: they are staged in the communal house at night; the dancers are elaborately costumed; the songs concern people's lands and evoke grief, crying, and burning from the hosts for which the dancers offer compensation. They seem to be alternative ways of expressing the same things.

Kaluli ceremonies are not connected with any particular season or time of year, so long as there is sufficient food available to feed the guests. Any ceremony may be performed in connection with any important occasion that people wish to mark. The one exception is that ceremonies are not held at funerals, for Kululi feel it is improper to jiggle a dead person with dancing. Besides, after a death people are grief-stricken, somber, and angry and are more in the mood for murder than for ceremonial dances. Which ceremonies will be performed depends largely on practical considerations, such as how elaborate the occasion is going to be, how long a time there is to prepare for it, and what people wish to do.

Ceremonies such as Gisaro are striking to an outsider at first because of their dramatic qualities; but, more important, one perceives that the people are deeply moved, in their grief and violence, and for that moment one glimpses something fundamentally important about their lives. Gisaro fascinated me while I was in Bosavi because I felt that, if I could grasp what it was about, it would provide a way to understand the people who performed it.

Ceremonies and Reciprocity

The occasions Kaluli celebrate with Gisaro are nearly always bound up with important transactions of social reciprocity in their relationships with one another. A bride is brought in procession to the house of the groom, the bridewealth is exchanged, and the visitors

[4] The other ceremonies are Ilib Kuwɔ, Sæbio, Kɔluba, Iwɔ, and Heyalo (or Feyalo). They are described in detail in the appendix.

perform a ceremony at night. Pigs are to be gathered for a forthcoming distribution. Those who are to receive them are invited to the donors' longhouse to celebrate and perform a ceremony at night. A garden produces an unexpected abundance; relatives and friends from other longhouses are invited to help themselves to it, and they perform a ceremony that night.

This kind of social giving and exchanging is basic to the Kaluli way of life. Friends and relatives in the same longhouse community normally expect to be able to borrow food and tools or request gifts of wealth from each other if the need arises. Among people in different longhouses, this sort of reciprocity is even more visible because it tends to be carried out in a formal and conspicuous way. The exchange of women and wealth in marriage provides the basis for the provision of hospitality for visiting, support in conflict, invitations to hunt and fish, mutual assistance in garden labor, and occasional ceremonial prestations, which are formal, customary gifts of food, especially meat.

It is difficult to give an adequate impression of the pervasiveness of this sort of social reciprocity in Kaluli life. A man's relations with, interactions with, and affection for his affines, for example, are so bound up with situations of reciprocal gift-giving and mutual help that he tends to think of his life with his wife, on reflection, in terms of the situations in which he worked cooperatively with her and reciprocally with her relatives and exchanged countless minor gifts of food. Sialo, an older man of clan Bonɔ, recalled his romance and young marriage to a girl from Tusuku in the following terms:

> We held a Gisaro at Tusuku [longhouse], and I was one of the dancers. After the ceremony, lo! a woman followed me home! I told her to wait. Later Tusuku [people] brought her to Bonɔ for a formal wedding.
>
> Well, we went down and planted pandanus and bananas. Then my brother-in-law Kiliyæ called us to plant bananas. We went to Tusuku and planted many, many bananas, and cut many trees.
>
> Later Tusuku brought a cassowary. I brought them bananas I cut from my garden. I went to Bosavi and hunted for animals. I got many, many animals, and also sago grubs and brought them to Tusuku. Then Tusuku went to Bosavi and hunted animals and

got sago grubs and brought them to Bonɔ as return. That's the way it was!

Well we went down to Alimsɔk [a garden place]. We planted Okari nuts. We called Tusuku, "Come plant bananas!" We planted bananas one day, two days, five, six days. Then we cut trees. Being hungry we said, "You take this sago." "You go pick bananas and pandanus."

We were hungry for meat. We [invited Tusuku] to the Walu [stream]. We caught crayfish. We dammed the Isawa, and beat poison and caught many, many fish. We went to the gardens. Tusuku said, "Bring bananas!" So we brought bananas. "Bring more"; so we brought more.

At Balesawel the woman died. I gave it up. (Field notes)

Sialo gives no mention of battles that took place at the time, of movements of the longhouse community over several different locations, or of the birth of a son. He presents the chronology of his happy marriage as a continuous situation of cooperation and exchange. It is within this kind of interactional context, facilitated by gifts of food, that Kaluli affirm and develop their relationships with each other. Food gifts are a particular obligation between in-laws, but food as gift or hospitality is the main vehicle for expression of friendly relationship to anyone, kinsman or acquaintance. Kaluli celebrate their relationships with others formally in large-scale ceremonial prestations, when most of the people of one longhouse community distribute pork or smoked game to people in other communities. It is to celebrate these big occasions of food giving, or important stages in their preparation, that Kaluli most often stage ceremonies such as Gisaro.

Indeed, while celebrating occasions of reciprocity, Gisaro embodies some of its characteristics. Compensation (*su*) must be paid for feelings deeply moved, and one ceremony is explicitly given in return (*wel*) for another. A performance that has caused a lot of grief motivates the hosts to return an equally affecting one to their guests. Gisaro is itself, therefore, a reciprocal transaction in the esthetic domain. All this suggests that social reciprocity is not merely punctuated by ceremonies such as Gisaro but is deeply bound up with what they express. Gisaro clearly involves emotional or ideological matters of wider cultural significance than only the giving of the food. It points to ways that reciprocity may be bound up with other realms of cultural symbolism and social experience.

At the same time, ceremonies retain a character independent of the events they usually celebrate. Kaluli sometimes perform them in the absence of important social transactions,[5] in times of fearful portents, such as when the first airplane flew over the plateau, or at the approach of epidemic disease. In the latter case, the community may perform sickness-warding magic and invite another community to perform a ceremony that night. If sickness is already in the longhouse and there have been several deaths, magic is dispensed with, and, in a mood of panicky anxiety, people announce their imminent arrival to another community and go there to dance.

If Kaluli social life takes much of its form through processes of reciprocity, it is not surprising that reciprocity should be celebrated by ceremonies that express important human concerns in deeply moving ways. It is in ceremonies such as Gisaro that these wider concerns are focused and made visible. If we are to appreciate them, and what they mean for Kaluli people, we must learn what Gisaro is about. And for Gisaro to yield insight into Kaluli experience, we must also learn how to interpret it.

---

[5] Three out of fifteen ceremonies from 1966 to 1968 were performed without important social transactions.

Chapter 2

In the Shadow of the Mountain

Gisaro dancers sing about streams and garden sites and places in the forest. Kaluli relationship to their land—the way they perceive it and feel about it—is fundamentally important to understanding their experience.

The climate on the plateau is mild and humid, the temperature about 85° to 90° during the day, with rains in the late afternoon and at night. In the forest there are no natural clear spaces from which to gain a view of the landscape. It is only from some vantage point temporarily cleared by the work of men that one can get an overall glimpse of this vast, lonely country. A person standing on the veranda of the longhouse at Doba can see Mt. Sisa and the escarpment of the Karius Range about fifteen miles to the north. Ten miles to the south the landscape is dominated by the crumpled dark-green slopes of Mt. Bosavi. To the east and west, the land rolls away in a series of low ridges covered in vegetation.

To an outsider, the tropical forest has an immense anonymity. Away from human habitation, one may walk for hours among the galleries of trees, seeing everywhere the same spindly ground plants and crossing dozens of identical brooks and creeks.

To the eye of someone who has always lived there, however, the forest is full of the intimate signs of daily life. Kaluli can recognize individuals, and even pigs, by their footprints in the mud and tell what they are up to. A piece of charred log on the track indicates that someone has passed there at night. A fern leaf stuck at the entrance of a side trail blocks the escape of the souls of bananas. This means that a new garden is planted nearby. Freshly scattered feathers show where a youth has caught a small parrot in the early morning.

To a person on his own land, every large tree, cliff, hill, or swampy area is a familiar place. Kaluli know the course of every water and give a name to each, as well as to every area of land. Important landmarks have names of their own, such as Wilib, a prominent hill; Galamisen, where there is an enormous *ilaha* tree; or Sisande, a large pool in the Isawa River. Occasionally, a place is named after some event in the past—for example, Kušukini, where a large *kus* tree was cut down by someone long ago. But apart from important landmarks, Kaluli rely for sense of location and direction primarily on the many watercourses that flow northward through their country from Mt. Bosavi.

Accordingly, most places in the forest are named after the stream that gives the land its contours in that vicinity. A place is given the name of the water plus a suffix that indicates its character in that area. Thus, the area about the spring of the Kiden Stream would be called Kidenelip; Kidensawel would be the place where there is a waterfall; Kidensadugu would be the place where the stream levels out after a steep descent; and so on, down to Kidensɔk, the mouth of the stream at the Walu River, or Kidensagu if there is a waterfall there. The waters, as they turn and fall, generate new localities for every new configuration of the land. The name of a locality carries, in effect, its own geographical coordinates, which place it in determinate relation to the brooks and streams that flow through the forest.

Men know the resources of their longhouse territories in detail: where to find the right bark for flooring the house, ferns to cook with pork, nettles to rub on a stomach ache. Much of the attention people pay to the signs and qualities of the forest has an eye to the kind of game they are likely to find there. Kaluli know to which trees the birds will flock in which season and which berry bushes to set traps around for marsupials. Kaluli normally get game in quantity only sporadically as a result of lucky chance or successful hunting or fishing expeditions. However, when people are working or just passing through the forest, they are always alert for whatever may fall to hand. Any small animals, rodents, lizards, or unwary marsupials that appear by the trail are immediately pursued and dispatched, with stick or bushknife or simply stamped on with the foot. A person crossing a brook may pause to search with his hands for small fish or crayfish that are hiding under rocks and logs. These casually gathered morsels never amount to a significant part of the diet, but they do provide most of a person's day-to-day protein.

In more purposeful hunting, Kaluli chase animals with dogs, set deadfall traps, or construct blinds for shooting birds. The most common techniques, however, are simple. To catch arboreal animals, Kaluli simply cut down the trees in which they appear. Small birds are grabbed out of their nests at night. To catch such formidable animals as cassowaries or wild pigs, men discover the animal's nest during the day and then surround it at night. They then leap on the sleeping animal, pin it down, and dispatch it with an ax.

Kaluli regard the uninhabited precipitous forests of Mt. Bosavi as the true home of the animals. Game is particularly abundant there, including several species not available on the plateau. Despite the inhospitable cold, damp nights, difficult terrain, and various supernatural dangers, when a man needs a large quantity of smaller game for an exchange, he goes for several days to the mountain.

Apart from game Kaluli get meat occasionally from domestic pigs (kabo), which they keep in small numbers. As elsewhere in New Guinea, however, they kill their pigs only on infrequent occasions to make ceremonial gifts of pork to relatives and affines. The largest number of pigs I saw killed at such a time was twenty-eight.

For ordinary subsistence, Kaluli live primarily off the produce of extensive swidden gardens cleared in the forest and sago extracted from palms that grow in boggy places by the sides of streams. Sago is the staple starch of every Kaluli meal, and the word for it (mæn) is also the generic word for food.[1] Although

---

[1] Sago is the only food Kaluli can store for any length of time. Raw sago wrapped in leaf packets and buried in mud will keep for nearly a year.

the palms propagate themselves naturally in the wild from shoots put out by mature plants, each one is owned individually by someone in a nearby longhouse, who will work it for his family when the need arises.

Gardens, which are planted along the low ridges of the plateau forest, supply several varieties of bananas, pandanus, and breadfruit as principal crops, along with pitpit, sugarcane, taro, sweet potatoes, and a number of different kinds of greens.

The Longhouse Community

The most conspicuous group in Kaluli society is the local longhouse community, roughly those people who associate themselves with one longhouse, cr *aa*, as it is called. A Kaluli "village" normally consists of a single big longhouse, occasionally grouped with one or more smaller ones, situated within convenient distance of maturing sago stands and good gardening grounds. Each community builds its longhouses and plants its gardens on its own particular territory, about two to four square miles in extent, which is bounded on all sides by the lands of other house groups or by uninhabited forest used for hunting. Aside from the major longhouse, there are usually five or six smaller houses and numerous temporary shelters near scattered gardens and sago stands. These belong to one or two individuals from the main longhouse who inhabit them periodically with their families when these gardens are ripe or to families living apart from the rest of the community but still considered a part of it.

A big Kaluli *aa* is usually sixty feet long by thirty feet wide with a veranda at each end (Figure 2.1). The ridge of the roof curves downward in the front and back, giving it a humpbacked appearance, like an overturned boat. For defense against raids, the whole structure is raised five to twelve feet in the air on posts. In addition, it is traditionally built off the spur of a ridge so that the front door faces the forest track, with the rear veranda sometimes as high as twenty-five feet in the air. The forest of the surrounding slopes is then felled for good visibility. In the past,

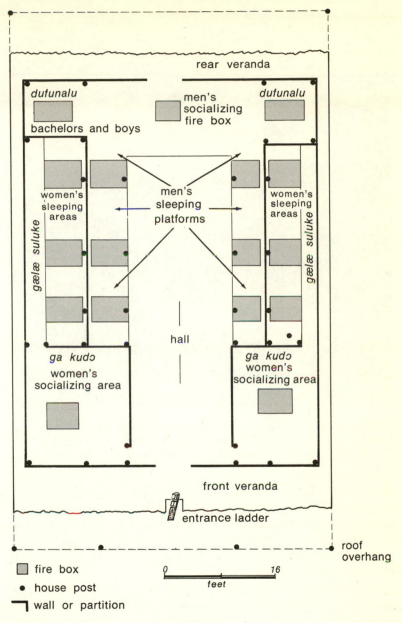

FIGURE 2.1 Plan of a Kaluli Longhouse

Longhouse (*aa misen*) at Muluma. This longhouse is built about five feet from the ground in front. The surrounding fenced garden, which has been cleared of fallen trees, is planted in pitpit, sugarcane, and bananas.

this was an effective fortress against the usual armament of bows and clubs. Six or seven men in a small, strategically placed *aa*, standing with bows at cracks in the walls and floor, could successfully hold off a much greater force. Domestic pigs sleeping beneath the house functioned as watchdogs, making noise at the approach of strangers in the night.

Big Kaluli *aas* are isolated in the forest, one or two hours' walk apart. One emerges from the shade of the forest into a sunli garden area several acres across amid a wreckage of fallen trees. On the opposite rise, the longhouse commands the view, smoke drifting slowly through the thatch.

The interior, which is lit dimly by the light coming through the doorway at either end, gives an outsider a first impression of being a single cavernous room (Figures 2.1 and 2.2). Once accustomed to the darkness, however, one can see a broad, bark-floored hall (*tigilip*), littered with sugar cane spittings and discarded cooking leaves, that runs down the center of the building. It is bordered on either side by a row of houseposts. Behind these, set back on each side of the hall and raised about ten inches off the floor, are bark-floored sleeping platforms, with fireboxes set into them at intervals opposite each housepost. Virtually everything is covered with soot. Blackened piles of firewood and smoked pork or game are laid side by side on wooden racks over each firebox to cure. Bags of sago and grimy bark-wrapped bundles of possessions hang nearby from stringers and rafters out of the reach of marauding rats. The houseposts are streaked with dried pandanus juice and grease where people have wiped their hands after meals.

The sleeping platforms along with the hall form the portion of the house inhabited by the men. The women, small children, and piglets sleep cramped in two dark, narrow passages down the sides of the house (*gælæ suluke*), separated from the men's area by partitions that run at about shoulder height down nearly the length of the building. Each firebox down the side of the hall is usually shared by two married men who own the sleeping places on either side of it. Their wives and small children sleep opposite them on the other side of the partition next to the corresponding fireboxes in the *gælæ suluke* (see Figure 2.1).

Unmarried youths and elderly widowers sleep together around fireboxes in the back of the house in corner areas (*dufunalu*) recessed into the space along the sides that is elsewhere part of the women's section. Important senior women and marriageable girls sleep in widened areas of the women's section (*ga kudɔ*) near the front, which extends into space that otherwise is given to the men's sleeping platforms.

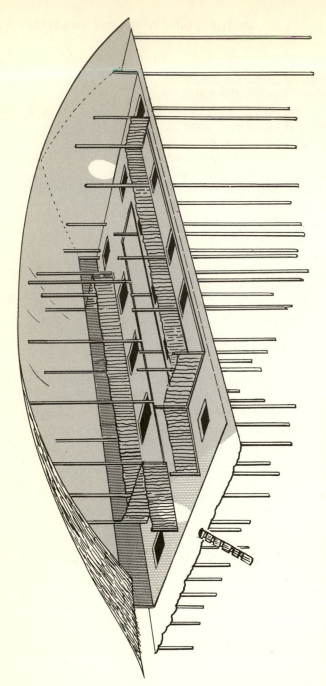

FIGURE 2.2 Cutaway View of a Kaluli Longhouse

Interior of aa *misen* at Sululib, showing the central hall (*tigilib*) flanked by the men's sleeping platforms (*wub*). The social fire box is in front of the rear door. The large packets are leaf ovens steaming fish. (Photo by B. Schieffelin.)

Kaluli people like to gather around fires, and fireboxes form convenient centers for conversation. The central firebox at the head of the hall belongs to no one and is reserved for general socializing. At odd times of the day, one can usually find two or three men squatting there to smoke and talk, silhouetted against the open back door. A man stays by the firebox at his own sleeping place when he wants to be alone with his thoughts or is not feeling well. He uses it to cook personal tidbits, informally entertains particular friends and relatives there in the evenings, and sleeps by it for warmth at night.

The *aa* is not meant to be only, or even primarily, a domestic residence. It is also a community meeting hall. When there is something important to discuss or when visitors arrive, the upper end of the hall is the floor for conversation. For funerals, bridewealth negotiations, and minor prestations of smoked game, the men gather around the socializing firebox or line the edges of the sleeping platforms as in a grandstand to watch and participate. The upper hall is also the stage for ceremonial dances and, occasionally, a battleground in the case of a raid.

The *aa* shelters about sixty people: the men of several patrilineal clans plus their wives and children, or about fifteen families. Kaluli clans are characterized by inheritance of the same clan name down the male line and by exogamous marriage. A particular group may have branches in different longhouse communities. The localized branch of a clan in a longhouse community commonly is made up of members of one or more unnamed *de facto* lineages who may or may not be able to trace genealogical relationship with one another.

The term for a large longhouse, *aa misen* (literally "head house"), is also the term for a clan. This does not mean that a longhouse community is made up of one clan. Most longhouse communities are made up of members of lineages of two or three clans, one of which may be numerically predominant.

Sometimes members of a house group depleted by deaths or pressured by raids will abandon their own *aa* and territory and go to live with another group to whom they are related. A few individuals leave their own lands for personal reasons and join their affines or mother's people. But most minority lines in a given *aa* derive from the descendants of women who married out to other communities, were widowed, and returned to their own longhouse with small, dependent children. The children are brought up by their mothers' brothers; girls are married out, and boys, if their fathers' people lay no claim to them, are given land and sago and, retaining their fathers' clan names, remain, along with their descendants, in the longhouse with their mothers' clan.

The people of any clan in a longhouse community generally consider their loyalties to be more closely bound to others in their own longhouse, especially age-mates, regardless of their descent affiliation than to members of their own clan in other long-houses. Indeed, people of a longhouse generally refer to themselves by the name of the place where their longhouse is located rather than by their clan affiliation.

Members of a longhouse community tend to act together in many domestic enterprises. They build the *aa* and plant their gardens together. They participate in communal hunting and fish-damming expeditions and provide songs, food, and labor for ceremonies. Most people in the *aa* contribute to the bridewealth when one of their young men is getting married, and if someone receives a prestation of meat, he shares it with everyone in the house.

Kaluli often refer loosely to the territory associated with a house group as if it is owned by the house group as a whole, but neither the house group nor the lineages of which it is composed have corporate control over it. Lands and sago palms are divided among the individual men of the community, who are free to give or leave them to whomever they wish. Usually a man passes his land and sago to his sons or, if he has none, to his brothers or their children or to his sister's sons. There is no shortage of land in Bosavi. A man may stay in his original house group or move to another as he wishes. If he is given land or sago on another longhouse territory, he will have no reason to use it unless he visits the area frequently or plans to move there permanently. Most men tend to stay in the community where they grew up and know the people, using land that they inherited from their relatives there.

Men sometimes use the sago they own on another longhouse territory to incubate grubs for prestations, but their land there usually lies fallow, and either they pass it on to someone else or the claim lapses after a generation or so of disuse.

A Kaluli longhouse is seldom fully or continuously occupied in normal circumstances. Kaluli do not like to travel even moderate distances to and from work areas. A family or two working sago at a place more than half an hour's walk from the *aa* usually builds a small shelter and camps there for about two weeks during the processing. Men often build small houses at garden sites some distance from the main longhouse, where they may live with their families and those of one or two close relatives or friends for extended periods of time. When their work is slack or they receive invitations, people go to assist in-laws and relatives in other longhouse communities with their sago and garden making. All these movements, plus other visiting, hunting, or trading expeditions of various durations, take people away from the main longhouse for extended periods. Unless a ceremonial occasion is in preparation or there is danger of raiding, only a few families will be in residence. The house may even be closed and empty for weeks.

The period of occupancy or use of an *aa misen* is strongly dependent on the supply of nearby sago palms and the productivity of banana gardens. Gardens become too exhausted and weed-choked to work efficiently after one crop, and people must plant new ones about twice in three years. (Old gardens return to forest on a fallowing cycle of about twenty-five years.) Some of the slack is taken up by the small gardens mentioned above, but as the gardens near the *aa misen* become exhausted and the building itself deteriorates after two or three years, the inhabitants construct a new garden and longhouse elsewhere. They alternate residence between the old *aa* and the new, until finally, as the old garden gives out entirely and the new one matures, they abandon the old house and burn it down.

The periodic shifting and regrouping of a longhouse community takes place within a limited area near the central portion of its larger longhouse territory. Gardens and secondary forest associated with occupancy of this vicinity do not usually extend to streams or ridgetops that mark the boundaries of the territory as a whole. This fact is related to considerations of defense in times past. While the longhouse itself was a reasonably effective fortress against enemy raids, it was still more difficult to attack if it was located deep inside its own territory. Bosavi longhouse communities were not customarily on hostile terms with one another, but disputes and accusations of witchcraft between them were not infrequent and sometimes led to violence. Thus it was best to situate one's dwelling cautiously.

Identification with Locality

The identity of each longhouse community is not primarily associated with the clan membership of the people who inhabit the *aa*. Rather, over a period of time the community becomes bound up with the area it moves about in and comes to be referred to by the name of the locality. Thus, for example, lineages of Gæsumisi and Wabisi whose communities' successive longhouses have been located in the vicinity of Bægolo Ridge are called Bægolo people. Less frequently, but more particularly, they may be referred to as Gæsumisi (the predominant clan) or Malosonɔ (the present site of the longhouse, in 1968). Similarly, a branch of clan Didesa, together with small groups of Wabisi and Ferisa living at Olabia in 1968, are known as Kagabesi people, after a local grove of *kagab* trees.

New communities come into being largely by extension of the normal movements of dispersal and regrouping of the community in relation to its sago stands and garden land. During the shift from one *aa misen* to another, one or two families who inhabited the old one may decide not to join the others and to live apart for a while. This is particularly likely if they have just completed a new small *aa* at another place in the territory. Alternatively, one or two families who have been living apart in this way may join the rest when they have built a new *aa*.

If, over time, the sago resources or garden land of one particular man or group of brothers becomes depleted in the area frequented by the rest of the community, they may gradually spend more and more time living apart from it until they become, in fact, a separate community. Alternatively, a group of younger men, feeling restive, may simply decide to leave and set up on their own.

About three generations ago, the people of Bonɔ clan lived near the Hɔndugu stream west of their present location and were known as Hɔndugusi Bonɔ. There was a minor dispute[2] in the community, and one of the parties and some of his age-mates decided to leave and build a small house and garden near the Yolo stream by the Isawa River. This land had itself been abandoned earlier by its original owners, clan Wasu, which had moved east to better fishing grounds on the Bifo River, and clan Sæsæn, which followed somewhat later, fleeing the depredations of witches in a time of severe epidemic.

The Bonɔ emigrants lived in a succession of *aas* in the vicinity of Desep Ridge near the Isawa until, over time, they became known as Desepæsi (those who stay at Desep). Shortly afterward, two elopements between the Desep and Hɔndugu branches of Bonɔ brought the groups into affinal rather than "brother" relationship. About this time, the Desep group was joined by refugees of the Wɔsisɔ clan who were abandoning their lands to the northwest under the pressure of raiding.

A generation after the founding of the Desepæsi community, a group of lineage brothers moved away to a place called Kolok, where they stayed with their families for about fourteen years. This was long enough for the younger people at Desep to begin thinking of them as another community and calling them Kolonesi (those who stay at Kolok). Older people at Desep still considered them as members of their own community, living apart for an extended period of time. About 1950 the Kolok community returned to Desep to cosponsor a *bau aa* ceremonial hunting lodge and decided to remain there after that. If they had stayed at Kolok for another generation, informants said, the name Kolonesi

[2] According to the story, a man found a pile of excrement left by a dog on his sleeping platform. The dispute was set off when he told another man to clean it up, blaming it on his child.

would have stuck and they would have become a separate branch of Bonɔ.[3]

As a community becomes associated with the locality in which it lives, its members use the name of the locality as part of their social identity in friendly interaction with people of other communities. In warfare, however, they used place names in an opposite manner, not to mediate identity but to intensify antagonism between opposing sides and throw the enemy into confusion. Most of the members of a raiding party that entered another longhouse territory for an attack would be traveling in a relatively unfamiliar country whose trails, ambush points, and other important features were not well known to them. Kaluli defenders were aware of this and turned the situation to psychological advantage by yelling place names from their home territory as war cries (*kamo salab*) when they projected themselves into battle. *Kamo* names were usually prominent landmarks—hills, ridges, and rivers—or important house sites with which people identified themselves, or after which the community was named. (Gardens, sago places, and small house sites were never shouted in battle.) These names were particularly potent if they were names of places where enemies had been killed or wounded in the past, and if a man wounded an enemy with an arrow in battle, he yelled after him, "One down at such-and-such a place!"

Defenders yelled *kamo* as they charged out of the longhouse in order to confuse and frighten the attackers. Kaluli explained: "They were afraid because they didn't come to these places and didn't belong here." Disoriented, it was thought, they would scatter and retreat. Attackers, for their part, yelled the names of their own localities to rally their courage and regroup in a dispersed battle in the forest.

The yelling of war cries not only named one's community identity but asserted it actively against other communities. When

---

[3] As old house groups split into new ones and people are renamed according to the areas they come to inhabit, original clan affiliations may in some cases be forgotten. Several present-day clan names, such as Gæsumisi (those who stay by the Gæsun stream) and Wabisi (those who stay at the Wab trees), seem originally to have derived from names of places.

the group of young men who were to found the Desepæsi branch of Bonɔ left their kinsmen at Hɔndugu, the latter mocked them saying, "You are going to the Yolo stream?[4] What will you eat? Yolo fruit?"

Later, the bananas of the first Yolo garden came up in such abundance that they ripened before anyone could pick them. The emigrants hastily gathered them in and invited their former housemates at Hɔndugu, along with people from other long-houses, to come and celebrate. When the visitors had made their ceremonial arrival and were lined up in front of the new *aa*, their hosts came rushing out of the house yelling "Yolo fruit! Yolo fruit!" and scattering bananas in all directions. The guests turned to each other in dismay, saying, "They are shouting *kamo!* They must be angry at us!" Their hosts said, "No, we are not angry. When we left to live here you asked, 'Will you eat Yolo fruit?' Well, this is Yolo fruit!" And they threw more bananas over the ground.

Here, *kamo* was shouted not in battle but at a food distribution —and not at enemies but at former housemates from whom the community had split. The unconventional use of food in a war cry reference mixed antagonism with hospitality, clearly serving notice that the people at the longhouse no longer thought of themselves as part of the Hɔndugu group, but as a new community altogether.

When Kaluli use their place names to identify themselves to others or to project their ferocity in battle, they are doing more than merely asserting membership in a residence group. Place names, including that of the longhouse vicinity, refer to familiar forested ridges, streams that are full of fish, house sites and sago stands where a person has lived most of his life. They are bound up with his sense of himself. "When a man lives somewhere for a long time," one informant explained, "his name is in the ground just like you put your name in that book." The subtle changes one sees in the forest regrowth reflect the presence and work of people one has known in the past. "These are the weeds of my father's garden," Jubi told me once as we descended to a part of

---

[4] At the time, uninhabited ground used for hunting.

the forest where the trees were somewhat lighter and thinner than on the ridge we had left. "We lived at Sulusawel up there. I was small like Seyaka." People would sometimes point out to me tangled areas of weeds or a burnt-off post in an old house site and remark upon who had lived or gardened there. These places are meaningful because they mark the contexts of one's past experience. Kaluli identify themselves with place names because they see themselves reflected in their lands.

Chapter 3

I'm Sorry, Brother,
I Don't Eat That

Places on familiar lands are significant because they are the context for relationships and shared activities. Most of the people with whom a Kululi person interacts daily, and upon whom he relies for assistance and support throughout most of his life, are those he counts as kinsmen and affines. The way Kaluli carry out relationships with these others in mundane situations of casual visiting, garden planting, and sago making gives their social interaction its particular quality and style. The focus here is not so much on the structure of social relationships—the relative statuses, rights, and obligations obtaining between kinsmen. Rather, the issue is the way Kaluli relationships are conceived and expressed in a system of metaphors and the symbolism of everyday behavior. We are interested in seeing how Kaluli frame and communicate their sentiments about each other and articulate their social relations in actual situations.

The set of social conceptions and expressive behavior is part of a larger system of cultural idéas concerning life and death, male and female, health and illness, the implications of which permeate every social situation and every domain of Kululi experience.

Food and Social Relationships

The basic theme in the expression of Kululi relationships is the giving and sharing of food. Thus, a man with nothing else to do wanders off to his gardens to check the progress of his pandanus fruits or have a look at his bananas. People walking through the forest point out to each other trees that have been felled along the way to catch arboreal animals, logs that have been split for grubs, birds' nests, places where wild pig or cassowary tracks have recently been seen. Kaluli also took an interest in the European foods that we brought into the field. I discovered quite early that men who refused to carry my supplies even for double the usual wages would readily consent to the regular price if I promised them a cup of rice or a tin of corned beef. Interest in food is not due to a lack of it; the Kaluli diet may be one of the most varied and. adequate in New Guinea. Rather, food is important because it is a vehicle of social relationship.

I became aware of this as soon as I entered a longhouse on the plateau for the first time. I sat down wearily on the edge of the men's sleeping platforms and was pulling the leeches out of my socks when a man approached with a blackened, loaf-shaped packet in his hand. He broke off a piece and handed me a chalky-looking substance covered with grayish, rubbery skin. There was a pause while the people of the longhouse watched to see what I would do. Reluctantly, I took a bite. The flavor was strongly reminiscent of plaster of paris. "*Nafa?*" ("Good?") asked one of my hosts hopefully, using one of the few Kaluli words I knew at the time. "*Nafa,*" I answered when I could get some saliva back in my mouth. "Ah," said my host, looking around to the others. They relaxed. Having eaten sago, I was established as a fellow creature.

Thereafter, whenever I, and later my wife, visited a longhouse where we were not familiar or a visitor came to the one where we were staying, I would overhear long discussions about what we ate. When the Kaluli realized that we really liked most of their local food, people went out of their way to bring us things we had not tried to see if we would like them. This was not simply a question of hospitality. Our common enthusiasm for such things as pitpit and breadfruit was a way we could come to understand each other, even if we could not speak the same language. At the same time it made us friends.

The giving and sharing of food among the Kaluli communicates sentiment; it conveys affection, familiarity, and good will. A toddler who burst into tears on seeing me for the first time was reproached by his father, who said, "Don't cry, he gives salt." The man then explained to me that one should give food to little children "so that they will know you and like you and not be afraid of you." The advice would apply equally to the whole range of Kaluli social relationships. Kaluli exercise it as soon as a child comes into the world.

A day or so after a child is born, his parents and a few relatives take him on an expedition to a forest camp where they spend a few days catching crayfish and sago grubs to feed him. The common concern is to "make the child strong" and to please him and make him feel welcome so that he will not "go back" to where he came from and die. It provides others beside the mother, who feeds the baby at her breast, with the opportunity to relate to him by giving him food.

Thereafter, the giving and sharing of food continues to be the social idiom in which close relationships and affectionate sentiment are given form. A young man smitten by a girl may try to slip her a small packet of salt or meat to let her know how he feels. A man expressing his grief over a friend's death will say, "He gave me pork!"

Within the longhouse community, each nuclear family gets and prepares its own food but readily gives to anybody who is short at the time and expects others to share in the same way with them. A person who does not have enough shoots to plant may ask for more from his relatives or in-laws in his own or in other longhouse communities; if he has too many shoots, he may give them away for the asking. Later, the favor will be returned. Beyond this give-and-take in garden produce, there is a particular obligation to share delicacies—especially meat. Anyone who receives a formal gift of meat at a prestation or who brings back some quantity of game from hunting or fishing is expected to share it with everyone else in the longhouse to whom it is not for one reason or other taboo.

Those who wish to eat a small animal by themselves or to share it with a select group of friends will prepare and eat it at a camp secluded in the forest, at the longhouse at midday when everyone else is off in the gardens, or late at night when others are asleep so that they will not be offended. Not to share meat with people to whom you are close is inconsiderate and will hurt their feelings. Two men who came furtively to my house to eat a meal of fish explained that that particular kind of fish was taboo to their wives and children. But their wives and children loved fish, and to eat it in front of them would only make them unhappy. Though they could not share with their families, they did not want to be thoughtless or unfeeling.

These sorts of social implications of giving and sharing food underlie the Kaluli sense of normal good manners. To startle or interrupt a person who is eating is extremely bad manners, and the usual noisy, animated talk around the firebox stops while people eat. Talking while eating, I was told, is likely to make a man choke on his food.

People become even more upset if food is made to seem repulsive or disgusting. Once I came upon a youth gathering edible tent caterpillars (*bidæli*) for a meal. Surprised, I asked him if Kaluli really ate caterpillars (*kægæbi*). His revulsion was as great as mine. "Don't say *kægæbi*," he shouted angrily, "People don't eat *kægæbi*; these are *bidæli!*" For the same reasons, one does not mention worms or leeches while people are eating fish (which eat worms and leeches) or red pandanus (which is the color of sucked blood) lest people revolt at their meal.

Such behavior is not merely graceless or irksome. Interfering or preventing a man from eating has implications opposite to those of giving him food. The force of the eater's outrage comes from the fact that one has taken food away from him, "taken it out of his mouth," as the Kaluli would say.

Consequently, mistreating food, playing with it, spitting it out, throwing it at someone is shocking behavior. I rarely saw even tiny children do it, and when it did happen, the horrified mother would tell the offender he was acting like a witch (*sei*). Among adults, mistreatment of food is often interpreted as a deliberate provocation.

Similarly, most domestic disputes in the longhouse, whatever their actual underlying causes, converge over mistreatment of food. A husband, irked at his wife, may tell her to have a meal ready early, delay eating it for some time, and then berate her for serving his food cold or for giving it to someone else. Women, annoyed with their husbands, may refuse to cook for them or, if extremely provoked, may deliberately step over their food, exposing it to their genitals and rendering it unfit to eat.

The sharing of food has a special positive significance. Two friends or kinsmen who wish to express special affection for each other may share a meal of meat. Thereafter, they may indicate this bond between them by addressing each other by the name of the food they have shared. If they share a bandicoot (*mahi*), for example, they may call each other "my bandicoot" (*ni mahi*) thereafter. This custom is called *wi aledo*, or "reciprocal name" and implies close personal identification and brotherly relationship between the two people who use it. Hospitality, the giving of food to a guest, differs from sharing in that it does not involve or imply a particularly special closeness between the people involved. Rather, the giving of food implies precisely the social distance—or opposition—that lies between people as host and guest.

People automatically offer food to their relatives from other longhouses when they come to visit and expect the same when they go to other longhouses. The failure to offer food to a visitor at the appropriate moment or to give meanly is bad manners, defaults on the relationship, and implies that the visitor is not welcome. If hospitality is not offered at all, the visitor is left in a social limbo—as a kind of intruder—and before European contact, he might legitimately have felt himself to be in danger. For this reason, men traveling to distant places usually went with a group that included at least one person with distant relatives there. The relatives would feel bound to feed him and his friends, and the size of the group would deter the possibility of trouble.

On the other hand, a welcome that is particularly hospitable, in terms of abundant food or the offer of meat, is remarked on and remembered by both host and visitor. Where it is unexpected, it may form the basis for the establishment of close relations and friendship. A man named Nokobe from the Etoro people came to our longhouse at Sululib to deliver a letter from another anthropologist. He had no Kaluli relatives, could not speak the language,[1] and his group had been traditional enemies in times past. At Bonɔ, a man named Seli, interested in developing ties with people to the north, shared his sleeping platform with Nokobe and fed him pork, an unusually gracious gesture under any circumstances. Later, when I went with five men (including Seli) to visit Nokobe's longhouse, Nokobe and his relatives appeared laden with enough food to feed the entire party for three days—for which he refused all payment. Seli later told me that in conversation they went so far as to discuss the possibility of arranging marriages between the Kaluli and Etoro, a historical first for these two peoples in about thirty years.

The manner in which Nokobe presented his food implied more than merely a return for Seli's generosity. It was a formal statement of the obligation of friendship he had incurred through Seli on his visit to the Kaluli. The distinctive quality of hospitality emerges most clearly on ceremonial occasions, when people of one longhouse play host to those from another. Here, it becomes a formal statement of the commitments of friendship between host and guests made through the medium of food.

Hosts are not supposed to eat at all at such times. They present a large quantity of cooked food to their guests and, sitting apart, watch them eat. The social distance maintained between host and guests allows the gift of food to be a public demonstration of good faith in the relationship. In this context, for the hosts to eat some of the food they present to their guests would be, in effect, to take some of it back and throw a cloud over the relation they wish to affirm. Thus, even when the hosts do get hungry and eat, they tend to do so furtively, after the guests have finished, and never from the same batch of food.

Kaluli who are hosts and guests to each other are usually related as kinsmen and affines. Indeed, it is on the basis of these relationships that food is most often offered and expected in the first place. The gift of food makes the relationship socially real and

---

[1] He came with two Onabasulu men, one distantly related to our community, to act as interpreters.

concrete. A man's total range of traceable kin provides the range of potential social relationships that may be most easily actualized.

Kinship Terminology and Relationships

Kaluli denote people at the fringes of their social field by the term *mæmu*. *Mæmu* specifically signifies "grandfather" or "grandchild," but it is also applied to people who live in distant longhouses or other tribal areas with whom they have no relationship at all. Kaluli, in moments of bravado and ethnic chauvinism, sometimes refer to the latter as *iko*, or "wild pig," implying that the distance is too great for extension of personal consideration or, more contemptuously, that they should be treated not as people but as food. Grandparents and distant, unrelated people both share the connotation that one does not usually know them personally. A person's grandparents are often dead before he is out of infancy; consequently, he is never acquainted with them and sometimes does not even know their names. It is not inappropriate, then, that the term *mæmu* brackets the Kaluli social field. Anyone removed from the speaker by two generations or more, in effect, tends to drop into the most distant relationship to him.

Within these limits, the terminology (summarized in Figure 3.1) is comparatively uncomplicated. An individual usually addresses his father as *do* but may also use the term *nawa*, which usually applies to his father's brother. Mother and mother's sister are both called *nɔ*. Father's brother's children and mother's sister's children are then classed as brother and sister (*ao* and *ado*). Father's sister (*nao*) and mother's brother (*babo*) are distinguished from parents, and their children are classed as cross-cousins (*nosɔk*). Mother's brother's daughter is in an anomalous position. Before she has children, she is classed, appropriately, as cross-cousin, *nosɔk*. When her children appear, however, unlike the children of other cross-cousins (which are classed as *mæmu*), they are classed as siblings, and mother's brother's daughter is moved up to "mother" (*nɔ*).

Kinship terms, like any other cultural-symbolic system, are a means by which people interpret and arrange social reality. The list of terms itself does not tell us, however, how one uses it to

FIGURE 3.1 Basic Kaluli Kinship Terminology

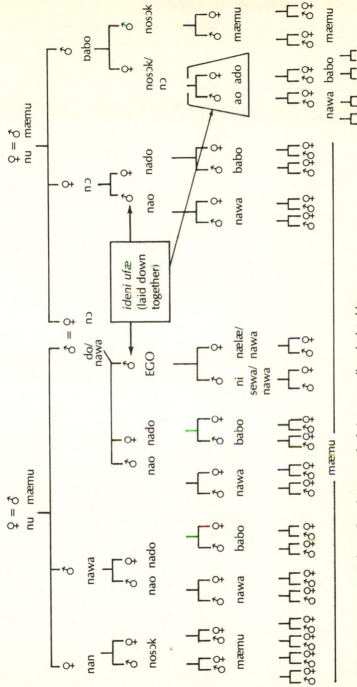

NOTE: Terms are arranged to reflect the range of relatives normally calculated by reference to genealogical connection (except those who are *ideni ufæ*). More distant relatives (that is, descendants of siblings of grandparents) are normally calculated by relative product calculation.

perform the interpretation and hence how one really calculates kinship relationships. For the Kaluli, there is more than one approach to thinking about kinship relationships.

The simplest, but most limited, way is in terms of genealogical relationship. That is, a person traces through his genealogy to see how he is related to someone else. This procedure is limited by the fact that the Kaluli are not great genealogists. As the connotation of grandparent as unknown person might suggest, they often cannot even establish links through people on the second ascending generation. But even if they can, in practice Kaluli do not usually trace links by genealogical reckoning beyond those linked through the parents' siblings. This is because Kaluli prefer to use other means of calculation. They may short-circuit genealogy by a classificatory, or "relative product," type of calculation. That is, rather than deciding to call so-and-so *babo* on the basis of his being FaFaBroSoDaSo, Kaluli simply explain that *babo* means sister's son and that since so-and-so is the son of someone called sister (*ado*), he must be *babo*. Similarly, a man will explain, "I call so-and-so brother [*ao*] because my father called his father brother." The actual genealogical connections of the latter to ego may be known, but just as often they are not—particularly as the geographical and social distance between their longhouse groups increases. In that case, if one presses for genealogical details, informants shrug and say something like, "A long, long time ago our clans [or grandfathers] must have married women from the same place."

The group of kinsmen that one calculates by genealogy are usually those kin of one's own lineage whom one has grown up with, knows best, and maintains the closest relationships with. They are his closest relatives in his own longhouse or (on his mother's side) those through whom he is most closely linked to other longhouse communities.

Within this group, close brothers (FaBroSo and MoSiSo) may pick freely from each other's gardens as do members of the same nuclear family. So may *babo* (MoBro/SiSo). Everyone within this circle, *babo, nao, nosɔk,* and so on, is expected to give and share food and wealth with each other freely with some expectation of future reciprocation, but no formal obligation.

This group of kin, calculated by genealogy, are often said to be *solo dowɔ*, or "together with each other" (particularly those who live in the same longhouse). Other kinsmen are also held to be relatives, but *heb dowɔ*, "to the side," and they make up the bulk of kinsmen known to anthropologists as classificatory. Kaluli who are tracing relationships to these people by relative product calculation most frequently invoke a sibling relationship as the link that explains the application of a term—"I call him brother because my father calls his father brother"; "I call him *babo* because he is my 'sister's' child [or 'mother's' brother]," and so on. This is basic to the way that Kaluli understand human relationships generally. A person will explain why he calls another person in his clan "brother" or "sister" by saying, "We are all Wabisi [or whatever the clan name], after all."

Similarly, he will explain that he was "laid down" (*ufæ*) by his mother's clan and that all people in his generation who were also "laid down" by that clan (that is, whose mothers came from that clan) are his brothers and sisters. This idea of *sharing* matrilateral or patrilateral descent[2] is the essential basis for the notion of siblingship and takes precedence in kin reckoning over the notion of siblingship calculated in other ways. Hence a man will say, "I call him brother because we were laid down together [*ideni ufæ*]" rather than "I call him brother because my mother calls his mother sister." The latter explanation obtains only if his mother's "sister" is of a different clan from his mother, and hence does not "lay down" her child the same. (Cross-cousins are, in effect, the inversion of the sibling situation by this logic. They are those of the same generation as ego who are members of ego's mother's descent group or were "laid down" by his own.)

This way of thinking illuminates the inconsistency in the calculation of relationships that results in the usual terminological switch played on MoBroDa. We recall that prior to her having children, MoBroDa is referred to as *nosɔk*, or cross-cousin, by ego. After she has children, she is called *nɔ*, or mother, by ego, and her chil-

[2] Note that Kaluli here are speaking of mother's line of paternal succession, *not* mother's (and ego's) line of maternal succession. Like mother, MoBroDa is a member of ego's mother's (and MoBro's) patriline, which through its women "lays down" people for other patrilines.

dren addressed as siblings instead of *mæmu* like the children of other cross-cousins. The reason, according to the Kaluli, is that MoBroDa's children, like the children of MoSi, are "laid down" by the same descent group as ego and hence become his siblings. Their mother, therefore, by this logic, must become *nɔ*, or mother, to him.

At this point, it becomes clear that Kaluli ties of sibling relationship are in contradiction to those traced by descent (by genealogical reckoning) and that the *sibling relationship takes precedence over descent* whenever the principles are in conflict.

The result of this way of thinking leaves us with more than merely an interesting solution to a problem of terminology. We are in touch here with a basic way that Kaluli conceive relationships. The underlying logic is the same as that by which two people are established as close friends through sharing food.

We recall that two good friends may express special affection for each other by sharing a meal of meat—thereafter calling each other by the name of the food they have shared. The reciprocal name (*wi aledo*) indicates a special identification between the people who share it. In the same way, if two people share the same patrilateral affiliation or matrilateral affiliation, they are siblings. Moreover, if they are of the same sex, they call each other by a reciprocal name, *ao* (brother) or *ado* (sister), and their children will be siblings.

In Kaluli thinking, the use of a *wi aledo* refers primarily to the reciprocal name used by people who have shared meat. But the tendency to identify two people on the basis of some shared substance or attribute is a general way that Kaluli tend to formulate relationships at all levels. To take one ridiculous example, some men remarked on a patch of ringworm that had sprouted on my leg. I replied that I had probably caught it from my cook, who had been doing my laundry. "Then he is your namesake!" one of them cried, and everyone roared with laughter. I was classed with my cook on the basis of sharing the same ringworm.

This kind of identification is not merely labeled by a shared name but may also be *brought about* by it. To take another case, a visitor from the Namabolo people to the east came to spend some weeks with relatives at a longhouse where I was staying.

He remarked that a man there named Hɔwæ resembled in appearance a man in his own homeland named Fagenabo. Not knowing Hɔwæ well, he took to calling him Fagenabo. The name caught on and soon everyone was referring to Hɔwæ as Fagenabo. Meanwhile, in a nearby longhouse lived another man, also named Hɔwæ, who bore no relationship to the Hɔwæ of the first longhouse other than accidentally bearing the same name. However, it was not long before he too was being called Fagenabo on this basis.

Kaluli most frequently use *wi aledo* to express closeness and affection. Even when not sharing food, people sometimes extend it idiosyncratically in a gush of feeling on some other basis. I once heard two old ladies invoke a shared feature by shrieking, *"Ni seuwayo!"* "My vagina!" in greeting one another at a ceremony. A father will occasionally address his favorite son or daughter as *do* (my father), using the same term to the apple of his eye that the toddler uses to him. The implication of intimacy means that *wi aledo* is never extended between the sexes except as a sweetheart term. Even then one usually hears such things as "my heart" (*ni himu*), "my eye" (*ni si*), and "my forest cabbage" (*ni kiwalo*) only between husbands and wives who have enjoyed longstanding affectionate relations.

Conversely people avoid speaking the name of a common object if the word resembles the taboo name of a close affine. To speak it would be to invite the same calamities as are believed to accompany the speaking of the in-law's name. Using similar logic, a man of my acquaintance named Okaba changed his name to Heani when he overheard a woman in a longhouse cursing a cob of pandanus (*oka*) that she had bungled in preparation. To curse food is a terrible thing, and Okaba changed his name to avoid the possible consequences of the curse falling on himself because his name was the word for the plant.

Men sometimes use a shared name as a basis for asserting rights or making claims over others. When Dowai of clan Dɨdesa was killed as a witch, the men of Dɨdesa, together with their allies, gathered to demand compensation. Among those who went to Dɨdesa's support was a fellow named Hemayo, who was not closely related to either side of the dispute. He claimed a place among those demanding compensation, on the grounds that he happened to have the same name as Dowai's wife's father (long dead) and that, consequently, he had called the wife "daughter" (*nœlœ*), and Dowai "affine" (*eso*). This tenuous claim was accepted, and he received a cowrie shell necklace from the settlement.

People use reciprocal names infrequently when the relationship is an ordinary kinship tie and usually address kinsmen (except *do, babo*) by their personal names. Kaluli use kin terms mainly for formal greetings at ceremonial occasions or when one person wishes to stress his link to another in order to secure a request ("Brother, give me some tobacco"). Reciprocal terms are obligatory, however, in affinal relations, formally established through marriage.

Marriage

Kaluli marriage, as marriage elsewhere in New Guinea, involves the exchanging of a woman for a negotiated payment of wealth. In ordinary circumstances, the exchanging or sharing of wealth does not normally entail the application of a reciprocal name, even though it often has many of the same implications for forming relationships as does the giving and sharing of food. For example, people who are already close sometimes exchange wealth between themselves as an expression of affection—as when friends exchange equivalent pearl shells with each other, or a man gives most of his shell wealth to his sisters and favorite relatives to wear and keep for him.

The affectionate connotations are phrased as concern for the health of the recipient. Every Kaluli wears some sort of necklace or pendant that hangs over the upper part of the chest just below the throat. This is the area of the body torn open invisibly by a witch (*sei*) seeking to take out a victim's heart. Kaluli feel naked and vulnerable when it is not covered. People give their wealth to others to wear because they do not want to see their relatives going about with bare chests and thus likely to get sick.

Aside from this, however, the implications of the transfer of wealth may range from the virtual neutrality of a business transaction (an exchange of an ax for a half-grown pig) to the resolution of serious antagonism between two groups through the payment of compensation for the injury that has set them against each other.

Marriage differs from all these transactions in that the important and enduring set of social ties that it creates are established both through the transfer of wealth and in the woman who is transferred from one kin group to another. It is over the woman, and later her children, that the continuing exchanges of meat and garden labor are carried out between her relatives and her husband for the duration of her life.[3]

The gathering and payment of bridewealth creates more or less formal relationships on both sides of the transaction. On the groom's side, friends and relatives chip in with contributions of axes, pearl shells, cowrie necklaces, and so on, to help him pay. After the marriage transaction is completed, each contributor may address both husband and wife by the reciprocal term *nœsu*. The use of a *wi aledo* is based on the fact that, once the marriage payment has been made, husband and contributor shared in paying bridewealth for the same woman.

Contributor and couple are thenceforth associated in a kinlike relationship in which they may expect hospitality and food from one another as kinsmen normally do. Moreover, the contributor retains a permanent interest in the welfare of the match and its offspring. He will support the husband in the dispute if the woman commits adultery and will join in retaliation on the witch responsible if she should die. If the husband dies, the *nœsu* has a say in the disposition of the children. Finally, he has a right to receive part of the bridewealth of the daughters, equivalent in amount to that he contributed for their mother.

In practice, most *nœsu* will claim hospitality at one time or another, but few will go so far as to speak strongly on such subjects as the disposition of the children after their father's death. Those who are outspoken and who have the most weight in these

---

[3] The preferred marriage arrangement for the Kaluli is between a man and woman who are of different clans and stand as *mæmu* to each other. The closest permissible marriage is between ego and FaFaSiDaDaDa, but there is no preference for this relative or any other particular *mæmu*—such as there is among the Etoro in the northern part of the plateau (Kelly, 1973).

affairs are usually those who are the closest friends or relatives of the husband and/or who contributed most heavily to his bride-wealth. Occasionally, a man of strong personality may use a *nœsu* relation based on a minor contribution as an avenue for major support of or claims on the husband if he feels his interest may be served by it.

The payment of bridewealth secures a woman to a man as his wife and hence places him in relationship, across the marriage bond, with her relatives. In part, it compensates her relatives for the loss of her contribution to their household economy, for the food and attention they gave her in bringing her up, for the loss of a daughter in their affections. The biggest items of bridewealth —axes, pearl shells—go to those people who nurtured her (her father, mother, and mother's brother). In the case of an elopement, the young man can take much of the heat off the situation by paying off this set of relatives.

A girl's unmarried brothers particularly stand to lose when their sister gets married because she performs many of the sago-beating and pig-keeping tasks for their domestic subsistence that would normally be performed by a wife. To adequately compen-sate for this, the Kaluli feel a man should provide a wife to replace the woman he takes in marriage. In principle, he should provide his own sister. Marriage by sister exchange does not occur very often, but the Kaluli make every effort to arrange it or the bridewealth demanded is higher.

In compensating a woman's relatives for her loss, the payment of bridewealth buys off their rights in her and places her in the custody of her husband. If she should later run away from him, her relatives will receive her at their longhouse but must give her up when her husband comes to claim her.

The relationship between a man and his wife's relatives con-tinues until he or she dies. If the woman dies, it continues, though somewhat more diffusely, between husband and in-laws through her children, who were "laid down" by her clan.

Payment of bridewealth also helps to define which of a woman's relatives will be counted by her husband as in-laws. After the bridewealth has been made, all of his wife's close relatives, and those of her more distant classificatory ones *who received part of the bridewealth,* become name-taboo in-laws. The husband and they must never speak each other's names. They may address or refer to each other *only* by reciprocal in-law terms,[4] lest harm come to the man's wife or to their children. The relationship among in-laws is supposed to be close and affectionate, but it begins in an atmosphere of formality, restraint, and mutual obligation. Though it is likely that a man would go to the support of his in-laws against men of his own lineage in a dispute, he would never share food with them. He gives it to them, and they, in return, give it formally to him. Here the implications of social distance contained in the manner of providing food undercut those of identification contained in the *wi aledo* reciprocal in-law terminology to express neatly the balance of closeness and restraint in the in-law relationship.

Affinal Exchange of Food

Once the bridewealth payments have been made, the marriage becomes the basis for an extended series of periodic visits, exchanges of garden labor, and prestations of meat between the husband and his wife's relatives, which lasts until the children of the match are well grown.

The husband initiates prestations when he begins having sexual relations with his new wife. This may not occur for as long as a month or two after the marriage, particularly if it was arranged by relatives. If the bride and groom have never seen each other before the wedding day, they are shy in each other's presence. There is a period of grace for several weeks after the marriage in which they live separately in the men's and women's sections of the longhouse, becoming accustomed to each other from a distance.

Eventually, the wife cooks some food and gives it to her husband over the partition and touches his hand. A day or so later, the husband takes his sago-pulverizing tool (*udɔ*) and marches out of the

---

[4] In-laws refer to each other by the term "my in-law," *ni eso* (between husband and wife's parents' generation relatives) or *nabas* (between husband and wife's real and classificatory brother and sister).

house saying, "I am going." His wife follows him to a secluded sago camp where they make sago together for the first time and begin sexual relations. If all goes well, the husband spends his free time in the forest hunting small animals for his in-laws. When he has smoked eighteen or twenty animals, he goes to his wife's longhouse to present them to his brother-in-law or father-in-law. This prestation is known as *ga læsu* (literally "little wife" or "little woman"). The woman's relatives reciprocate with a present of an equal number of smoked animals at a later date, a gift called *ga sigi*.

These periodic exchanges of meat are supposed to be carried out between a man and his wife's true brother—or her father. In practice this happens fairly often, but these affinal relationships are open to considerable manipulation by the groom and various other people to whom he is related by marriage. Other people, who are distantly related to the wife but who wish to develop their relationship with her husband, enter into the exchanges of meat with him in addition to—or instead of—her brothers or father. These people are usually in-laws by virtue of having accepted a piece of the bridewealth and now wish to capitalize on the relationship. As a result, both sets of in-laws may develop a wider and more complex network of affinal relationships than would otherwise be possible. The multiplication of ties between longhouses is based in this respect not so much on the marriage itself (although Kaluli phrase it that way) as on the exchanges of food that are carried out over a marriage.

This development of marriage ties through exchange relationships is clearly visible in one collective prestation (discussed in Chapter 4) in which eight gifts of meat were made in relation to six marriages. Of these, two gifts were made between the husband and the true brothers of the woman, three gifts between husband and wife's distant classificatory brothers, and one each between husband and wife's mother's brother, wife's mother's new husband, and wife's cross-cousin. Finally, there was one gift transferred over a complicated arrangement whereby the husband of the donor's half-sister had adopted the exchange obligations of the donor's wife's parents so that he and the donor could act as if they had married by sister exchange.

The marriage tie may be viewed, in effect, as providing the enabling conditions (in the form of the necessary social categories and obligations) for undertaking affinal exchange. Of the reasonably extensive range of affines whom a man must call *eso* (in-law), it is mainly with those with whom he exchanges prestations that he has a substantially close personal and supportive relationship and on whom he can most surely rely.

Food and the Manipulation of Social Relationships

The manipulation of emphasis among social relations through the exchange of prestations of food is not confined to affinal relationships but also may be extended to kinsmen in other longhouses. The giving or sharing of food represents the general mode of establishing or adjusting relationships among all people—friends and kinsmen. Though kinsmen have a general obligation to assist one another in garden labor, fights, bridewealth collection, and so on, a general obligation does not make a binding one. Outside the immediate circle of one's brothers, connections of kinship by themselves are not a sufficient basis on which appeals for assistance or support are automatically honored in a simple way.

Each individual must develop his own network of close associations with those kinsmen (especially in other longhouses) on whom he wants to be able to rely. These relationships are actualized through mutual visiting, help in gardening, bridewealth contributions, invitations to hunt and fish, and the like—but always fundamentally, in the Kaluli view, by giving and sharing of food. In this way classificatory relatives in distant longhouses may be emphasized over geographically nearer or genealogically closer relatives, age-mates over true brothers, one cross-cousin over another, wife's father over father's brother, and so on.

The giving and sharing of food does not merely express a social relationship; it validates and develops it. Kinship connections may be viewed as avenues of potential personal relationships—always open, perhaps, but not necessarily actualized. It is through giving and sharing food that the relationship becomes socially real.

If relations of kinship are realized through the passage of food, then those who offer food to one another become eventually like kinsmen. In one case, Seyaka, a boy of eleven, told me he picked some tomatoes from a garden belonging to his older "brother," Degera. I knew that one could not take from someone's garden without asking unless he were a true sibling or a close classificatory one. Degera, by the closest genealogical reckoning, was a distant classificatory father's brother to Seyaka. Seyaka explained that, since his own mother had died and his father had married another woman, Degera's mother, Wayabi, an elderly widow, gave him his food. Therefore, he asserted, he called her "mother," and Degera, by the same reckoning, was his brother. He pointed out that his true brother, Dægæli, got his food from another woman and, hence, did not hold as close a relation to Degera and could not pick freely from his gardens.

A person's mother is thought of less as the person who brought him into the world and more as a person who gives him food. Thus, a woman who feeds a child comes to be thought of as his mother after a time, and her children as his siblings. This becomes particularly apparent when the child gets married. Claims for a piece of the bridewealth are in part based on the contribution a person made to "giving the child food." After marriage, an avoidance relation is observed between a man and his wife's mother. If for some reason the girl was brought up principally by some woman other than her mother, it will be that woman to whom the avoidance is extended, even if the real mother is alive and present in the same longhouse community. In cases like this, "feeding" amounts approximately to adoption.

Food Taboos

Kaluli see food as the appropriate medium for shaping social relationships and communicating personal sentiment because it is the basis of all human life. Food is closely bound up with conceptions of birth and death, personal strength, sexuality, illness, and the unseen. The kinds of food a person can eat are restricted, or tabooed, in connection with these things over a wide range of circumstances.

Some foods are restricted because of the supernaturally dangerous nature of the area in which they are found. Fish taken from the Isawa River can be eaten only by healthy adult men belonging to groups living along its banks, but not by their women, small children, or people from other places. The river, along with a few other places in the Bosavi area, is known to be *hungɔ* (roughly "dangerous with supernatural force"). Others who eat of it will die of a wasting sickness.

Similarly, food restrictions are associated with mourning, illness, pregnancy, and care of infants. In pregnancy a woman avoids eating pumpkins, papayas, and eggs (including crayfish eggs) lest her belly get too large or the child become potbellied and not develop properly. Food restrictions also may protect resources. One avoids eating breadfruit together with *okari* nuts for a season lest the breadfruit trees cease bearing. One avoids eating sago with cucumbers lest the sago trees fail to grow.

Other restrictions are connected to subsistence activities. People making a garden must avoid eating cassowary or the eggs of megapodes and crocodiles, for a brief period before, during, and after the planting lest the garden be unproductive.

The man who catalyzes the growing process by magically calling the garden spirits must observe these taboos the longest as well as a number of additional ones. For gardening, food taboos are only part of a wider set of restrictions on the activities of the garden makers, who may not have sexual intercourse or visit other longhouses until the trees over the garden are cut. In addition, everyone avoids entering the garden for a day or two if he has eaten pork (lest pigs ravage the crops) or if a woman in the longhouse is having her period.

These examples are by no means exhaustive, but the miscellaneous and complicated character of the system should already be apparent. The consequences of breaking these taboos does not involve any kind of pollution. Rather, the Kaluli invariably explain that a person who eats or does the wrong thing will develop a cough or become emaciated, his wife or children will waste away and die, his hunting will be fruitless, or pigs will devour his garden.

The ideas underlying this situation are simple. Bosavi people practice these taboos because food mediates not only different social relationships but also different domains of experience. Pumpkins and pawpaws bring swollen, bulbous shapes together with bad pregnancies and stunted children. Fish from the Isawa River mark the distinction between those who are traditional residents of the *hungɔ* area and those who are not. Animals forbidden to those in mourning are forms often taken by the spirits of the dead, while animals forbidden to the garden magician are those whose forms are taken by the garden spirits he appeals to. Similarly, to enter a garden with a stomach full of pork is tantamount to letting a pig inside the fence.

Bananas, pandanus, and other garden products are tabooed under certain circumstances, but the most conspicuous, burdensome, and longest lasting taboos on food apply to meat. Taboos on meat follow the Kaluli in one way or another virtually all the days of their lives. From the time a person is a toddler until he is about twelve years old, he can eat any kind of fresh meat except for a small group of birds and snakes known as *nɔ mal*, which are felt to be "too strong" for him. When a girl has her first menses, however, she must give all this up and, except for cassowary and domestic pig, may eat only meat that is smoked and dry. Boys, on the other hand, at about the age of twelve, abandon even the *nɔ mal* taboos and, if not enduring mourning restrictions due to the death of a parent, may eat whatever they please. These days of good eating are over, however, when a young man gets married. Thereafter, he must give up all fresh meat and, like his wife, eat only smoked. If he does not, his wife or children will die. This situation continues until the children of the match are well grown and a man is into advanced middle age. At that point, he may begin to gradually relinquish his taboos until, when he is old and his wife reaches menopause, the two of them may abandon nearly all their residual restrictions and eat fresh meat as they did when they were young.

Kaluli men often speak of this situation with an air of resigned family responsibility as one of the burdens associated with age, marital status, parenthood, and the like. However, this refers to the personal consequences of the restriction, not the reason for it.

Women cannot eat fresh meat, the Kaluli point out, because the juices (*nɔ hɔn*, literally "animal water") running down her throat would cause a phlegmy chest cough and make her ill. Smoked meat, on the other hand, has no juice and is safe. The reasoning is exactly that which we have already discussed for taboos—which often gives them a sort of folk-medicinal quality. If one is suffering from a stomach ache (*kuf hɔn*, stomach water) or diarrhea (*idɔ hɔn*, shit water), he should not eat watermelon, pawpaws, ripe bananas, or New Guinea cabbage because they contain a lot of water and will only aggravate the condition. Women are permanently in this sort of sickly (or runny) state since they menstruate. In fact, when in their period, they are forbidden even the few fresh meats they *can* eat along with ripe (juicy) bananas, red pandanus (associated with the myth of first menstruation), and certain forest fruits of blood-red color. If women eat these foods, it is feared that their menstrual flow will drastically increase and they will be likely to bleed to death.

Even worse, rather than the food affecting the menstrual debility, the menstrual debility can infect the foods. If a menstruating woman eats a fresh animal caught in a trap, future traps will not fall; if the animal was caught with a dog, the dog will lose his ability to find a scent. Similarly, bananas and pandanus, if eaten by a menstruating woman, will cease to bear. Other people in the longhouse avoid going to their gardens if they hear that a woman has come into her period, and the woman herself must leave the longhouse and move to a shack some distance away for the duration. If she should cook or step over food, those who eat it, particularly her husband, will become ill with a cough and possibly die.

Menstruating or not, women are considered weakened people, and prolonged intimate contact with them or their things is detrimental to men's health and stamina. This is the primary reason why the women sleep separately from the men in the longhouse. It is also the reason why, when a man marries and comes into close sexual contact with a woman, he must, in effect, take up her taboos and eat only smoked meat.

The taking up or releasing of taboos is not associated with any particular ritual observance. Taboos are usually dropped on the initiative of the individual himself when he feels the time is appropriate. The relinquishing of a number of prohibitions is undertaken gradually—some prohibitions being given up first and others following in a conventional order over an extended period, usually a few years. If a man marries a second wife after relinquishing his taboos, they must be taken up again and they must also be resumed for each child if dropped in between. If a man marries a widow, he must assume, in addition, her mourning restrictions. The social and cultural consequences of this fairly simple set of ideas and practices in Kaluli life is profound.

Most Kaluli associate the meat taboos with various stages in the life cycle and regard them as a burden. However, it is not the deprivation that food restrictions represent to the individual that is of interest but the bearing they have on social relations. If a certain food is tabooed to one man and not to another, they cannot share it. Neither can one receive it as a gift from the other.[5] It is difficult to give an adequate impression of the impact this has on social relations.

On the individual level, the effect is most visible in the plight of a young man at the time of his marriage. Youth is a time of independence, a time when close friendships are formed between young men. Teenagers hunt, fish, and hang around together in informal groups of brothers and cross-cousins between longhouse communities. They hunt animals and share them among themselves. It is around these meals and their mutual activities that close friendships develop. This kind of experience had its highest expression (prior to foreign contact) in the *bau aa* ceremonial lodge, where youths and boys of several longhouses would live together for over a year, spending most of their time hunting.

When a young man marries, his concerns tend to be gradually removed from his circle of close associates as life as a husband and father orients his duties toward his wife and in-laws. But the imposition of taboos against almost every kind of fresh meat brings this situation home dramatically by preventing him from sharing with his age-mates what was formerly one of their most intimate

---

[5] Kaluli are to some degree aware of this situation and occasionally may turn it to their own advantage. While my wife was making popcorn one day in the cookhouse, a group of small children gathered to watch. Our cook, Gigio, a boy of about thirteen, was stuffing as much popcorn into his mouth as he could, and the children asked for some. Gigio, not wishing to share it, said, "Hey, you are too small. If you eat this, you will burst." As the popcorn popped in the pan he added, "There! There! Do you see that?" The children were obviously put off.

experiences. The newlywed sits by the cooking fire eating sago and greens while his buddies cut up a tasty marsupial. For people who relish meat the way the Kaluli do, this is a paradigm of social isolation. The next time his friends are likely to eat without him out of consideration for his hungry discomfort. Friendships do not cease in this way, but they are rendered awkward and difficult in some of their most important contexts because an important mutual interest has been removed.

The discussion may be summarized by reference to the restrictions placed on bandicoot (*mahi*) over the duration of a person's life. Kaluli nearly always mention *mahi* first when speaking of forest animals or game that is particularly good to eat. One quickly gets the impression that this particularly meaty and delicious little marsupial in some way typifies for them all forest game. Not only is it more available than other kinds of animals in the Kaluli area, but in terms of tenderness and flavor it is so much superior to other forest animals that it stands in a class by itself. One is tempted to believe that it is for this reason that *mahi*, while nearly always tabooed along with other forest game at appropriate times, is also the one animal permitted again relatively quickly.

In any case, the fact that restrictions on *mahi* are given up more quickly than taboos on other forest game allows its systematic effect on social relations to emerge the more clearly (Figure 3.2). The juiciness of *mahi* meat in relation to menstruation is the explicit issue. Hence, the major line drawn by restrictions on *mahi* falls between those who do not menstruate and those who do menstruate or who are closely associated with those who do. In this way, they avoid passing the debility to which they are exposed on to others who have not been exposed to it. However, women who no longer menstruate, or men who are no longer married, form an intermediate group that may share with both, though not both at the same time.

With respect to solidarity established through *mahi* sharing, youths and unmarried men form one group, middle-aged established married men form another, while newly married men and fathers of small children are isolated from both and from each other.

Since fresh meat is the mediator of the passage of the debility

FIGURE 3.2   Social Consequences of Taboo on *Mahi* (Bandicoot)

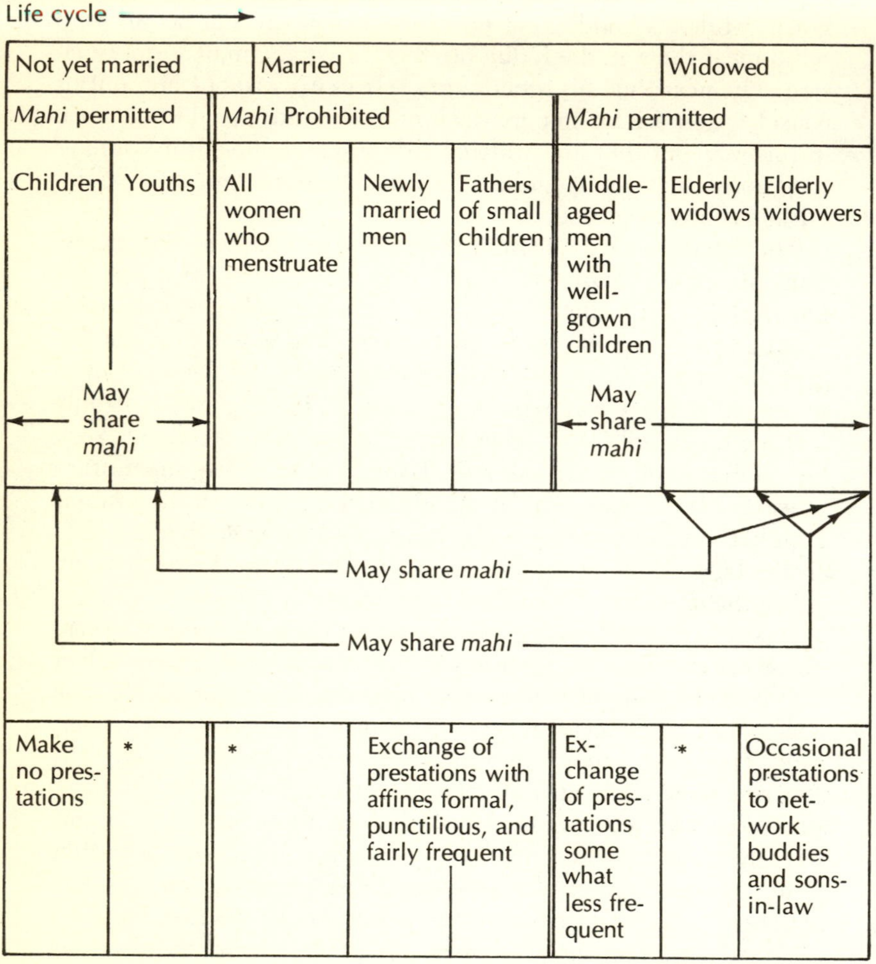

Life cycle ───────────▶

Not yet married		Married				Widowed	
Mahi permitted		*Mahi* Prohibited			*Mahi* permitted		
Children	Youths	All women who menstruate	Newly married men	Fathers of small children	Middle-aged men with well-grown children	Elderly widows	Elderly widowers
	May ◀── share ──▶ *mahi*				May ◀─share─ *mahi* ──────────────▶		
			── May share *mahi* ──				
		────────────── May share *mahi* ──────────────					
Make no pres- tations	*	*	Exchange of prestations with affines formal, punctilious, and fairly frequent	Ex- change of pres- tations some what less fre- quent	*		Occasional prestations to net- work buddies and sons- in-law

*Youths, middle-aged married women, and elderly but spry widows occasionally make prestations to relatives and friends on their own behalf, if they own a pig or are willing to trap their own game. (See Hɔidɔ's prestation to Yɔwa and Kiliyæ in Chapter 4.)

implicit in the menstruation of women, the result is the inhibition of the passage of fresh meat between those who are associated with menstruation in some direct way and those who are not.

The primary impact of these food restrictions among men is to inhibit relationships between newly married men and their kinsmen and age-mates within the same longhouse community. At the same time, they encourage pursuit of certain relationships outside it—namely, with affines. One never smokes meat for himself but only as a gift for someone else. The major source of smoked meat for the married couple is that presented to them periodically by the relatives of the bride in return for similar prestations of smoked meat made to them by the groom. Hence, if the married couple is to eat any forest game at all, it is only by making gifts of smoked meat to the wife's relatives. These mutual gifts at the same time develop the relationship between the particular affines involved. From a situation in which fresh meat may be shared with kinsmen, one moves to a situation where smoked meat is reciprocally exchanged with affines. This shift in food orientation not only parallels the shift in social orientation but at the same time contributes to effecting it.

Summary

At this point we may summarize our discussion of food, reciprocity, and affection in Kaluli relationships. Hospitality, giving and sharing of food, establishes personal closeness between individuals. If food is shared, the relationship may be marked by the extension of a *wi aledo* reciprocal name. Taboos on food operate by the same notions in reverse: while food is given or shared to establish relationships, it is prohibited in order to prevent relationships between cultural domains that must not be mixed. Women, weakened through menstruation, must not eat fresh meat. Those married to women and exposed to their weakening influence must also give up fresh meat, inhibiting their relationships with others. Smoked meat is allowed but available only through affinal exchange. Affinal exchange is thus encouraged, and, along with the gifts of food, close personal relations form.

Food is the mediator between male and female, sickness and

health, social relationships, and cultural domains. It is by managing food that the Kaluli adjust their relationships in regard to these things. The point is partly epistemological: in effect, food is not only good to eat, but, as Lévi-Strauss has remarked, good to think. It doesn't only mediate social relationships; it comes to stand for them as well. To be hungry, therefore, implies more than merely a condition of physical need. It also implies isolation from companionship.

Chapter 4

Organizing Actions: Those at the House and Those Who Came

Kaluli may gather with relatives and friends to eat and converse around a firebox in the big *aa misen*, but there are usually other people around and the atmosphere lacks the relaxed informality that prevails in a small sago camp or garden house. These places— the small *aa* built by one or two men for their families at a garden some distance from the *aa misen* or the temporary shelter near sago-working—provide a person's most intimate social contexts. People look back on the months or weeks spent working there with nostalgia long after the sago has been cut and the garden is in weeds.

Formation of Cooperative Groups

These small groups of people are formed around mutual coopera- tion in the production of food. The minimal unit of domestic economy is the "household"—typically, a man, his wife (or wives) and dependent children, plus unmarried brothers and sisters or a widowed mother. Alternatively, an unmarried young man may head up a household with his widowed mother and younger sib- lings. Kaluli like to work together, and usually a person who plans to work a sago palm will invite one or more other people and their families to join him.

The short-term groups formed for sago making are not based on any specific kinship groupings; they are simply recruited from those in the community whom an individual wishes to invite at a given time and who wish to join him. Affines or matrilateral relatives of the sago owner may be occasionally invited from other longhouses.

For the job of processing, the trunk of a sago palm is usually divided into sections about seven feet long, each of which takes two people three days to work. Two families take a leisurely two weeks living and working together at a sago camp to process a good-sized palm (though an entire longhouse community, barricaded in their *aa* in the expectation of an attack, could finish off the same tree by torchlight in a single night). It is the man's job to cut the palm, divide and split the trunk, and pulverize the pith. The lengthy, back-breaking job of beating and leaching the edible starch out of it is given to the women. Hence the only major consideration for a man recruiting a sago-working group is to ensure that it includes some women. An unmarried man or a widower will recruit his mother or sisters or invite a friend with a wife to help with his palm.

Assistance in sago making or any other cooperative subsistence task is extended partly in the expectation of a share in the fruits of the labor. Usually, the owner of the palm keeps out one or two bags of fresh sago for immediate consumption, gives one to each of the families that has assisted him, and buries the rest in the mud of a stream to store for future use. Similarly, anyone who joins an organized fishing expedition, whether or not he owns the fish dam or that section of river, gets to keep whatever he catches. People do not share the labor if they do not expect to get some of the proceeds of it.

Garden making requires the heaviest short-term outlay of labor of any subsistence task. Gardens for sweet potatoes and root crops, which are usually planted on the level areas on top of ridges (and are not more than half an acre to an acre in size), must be cleared of trees and fenced against pigs before they can be planted. Bananas, breadfruit, and pandanus are planted on the slopes down the sides of a ridge. Men first clear the underbrush from beneath the canopy and plant the shoots with a digging stick. Then, after four or five days, groups of men fell the canopy on top of the crop. The plants find their way up between the tangled wreckage of fallen trunks and grow normally. (For a more detailed account of this swidden technique, see Schieffelin, 1975.) These gardens may be of impressive size. Ivan Champion, in 1938, at a time when steel was rare in Bosavi,[1] reported an area of new and abandoned gardens that he estimated at two hundred acres (Champion, 1938, p. 200). My own impression is that the largest gardens today do not exceed forty acres. The group that works an area of this size is generally made up of most of the members of a longhouse community. Communal gardening has the advantages of opening a large area of sunlight to the crops and of accommodating a work force large enough to defend itself against a raid.

Whether the garden is to be a large one serving most of a longhouse community or a small one serving one or two families, the owner of the land invites the others to plant there with him and allots each family a plot in the area to use for the duration of the garden. However, though the garden is built jointly, once the planting holes are dug and the trees felled, the rest of the work of caring for the crops is performed by individual gardeners working only on their own plots. For the spurts of heavy work, such as tree felling, a substantially larger labor force is needed. Kaluli gardeners do not rely on relatives in their own community who are not working the same garden but call in in-laws and sister's sons from other communities while their own able-bodied lineage brothers sit on the veranda of the *aa* weaving armbands. "I will not eat from that garden," one such man explained to me, "so I don't cut the trees. But those people's in-laws are helping them because they will get food from it when they come to visit."

The way sago- and garden-making activities are organized suggests that cooperation and mutual support are not based primarily on internal solidarity of the longhouse community or the lineages of which it is composed. This becomes even more apparent when people in two different longhouses become involved in a dispute. As the issue becomes more heated, members of lineages and longhouse communities, far from falling into line with one another,

[1] The steel ax was initially preferred because it did not have to be sharpened as often as stone and, in general, stayed hafted better. Men complained that in the old days they would come to cut a garden site carrying several newly sharpened, polished stone adz blades in a net bag.

split to support different sides, while other members of the communities remain neutral.

Although a house group sometimes appears to act as a group (particularly for prestations), neither it nor the lineages of which it is composed are corporate units of Kaluli society, whether for ownership of land, cooperation in subsistence tasks, or even for fighting. Membership in a community, or lineage, is only one factor in enlisting support for one's projects. What are important are close individual ties.

For a young man, the people on whom he can most rely in his own longhouse before he is married are his own unmarried brothers and age-mates and, to a lesser extent, his father and his father's brothers. Outside his longhouse community, his most dependable ties are with his close matrilateral relatives—his mother's brothers, cross-cousins, and those matrilateral "brothers" (mother's sister's sons) "laid down" in the same way that he is. A young man usually forms close friendships with these people.

When he marries, however, these matrilateral relationships (and also those with his own lineage "brothers") become overshadowed by his affinal ones, which usually stretch to different longhouse communities and involve more extensive, obligatory prestations. Moreover, when his sisters, and later his daughters, marry, he becomes involved in exchanges with their husbands and is mother's brother or grandfather to their children. This way, without going beyond these immediate matrilateral and affinal ties, a person may involve himself in friendship and prestation relationships with people in six other longhouses. If he chooses to develop relationships with more distant kinsmen and affines, the range can be much wider.

Formation of Groups in Opposition

Kaluli recruit people and organize groups for basically two purposes: to participate mutually in some task or enterprise (usually involved with subsistence or trade) or to oppose another group. Oppositions between groups are formed over some temporary issue between them and, at least for weddings and prestations, do not necessarily imply hostility. But it is the situation of conflict be-

Dispute over bridewealth. Kabano aa, March 1967. (Photo by B. Schieffelin.)

tween people in different longhouse communities that best reveals the way Kaluli must sort out their relationships and loyalties within and between their communities. When conflict arises, each individual must decide for himself, on the basis of his own particular relationships to the principal protagonists in the issue, the side that he will stand with and how active a part he will play. The decision may be complicated because a man's ties with his in-laws or close matrilateral kin (though not to their communities as a whole) override the significance of all but his closest relatives in his own longhouse. In addition, resentment over old grievances and injuries, long settled (at least formally), may play a part in affecting how a man will act.

Opposition in Conflict: The Scenario of Retaliation

Kaluli conflicts usually arise over stolen wealth, women (adultery, bride payments, and so on), or death. By far the most serious is death. Every death is caused by a witch (*sei*). A *sei* attacks his victim invisibly, but a man who is very sick is sometimes able to perceive him while in the liminal consciousness of high fever. If the patient thinks he is going to die, he will whisper to his close kin the identity of the person he thinks he sees. When a person dies, he has in effect been murdered. If he was a beloved or important person, his kinsmen are furious, and in response, traditionally, they would organize a raid to kill the *sei*.

The Kaluli recognized a standard scenario for this kind of retaliation. Though retaliatory raiding had stopped by 1966, the details were still clear in people's minds. Not everyone from the *aa* of the dead person participated. Some who had close ties with the *sei* or relatives at his *aa* were not told about the raid at all. Others knew about it but remained neutral. The force was then drawn from those who were particularly angry about the death and wished revenge or who felt sorry for the grief of their kinsmen. Finally, there were usually youths and young men who were unconcerned with the issue but wanted some excitement. Often more than half of the supporters were recruited from other *aas*. When the forces were ready, two men were sent to spend the night at the house of the *sei*, ostensibly on some legitimate errand, to ensure that he didn't escape. During the night the attacking force surrounded the *aa* and at dawn rushed in and killed the *sei* by smashing his skull with a stone-headed club. They then dragged the body out the door and retreated to the forest edge.

Fighting inside the *aa* was done at close quarters with clubs. Outside, the attackers tried to contain the defenders with bows and arrows. Those in the house were greatly outnumbered by the surrounding force and rarely came down off the veranda to the ground.

Meanwhile, the body of the *sei* was cut open and his heart removed and examined. The heart of a *sei* was supposed to be a yellow color and soft to the touch, while that of a regular man was dark and firm. If the heart was pale and soft, those who cut it out held it high and yelled: "Give it up! Lo! This is a *sei!*" The fighting was then suspended as a man from the *aa* who was not closely associated with the victim came down to examine the heart for the defenders. If he agreed, the defenders broke off fighting but announced that they would demand compensation. The attackers then left. On their way through the forest, they cut up the body of the murdered man, discarding genitals and viscera, and the leaders of the raid distributed the meat to their supporters from other longhouses. (They did not eat the body themselves lest another *sei*, angry at his brother *sei's* death, retaliate by making another man in their community sicken and die.) The heart of the dead *sei* was kept aside, and when the leaders of the raid returned home they fastened it to a pointed stake that was planted in front of the *aa* near the exposure coffin of the *sei's* victim. Then they barricaded themselves in the longhouse to await the arrival of the *sei's* relatives.

On an appointed day, the relatives of the murdered man and their supporters arrived to view the heart; this way they could see for themselves that the man was really a *sei*. They agreed to settle without killing someone in return and named the compensation they would settle for. The largest items of wealth, pearl shells and axes, were demanded by the closest relatives of the murdered man and, if possible, paid on the spot to take the heat off the situation. The wealth items were either handed out to the recipients through a small hole cut in the side of the *aa* or brought down to them by a neutral inhabitant who did not participate in the raid. Other supporters then named their demands house group by house group, and those barricaded in the *aa* got the payment together in the next week or so. When the payments were all made, the closest relatives of the murdered man stayed the night at the house of those who killed him and shared food. Later, they returned the hospitality to the killers in a show of mutual trust and good will.

Actual raids and killings did follow this scenario in a general way but were quite complex or even idiosyncratic in the details of their organization. Since retaliation against *seis* had been ended by the time I got to Bosavi, I was not able to collect an account of any single raid with an exhaustive list of those who had participated along with their motivations and relationships. Nevertheless, for most raids, the principal figures stood out clearly in people's memories. The following case, described to me by four of the major participants, will serve for analysis.

In Revenge: Wanalugo Kills Hagabulu

About 1954, when the *aa* of clan Bonɔ was at a place called Dubia, Wanalugo married a woman named Gisa, of clan Walisɔ at Wabimisæn. In the course of events, Gisa's mother, Fali, called Wanalugo and his wife to come to Wabimisæn to help plant bananas. While they were there, Gisa got sick. They tried to hide her from further attacks of the *sei* by taking her secretly to a place by the mouth of the Wano River, but he found her anyway and she died. They hung her body on a pole and brought it back to Dubia for the funeral. The body was hung in the *aa* to be viewed, and though most of Gisa's relatives could not be located, friends of Wanalugo in other longhouses came to the funeral one longhouse at a time.

In the meantime, sickness was prevalent in the area and other people were dying. A woman named Healu, the wife of Kiliyæ of the nearby *aa* of Wabisi at Doba, had died while on a fishing trip with her husband. She named Sidawɔ of Wasu as the *sei* responsible, and when Sidawɔ, ignorant of this, came to the funeral, he was murdered as he walked in the door. Wanalugo thought to himself, "My wife died also. Why shouldn't I kill too?" After discussing this idea with his friends at the funeral, who gave him angry encouragement, he determined to kill the *sei* responsible for Gisa's death.

When she was dying, Gisa had told her mother that the *sei* was one Hagabulu, of the branch of Wabisi staying at Heyabisi. Unhappily, Hagabulu happened to be Wanalugo's close classificatory mother's brother. It is an extraordinary and horrible thing to kill as close a relative as one's mother's brother, but Wanalugo was very angry and would not be dissuaded. While his friends waited at the funeral, he went to scout around the house where Hagabulu lived. In the area, he met Ola and Hæmindæ, two men of other clans who lived in the same *aa* as Hagabulu. Ola saw that Wanalugo was up to something and asked him what it was. Wanalugo said that he was looking for Hagabulu to kill him. Ola said, "Good. He is in the *aa*. I won't tell him. You kill him." Ola was not unhappy to see Hagabulu killed, since Hagabulu had killed his classificatory brother Edi for being a *sei* some time before. (The incident had been settled with compensation.) Hæmindæ also kept quiet.

When Wanalugo returned to Dubia, his friends set out to round up support from among their connections in the various surrounding longhouse communities. Wanalugo asked Bugamia and Meyɔ from Malosonɔ to visit Hagabulu's house to admit the attacking party and prevent his escape. The attacking forces gathered after dark in the forest. Up to this point, Wanalugo had told only a few trusted people whom they were going to kill for fear word would get out and Hagabulu escape.

The party, which may have numbered as many as thirty-five, then proceeded to Hagabulu's *aa* and surrounded it at dawn. At a signal from Wanalugo, Meyɔ opened the door, and the raiding party rushed in. Bugamia grabbed Hagabulu and Wanalugo swung at him with an ax. Hagabulu, an experienced older man, reacted quickly, even though he had just been awakened, and Wanalugo only hit him a glancing blow. In the next instant, Hagabulu dived over the partition into the women's section, dragging Bugamia with him. Wanalugo followed immediately and swung again, this time killing him.

Amid the shouting, stamping press of angry men and terrifying confusion in the dark, a few other people were hurt. Those who had been warned of the raid made a lot of noise and waved clubs and axes but did not really fight. However, Ilibesi, Hagabulu's brother, struck down Gurambo, one of the raiders, with a club in retaliation for his brother. But before he could kill him, Ilibesi was knocked unconscious in return by Meyɔ with an ax. Gurambo was able to escape from the house with a six-inch scalp wound. Hæmindæ, who had known the raid was coming, fled out the back door, but he was shot with an arrow in the buttock by Seli, a bold youth of about fourteen, who had stationed himself underneath the *aa*. Retreating back inside, Hæmindæ retaliated by shooting another Bonɔ youth in the arm.

Hagabulu's body was by this time thrown off the veranda, and the raiding party retreated to the edges of the garden surrounding the house to shoot at the *aa* with bows. It was fairly dark, and people could not see very well to shoot. However, as it rapidly got brighter, a man who was not closely related to either side shouted, "Leave it off. It is getting bright. Leave it off." By now, someone had torn out Hagabulu's heart and called to the others that he was indeed a *sei*. Tiago, one of the men in the *aa* who had been warned by Ola of the impending raid, came out and examined the heart to confirm. Those of the *aa* then declared they were unwilling to fight any longer, and the raiding party departed for home, dividing up Hagabulu's body on the way.

Back at Dubia, the people set the heart up on the stake and barricaded themselves in their house to await developments. Meanwhile, the sickness in the area continued. Within four days a Bonɔ youth who had been ill died, and the Dubia people, regarding this as the work of another *sei* taking retribution for his "brother *sei's*" death, were once again fighting mad. Learning of their anger, Hagabulu's supporters did not show up to ask for compensation. Shortly afterward two other people died, and there was no intercourse between Bonɔ and the people of Heyabisi for over a year.

Finally, Mage, a Bonɔ woman married to one of Hagabulu's brothers, arrived by herself at Bonɔ one day with her two children, saying that she was tired of not seeing her relatives. Moved by sentiment, the people of Bonɔ collected several wealth items and gave them to Mage to distribute, on her return to Heyabisi, to those people who were most closely related or most upset about Hagabulu's death. She did so, and Bonɔ and Heyabisi resumed friendly relations. Shortly afterward the branch of clan Didesa at the Heyabisi longhouse community offered a woman in marriage to Mei, Wanalugo's brother, who had not participated in the raid. This was regarded as cementing the peace.

In organizing this raid, Wanalugo obtained his principal support from his friend Meyɔ of the Malosonɔ community, to whom he later married his sister. The members of his own house group were divided. His own father and brother refused to join him in killing their relative, although they did not warn Hagabulu and remained neutral. Others were unavailable because they had gone to support another longhouse against an expected attack, were ill at the time, or had affiliations at Heyabisi that they did not wish to jeopardize. Some remained neutral because they were "unwilling or afraid" to go. Of those who joined the expedition from Wanalugo's own *aa*, a number were unmarried teenage youths looking for excitement, and others were Wanalugo's age-mates and classificatory brothers who had been with him in the same *bau aa* several years before. (For a summary, see Figure 4.1.)

The composition of the support from outside groups was in part a circumstantial result of those present at the funeral. Of those who attended, the mourners from the *aa* at Malosonɔ—which was composed of lineages of three clans: Gæsumisi, Tæmæsi, and Wabisi—provided the most encouraging support. Some people of Gæsumisi and Wabisi were married to Bonɔ women, while those of Tæmæsi, particularly Meyɔ, were merely close friends.

It was through these Malosonɔ connections that other people were recruited for the raiding party, including some from the distant community of Uruše whom Wanalugo didn't know. At the same time, another age-mate, Uweli of clan Wɔsisɔ, who lived in the same house group with Wanalugo, went to Olabia and Wanagesa, where he picked up several supporters among his connections there. Finally, Wanalugo obtained a certain amount of cooperation from the people of the *aa* of the victim himself. Of the

FIGURE 4.1 Composition of Raiding Party

Men, Recruited from Dubia *Aa*

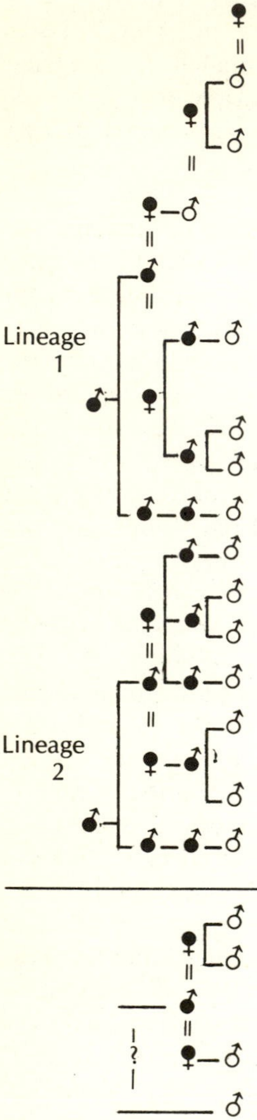

Clan	Genealogical Relation	Role in Raid
Bonɔ	♀ Gisa	Death caused by *sei*
	♂ Wanalugo	Aggrieved in death; led raid; killed *sei*
	♂ Mei	Nonsupporter; unwilling to kill MoBro
	♀–♂ Sogobaye	Nonsupporter; unwilling to kill his brother-in-law
Lineage 1	♂–♂	Age-mate and close friend of Wanalugo; participated despite distant affinal connection to victim
	♂ Seli	Participant; youth about 14
	♂	Nonparticipant youth; ill, died shortly after raid
	♂–♂–♂ Gurambo	Participant; wounded on head
	♂–♂	Participant; youth about 15
	♂	Participant; age-mate of Wanalugo
	♂	Participant; age-mate of Wanalugo
	♂–♂	Nonparticipant; ill
	♂	Not present; supporting affines at another *aa*
Lineage 2	♀–♂	Nonsupporter; said to be "afraid"
	♂–♂–♂	Participant; age-mate of Wanalugo
Wɔsisɔ	♂	Nonsupporter; remained neutral
	♂	Nonsupporter; visited Heyabisi frequently, though not related there
	♀–♂	Participant; friend of Wanalugo
	♂ Uweli	Participant; recruited supporters from Olabia and Wanagesa

Supporters from Other Longhouses

Aa	Clan	Genealogical Relation	Relation to People in Dubia Aa	Role in Raid
Malosonɔ	Wabisi	♀—♂	—	Recruited by his brother from sago camp; supported raid
		♂ Sigese	Friend of Wanalugo	Attended funeral; recruited men from Malosonɔ and Uruše; pulled out victim's heart
		♂	Married to Bonɔ woman	Recruited from sago camp; supported raid
	Gæsumisi	♂	—	Attended funeral; supported raid
		♂	Married Wanalugo's half-sister	Attended funeral; supported raid
	Tæmæsi	—♂	—	Attended funeral; recruited men from Uruše; supported raid
		♂ Bugamia	—	Sent ahead to hold victim; later paid a cowrie shell necklace
		♂ Meyɔ	Close friend of Wanalugo	Attended funeral; sent to open door of victim's aa
		♂	—	Attended funeral; supported raid
Olabia	Dɨdesa/ Kagabesi	♂ Daibo	Cross-cousin of Uweli at Dubia	Helped Uweli recruit men for raid; participated
		Etoro man	Visitor at Olabia	Recruited by Uweli; urged fighting to stop at daybreak
		Others	—	Supported raid but remained outside aa
Wanagesɔ	(various)	Several men	Distant classificatory relatives and people not well known to Wanalugo	Recruited by Uweli and Daibo; supported raid but remained outside aa; received the head and legs of victim
—?—	Uruše	Several men	Distant classificatory relatives and people not well known to Wanalugo	Recruited by Išiba and Sigese; supported raid but remained outside aa; received trunk and arms of victim

People Present at Victim's Aa at Time of Raid

Clan	Individual	Comment
Dɨdesa	♂ Ola	Met Wanalugo scouting; warned of raid; revealed presence of victim in aa
	♂ Tiago	Warned by brother Ola of raid; came down to examine heart after killing
	— ♂	Married to a Wabisi woman, hence in-law of victim; not told of raid lest he warn him
Wasu	♂ Hæmindæ	Warned by Wanalugo of raid; shot in buttock while trying to escape out back door of aa
	— ♂	Youth, unimportant; not warned of raid
Wabisi	♂ Hagabulu	Victim, killed in raid; afterward eaten
	♂	Not warned of raid lest he alert his brother; struck down Gurambo of Bonɔ in attempt to retaliate
	♂	Not present during raid
	‖ ♀ Mage	Bonɔ woman; not present during raid but later instrumental in achieving settlement between Bonɔ and victim's relatives
Sæsæn	— ♂	Not warned of raid because he was away; present night of the attack
Gæsumisi	— ♂	Also present during attack; not warned

♂ ♀ = dead; ♂ ♀ = living

nine men who were present in the *aa* at the time of the attack, three knew it was coming but did not tell the victim and only made a show of a fight. This reduced the effective defending force to five, once the victim had been killed.

A conflict within the same longhouse community rarely involves people from other longhouses. But conflicts between different *aas* draw members of the surrounding communities to support the opposing sides, each man participating according to his affiliations to the protagonists in the dispute. Though everyone is theoretically expected to come to the defense of his own longhouse when it is under attack, external relationships may sometimes place the social allegiances of the various members of the house group in opposition to each other and mitigate their actual effectiveness.

The Kaluli themselves are well aware of this situation in the recruitment of support in conflict.[2] Their term for the division of a house group during times of dispute is *alɔ bana hanan*, literally, "the house splitting goes," which means that some people go to one *aa* in the dispute and some to the other, while others stay neutral. This did not lead to dissension within the longhouse community. Supporters of opposing sides would be antagonistic to each other only when they were at the *aas* of the protagonists they supported. If people had ties to both sides, their conflicting commitments were adjusted by sending brothers or other close relatives to support both parties in the dispute.

Relatives on opposing sides would not club or shoot at each other in battle but would aim instead at other supporters of the opposition to whom they were not related. If someone was killed in battle, no attempt was made to obtain compensation. Rather, the side that had suffered the loss would try to kill someone in return immediately. At times of comparative quiet in the dispute, supporters who had relatives on the opposing side would sometimes try to exert their influence to achieve a peaceful settlement without further resort to violence.

---

2 They sometimes will phrase a conflict as if it were a dispute between clans, but it quickly becomes clear that the clan names designate those clans to which the protagonists happen to belong or whose lineages in a particular house group give them the most support.

Opposition in Friendship: Weddings and Prestations

Weddings and prestations are the other principal occasions on which Kaluli oppose one another in groups. For weddings the opposed groups are formed in much the same way as for a fight. The bride's longhouse community together with a large group of supporters bring the bride in procession to the groom's *aa*, where, after receiving the bridewealth, they give over the bride and present a ceremony at night. Supporters from other communities split to one side or the other depending on their relations to the bride and groom and to the bridewealth negotiations. Those who have donated to the groom's bridewealth accumulation tend to stand with the groom, whereas those, however distantly related to the bride, who expect to receive an item of bridewealth tend to go with the bride's party. Those who have no predominant relationship with either side will simply stand where it is convenient.

Groups that form to oppose each other over a prestation are recruited in the same way as those recruited for weddings and disputes but with different results. In conflicts between different longhouse communities, lineage brothers and housemates in each nearby community are divided and opposed to one another as they move to support their relatives and connections on opposite sides of the issue. In prestations, however, members of a longhouse community stand together against their various relatives and affines in other communities in making gifts of meat. These gifts are not made only in fulfillment of affinal obligations; people in the donor's community who have matrilateral or classificatory sibling relationships among the proposed recipients may decide to honor those relationships with gifts and join the prestation also.

The result is to generalize a number of small gifts of meat given individually by one man to another in response to a particular obligation into a group of gifts of meat presented by the opposed communities. This outlines the nature of relations between longhouse communities in Bosavi: they are the summation of the overlapping ties between individuals in each of them.

The situation may be illustrated as follows. A gift of smoked game was prepared by the people of clans Bonɔ and Wɔsisɔ at Sululib longhouse in 1968. At different times during the previous weeks, they had received presents of smoked game from people of branches of clan Wabisi residing at Muluma and at Doba. The recipients at Sululib decided they would make their reciprocations all at the same time. They were joined by other housemates who had not received anything from Wabisi but felt it was a good opportunity to make a prestation to their nearby affines of another clan, Gæsumisi, at its branches at Kæsi and Wahalib.

After six weeks of hunting, those making the prestation (about half the population of Sululib longhouse) shouldered net bags of smoked game and headed in separate expeditions to three different *aas*. Figure 4.2 lists those who went, those they brought presents to, and why. Married men brought along their entire domestic households, women and children, for the visit. Aebi, having prestations to make at both Muluma and Dubia, sent his wife, Dayame, to one place and went to the other himself. Sialo, a widower, who had the same problem but no wife, had to go to two different houses on successive days. Jubi, who was away, sent his bag of meat in care of his small son, Seyaka. Since Wanalugo had no personal obligations himself, he decided not to accompany his wife, Hɔidɔ, when she went to settle hers.[3]

Here the people of Sululib made their prestations all at once but then split up (*alɔ bana hanan*) to make them to the various *aas* of the recipients. A recent death at the *aa* of some of the recipients and the small size of the parties of donors made the presentation of a ceremony inappropriate. (For a description of this prestation occasion at Doba, see Chapter 8.)

Large-scale ceremonial distributions of pork or sago grubs are analogous to this prestation of smoked game, except that they are larger in scale, and instead of the donors' taking the meat to the various *aas* of the recipients, the recipients gather at the *aa* of the donors to receive it. The opposition between donors and recipients

---

[3] Hɔidɔ had received a gift of animals from her cross-cousins and trapped animals for the return gift herself, an unusual procedure for a woman among the Kaluli. Wanalugo was away when she received her gift and did not return until shortly before the return prestation was to be made. Hence, if she were to make a prestation, she would have to prepare it herself. By the same token, Wanalugo had not shared any of the meat that she had received. Hence, he did not feel he needed to help her trap the meat for the return or accompany her to Dubia when she went to make it.

Delivered to (clan and *aa*)	Donor	Recipient (relationship)	Number of Marsupials	Type of Gift

Clan Wabisi at Doba

	♂–♂–♀ (Heyeli)			
♀ ‖	♂–♂ Æbi ⟶	♂ Hiilo (husband of Heyeli)	15	Affinal prestation (*ga sigi*) for classificatory daughter; return *(wel)* for previous gift
♂ʼ ‖				
♀— ♂–♂ ⟶			17	(As above)

	♀ Ulahi ‖			
	♂–♂ ⟶	♂ Yɔwa (cross-cousin of Ulahi)	5	Affinal prestation (*ga læsu*) to wife's cross-cousin; return *(wel)* for previous gift
	♂–♀ Hɔidɔ ⟶	♂ Yɔwa (cross-cousin of Hɔidɔ)	5	Gift to cross-cousin; return *(wel)* for previous gift
		⟶ ♂ Kiliyæ (cross-cousin of Hɔidɔ)	2	(As above)

	♀ (Suaga)			
	♂ ⌐ ♂ ⟶	♂ Kiliyæ (husband of Suaga)	18	Affinal prestation (*ga sigi*) for sister; return *(wel)* for three previously not reciprocated
	♂–♂ ⟶	♀ Suaga (classificatory sister)	6	Gift to classificatory sister; return for previous gift

Delivered to (clan and *aa*)	Donor	Recipient (relationship)	Number of Marsupials	Type of Gift
Clan Gæsumisi at Kæsi	♀—♀ (Eyobo) ♂ →	♂ Baidæ (husband of Eyobo)	?	Affinal prestation (*ga sigi*) for sister's daughter; opening gift
Clan Wábisi at Muluma	♀ (Oame) ♂ Degera →	♂ Bibiali (husband of Oame; brother of Wadeo)	9	Affinal prestation (*ga sigi*); opening gift
				Baseo and Bibiali married each other's sisters and so could not exchange *ga læsu* and *ga sigi*; Bibiali exchanged with Oame's other brother, Baseo with his wife's stepfather
	♀ Wadeo ‖ ♂ Baseo →	♂ Hɔwæ (Wadeo's stepfather)	8	Affinal prestation, (*ga læsu*); opening gift
	♀ Kɔlu			
	♀ ♂ Hɔwæ ‖ ♠ ‖	♂ Waibo (no traceable relation)	12	Affinal prestation (*ga læsu*) for Kɔlu; Waibo took over exchange relations in absence of others to gain relations with Hɔwæ
	♀+♂ (Æbi) ‖ ♀ Dayame → ♂	(—?—)	18	(Absent; went to Doba) Affinal prestation (*ga læsu*) from Dayame's husband to her relatives at Muluma

♂ ♀ = dead; ♂ ♀ = living

as such is dramatized when the groups of recipients mass together in the forest beforehand and then enter the clearing before the donors' *aa* in a single procession.

These groups, enlisted for performance of tasks or support in oppositions, for the time they are in existence are best understood as "action sets" (Mitchell, 1969, p. 10), temporary groupings gathered for a particular purpose and recruited from personal networks of individuals across diverse structural lines. The relevant question, then, is not how groups come into opposition to each other, but how oppositions bring about the creation of groups. It is precisely to this issue that Kaluli refer when they say that the "house splitting goes" (*alɔ bana hanan*).

Although the longhouse community does not necessarily act as a social unit, Kaluli think of people gathered at an *aa* as an important and special grouping in a particular sense. We recall that the house itself (or the yard in front) is the stage *par excellence* for nearly all Kaluli social discussions, confrontations, ceremonial activities, dramas of conflict, and reciprocity. Not only is it the usual arena in which issues are joined and the principal events take place, but it is to some extent the place to which they are restricted.

When an issue arises that sets up an opposition and the people of several house groups split to support opposing sides, the various fragmented groups reassemble themselves into action sets in the form of two groups, one that is gathered at a longhouse (*aa bišɔ*) and another that comes (*miyɔwɔ*) to confront them. The Kaluli are conscious of the staging of this situation and set aside a special day (*dægi*, or gathering day) to accomplish it. The supporters of the opposing sides (or the raiders) gather at different *aas* and then on the following day one group goes to confront the other at its *aa* as guest to host, bride's party to groom's people, or attackers to defenders, as the case may be. The action is staged between *aa bišɔ*, or "those at the house," and *miyɔwɔ* or "those who have come." *Aa bišɔ* may refer incidentally to a house group as a residential unit, but its significance really refers to "those who are gathered at an *aa* on a particular occasion"—and may include many people who are not members of the residence at which they have gathered. However, the *aa bišɔ* acts more or less as a unit in relation to the *miyɔwɔ* during the time the particular social drama is in progress. *Aa biśɔ* and *miyɔwɔ* are defined not only by the issue over which they are opposed but also by their presence on the stage where the issue is most alive and the opposing roles are to be enacted. Accordingly, the terms define these groups according to where the action is, rather than by social function or composition. They outline a type of ad hoc opposition, not one that is latent and enduring between groups. It is to this that most important Kaluli oppositions assimilate themselves when the issues are to be publicly enacted and resolved, and most Kaluli acts of reciprocity and ceremonials are staged in this manner.

Chapter 5

The Unseen World and
the Opposition Scenario

The significance of *alɔ bana hanan*—the splitting of the house—runs deeper than simply the members of a house group splitting to support opposite sides in some dispute. It also refers to the fundamental relationship among all things in the world. The Kaluli believe that all things had their origin at a time in the distant past known as *hena madaliaki* (roughly "when the land came into form").[1] At that time, according to the prevailing story, there were no trees or animals or streams or sago or food. The earth was covered entirely by people. These people soon began to get hungry and cold as they had nothing to eat or to build houses with. One man[2] got up and said, "Everyone gather around here." When everyone had assembled, he said, "You be trees," and one group of people became trees. "You be sago," and another group became sago. "You be fish. . . . You be bananas," and so on, until all the animals and plants and every other being and natural feature (rivers, hills) in the world were divided each to his own kind. The few men who were left became the human beings of the day. The Kaluli term for this myth is "the time when everything

[1] *Madaliab* is a verb sometimes used to refer to the process of a child taking form in the womb.
[2] This individual (sometimes two individuals) did not have a name. Since the arrival of the missionaries, Kaluli have tended to identify him with "Godeyo" (God) and/or "Yesu."

alɔ bana ane" (*ane* = past participle of *hanan*), and it is from this original "splitting of the house" that all things have attained their present form of existence.

The myth suggests that the Kaluli perceive the relation among the various species and objects in the world as being of the same nature as that which obtains between two groups of men divided over an issue. The various things in the world attain differentiation not by separate creation but by being set against one another in a complementary opposition. Animals, plants, and people are fundamentally related (all were originally men) but opposed (they are now separate species).

Moreover, it is precisely through these oppositions that life can proceed in the world at all. Men have food and shelter by virtue of the plants and animals. Animals live somehow in a corresponding manner. Indeed, they are fundamentally "men" also, though in a different way, as we shall see.

While the basis for the forms and processes in the world is to be found in the opposition between man and man, and species and species, their identical but opposed natures are most clearly revealed in the relationship between the visible and invisible in Kaluli experience.

In the forest it is impossible to see very far through the trees. However, things that are out of sight announce their presence and identity through the calls and the sounds that they make. The creaking of wings over the top of the canopy reveals the presence and direction of a flight of hornbills. The flapping and screeching of a white cockatoo as it bursts into flight announces the approach of someone along the path near the *aa*. In Kaluli thinking, day begins with the sound of the first birds singing, not the appearance of the sun. Evening is characterized by the singing of the cicadas, not the fading light. Kaluli tend to identify animals and birds more by the sounds they make and the way they move than by their appearance. The *hi fun*, a large pigeon, is named after the nature of its call: "hmmm-hoo, hmmm-hoo." *Hi susulubi*, another pigeon, is also named after its call, which can only be written "susulubi." A man will never characterize a rat as a small, furry animal with a pointed nose and sharp teeth. Rather, he will make a squeaking noise, pinch himself gingerly to indicate a small, cautious, fast animal biting him, and follow up with a remark about how rats ruin net bags or eat people's bananas. Picking up on this, I once tried to describe a bird I had seen in the forest to a knowledgeable man. He was unable to figure out what kind of bird it was until I recalled that its wings made a peculiar rattling noise when it flew. I rumpled some paper as an example, and he identified the bird immediately.

The perception of creatures by their voices and movements in the forest gives a peculiar sense of presence and dynamism to things that are unseen, to surrounding but invisible life. Sound brings to awareness not objects, but movements, activities, and events, to which the Kaluli are ever alert. For practical purposes, like hunting and defense, these locate the individual at an approximate distance and direction, even if it is remote.

It is important to realize the remarkable impression of immediacy of sounds and creatures heard amid the pervading stillness and immobility of the forest. The calls of the birds have the sudden and curious appeal of a spoken voice. A man walks along, hearing only the slight crunch of his own footsteps, when the self-satisfied, declamatory squawk of a hornbill suddenly comes clapping, as though someone had shouted a greeting right at his shoulder. Kaluli remark on this sort of thing spontaneously again and again. Out hunting with Wanalugo, we heard the plaintive "juu-juu-juu" of the *kalo* (a small pigeon). Wanalugo turned to me with a wistful expression and said, "You hear that? It is a little child who is hungry and calling for its mother." It is through remarks such as this that we can best understand the Kaluli perception of the unseen world of spirits.

The everyday Kaluli world of gardens, rivers, and forests is coextensive with another, invisible side of reality. The remark that the voice of the *kalo* is a little child is not merely a metaphor. The *kalo* may actually *be* the soul of a child. "Do you see that huge tree?" another man asked one day on the path. "In their [the birds'] world, that is a house. Do you see the birds? To each other, they appear as men." Similarly, houses in our world appear as exceptionally big trees or as river pools to them, and we as animals there.

In talking about the people of the other world, the Kaluli use the term *mama,* which means shadow or reflection. When asked what the people of the unseen look like, Kaluli will point to a reflection in a pool or a mirror and say, "They are not like you or me. They are like that." In the same way, our human appearance stands as a reflection to them. This is not a "supernatural" world, for to the Kaluli it is perfectly natural. Neither is it a "sacred world," for it is virtually coextensive with and exactly like the world the Kaluli inhabit, subject to the same forces of mortality. They do not regard it with particular awe. In the unseen world, every man has a reflection in the form of a wild pig (women appear as cassowaries) that roams invisibly on the slopes of Mt. Bosavi. The man and his wild pig reflection live separate existences, but if something should happen to the wild pig, the man is also affected. If it is caught in a trap, he is disabled; if it is killed by hunters of the unseen, he dies.

When a person dies, his wild pig aspect disappears from the *mama* world. His personal life virtue, which animates his living body and is manifested in his breathing and conscious awareness, escapes with his last breath and takes on human form in the *mama* world where it continues a life very much like the one he left. In the visible world, the person now usually appears in the form of a bird or a fish, and his longhouse as a tree or river pool.

Inhabitants of the Invisible

The invisible is inhabited by various sorts of people. Most familiar to the Kaluli are the *ane kalu* (gone men). These are the spirits of the dead, together with others (also called *ane kalu*) who are just like them except that they have never been alive. According to mediums who have seen them, the *ane kalu* appear just as men but wear no shell ornaments. They build their *aas* (trees and pools) on the same ridges and plateaus as the Kaluli *aas.* Their trees and pools are well known to the Kaluli, who will point them out and name some of the *ane* who live there. There are no restrictions on hunting or fishing in these areas, for, although the *ane kalu* take the forms of birds and fish, not all birds and fish are *ane kalu.* Kaluli say, "To us they appear as just [ordinary] birds and fish, and how are we to know the difference?" For those animals that are really *ane kalu,* Kaluli like to think there is a certain apt continuity between their animal manifestations and their underlying human ones. Birds with masklike face markings are said to be *ane* Gisaro dancers; the palm cockatoo with its large crest is an *ane* wearing a headdress; a hornbill is a man with a big nose. Men who were murdered become a form of solitary parrot with blood-red plumage.

The Kaluli relations with *ane kalu* are generally cordial. This is because in the case of the dead (*sowɔ mama*), the people were acquainted with some of them when they were alive. There is none of the antagonism and resentment between the dead and the living in Bosavi that is commonly found in other parts of New Guinea. It is inconceivable to the Kaluli that a dead person would wish to harbor resentment against the living. One does not injure his relatives and friends.

Knowledge of and access to the invisible world occasionally comes to individuals in special dreams (never in myths or tales), but for most purposes the Kaluli rely on mediums. The medium is always a man who is married (in a dream) to a woman of the invisible world. When he has a child by her, he is able to go to sleep, leave his body, and walk about in the *mama* world. At the same time, the people from the invisible world may enter his body as they would a house and converse through his mouth with people assembled for a seance.

All the men, women, and children of the longhouse are present. Gathered about the prostrate form of the medium in the darkened *aa,* they can talk with their dead relatives. The conversations are held in an atmosphere of noisy excitement, and the affection of the people for their dead is apparent in the tone of their talk. They often ask where their dead friends are staying, what form they have taken, and if they have enough to eat. People also ask about those among the living who are sick (*ane* can see what is wrong and help to cure it), the whereabouts of stray pigs, and the identities of *seis* who may be creeping about at the time. *Ane kalu,* who are spirits of the dead, are concerned for their living relatives and sometimes block the door of the *aa* if a *sei* wishes to enter. Other *ane kalu,* who have always lived on the invisible side and never been alive (*hen bišɔ,* or "those of the ground"), also come to seances and speak. They are usually spirit in-laws or acquaintances of the medium, since it is ·a *hen biŝɔ* woman (not a spirit of the dead) whom he marries.

Besides the *ane kalu* in the *mama* world, there are the *kalu hungɔ*, which may be roughly translated as "dangerous, forbidden men." These individuals inhabit a few well-known localities in Kaluli territory. Those who have seen them say that they are generally light-skinned and of larger than average size. *Kalu hungɔ* are characteristically more bad-tempered than *ane kalu* and generally keep to themselves unless they are provoked by someone trespassing to fish or plant gardens in their area.

The Sɔlɔ Stream near Sululib on the lands of Bonɔ clan is owned by a *kalu hungɔ* named Hɔwæ; he lives invisibly in a huge tree near a waterfall with two of his brothers. The people of Bonɔ are forbidden to plant the banks of the Sɔlɔ for the entire length of the stream or to drink or fish its waters. A man crossing the Sɔlɔ first throws a stick or rock into the water to scare away the fish and then crosses without looking at the bottom of the stream. If these precautions are not observed, the *hungɔ* will be angry. An angry *hungɔ* rumbles like distant thunder, his voice coming from somewhere in the further canopy. Sometimes he affects the weather. If he is really provoked, he is likely to strike a man who has offended him and make him sicken or die. Early in my stay, I made the mistake of bathing in the Sɔlɔ and pulling a dead fish out of it. This act created considerable consternation among the Kaluli and shortly afterward was followed by a rainstorm. Occurrences such as this lead Kaluli to avoid the *hungɔ* areas as much as possible.

Finally, in the unseen world there are the somewhat mysterious *mamul* people, who live in big invisible *aas* on Mt. Bosavi. The *mamul* seem to be considered more powerful and different culturally from the other inhabitants of the invisible world, a friendly but distant neighboring people. While they are not ill-disposed to the Kaluli, they remain aloof and do not often speak through mediums. The Kaluli do not think of the *mamul* as reflections, *mama*, in the invisible world; rather, they think of *mamul* reflections as being found in our world. The *mamul* appear in the Kaluli world mainly in the form of the most formidable animals of the forest, the cassowary and the wild pig. The noise of their ceremonies and raiding expeditions can be heard as a tremendous crashing of tropical thunder that shatters the air and shakes the *aa*.

The Kaluli visit the area frequented by the *mamul* on the thickly forested slopes of Mt. Bosavi on hunting expeditions, but they always observe certain ritual precautions. No woman may accompany them, and they must use a special secret language among themselves and observe a special kinship terminology. If they do not, the *mamul* may be aroused and attack the hunting party with terrific tropical rainstorms and cause huge rocks or trees to roll down the mountainside.

The *mamul* and the Kaluli stand in a particular complementary relationship, for it is on *mamul* grounds that the wild pig reflections of the Kaluli roam, and the wild pigs on the Kaluli ground are often the reflections of the *mamul*. Because of this, the life and death of each is bound up with the other: as the Kaluli kill wild pigs, so do the *mamul* die; as the *mamul* kill wild pigs, so do the Kaluli die.

Further, because the *mamul* live in places accessible only to men, they have a peculiar relation to the celebration of maleness. While nearly all aspects of Kaluli life emphasize maleness to some degree, the highest celebration of the masculine came in the *bau aa*. The *bau aa* was a ceremonial hunting lodge to which all the virgin youths of several clans would retire for a period of about fifteen months. During this time they would hunt large quantities of animals that would be smoked and distributed with exuberant ceremony at the end of the period of seclusion.

The cycle of Kaluli *bau aas* was directly linked to the cycle of *bau aas* held by the *mamul*. From time to time, the *mamul* held a *bau aa* to hunt animals on one or another big hill in Kaluli territory. This would generally be discovered by mediums who went out into the invisible side to find out why there were so many thunderstorms at a particular time. When the *mamul* had a *bau aa*, it resulted in a kind of epidemic among the Kaluli, whose wild pig reflections the *mamul* hunted. Many people died. When the *mamul bau aa* had run its course, the Kaluli would themselves hold a *bau aa*. This was both to strengthen themselves against further death and to take retribution, for as the Kaluli youths hunted, so the *mamul* died.

There was no feeling of enmity between the Kaluli and the *mamul* over this, for how was one to know when he killed a wild pig that it was the reflection of someone else and not just an animal? Kaluli seemed to look on this as one of those tragic facts of life that must simply be accepted. "We asked the *mamul* to hurry up and finish their *bau aa* because we were afraid. But we were not angry, for a *bau aa* is a good thing. Anyway, we would soon after have a *bau aa* and kill them." This reflects a deepseated attitude that the Kaluli have about gratuitous misfortunes in their lives. It is the same as that reflected in the words used to hush a child who has hurt himself: "It is like that, don't cry." There is a more or less cheerful acceptance of the fact that everything in life is paid for by somebody somewhere and that from time to time one must receive the lumps himself.

The Kaluli die when the *mamul* kill their wild pig reflections, but this is never felt to be the important or immediate aspect of the matter. The *mamul* are remote, and their contribution to death is unwitting by virtue of the internal nature of things. It is the *sei*, who attacks individuals out of personal malice and hunger, who is felt to be primarily responsible for a death. Most of the killing among the Kaluli themselves was in angry retribution against *seis*.

All deaths, whether due to illness, old age, or violent accident, are caused by a *sei*. A *sei* is a living man (occasionally a woman) who, often unknown to himself, has an evil aspect, a kind of shadow creature (*sei inso*, witch-child) dwelling in his heart. When he is asleep, this creature takes his form and creeps invisibly out of his body and abroad in the night, looking for victims. A *sei* is supposed to attack only those people to whom he bears no kin or affinal relationship—his *mæmu*—but a very hungry, angry *sei* may be indiscriminate and go after relatives as well. A *sei* can be seen in its human form only by people who are deathly ill or have the special ability to see into the invisible. They describe a *sei* on the prowl as a crouching, creeping figure with glowing eyes, clutching hands, and a face distorted in a hideous grimace. *Seis* are malicious, irrational, voracious, disgusting, dangerously violent, and tremendously strong. They are the incarnation of implacable evil.

Physical disability and high fever are the marks of a *sei* attack.

The Kaluli say that most of the time a person's body is "dark" to the *sei* so that he cannot see it well. But if a man is excessively angry and upset, if he is ill in a minor way, or if his wild pig reflection has been trapped or wounded, his body becomes "bright" to the *sei*, so that he can see it easily to attack. The *sei* attacks by injuring or dismembering his victim's body, but the body looks the same afterward. The damage is visible only in the *mama* world, although the effects are manifested in this one. Thus, a man whose legs have been cut off by a *sei* is unable to walk; his legs are visible but not really there. A man in whose stomach a *sei* has placed a big stone gets a distended belly. To say that a *sei* attacks a man's body but not the body that is visible is paradoxical, and my informants were perplexed as to how to explain it. The closest analog in Western thought is perhaps the concept of the spirit body, the spiritual double of the corporeal body, which is still not the same as the soul. For the Kaluli, it is really a question of the same body viewed in two aspects—one from the *mama* side, and one from this one.

When his victim has been seriously weakened by illness, the *sei* returns to pull out his heart and cause his death. Afterward he sits invisibly on the edge of the exposure coffin and dines on the decomposing corpse. It is to this that Kaluli attribute the disappearance of the decomposed flesh.

One is very wary about revealing the name of a *sei* unless he has actually been responsible for a death, for to call someone a *sei* is a damning insult, and he may come out in his *sei* aspect some night and attack his accuser. Indeed, if a man who is sick but not dying perceives a *sei* in his fever or if a medium sees him creeping about, they take care to identify him only by clan or longhouse community. A relative then visits the *aa* in question (or, more cautiously, shouts from a nearby ridge) to tell the inhabitants that one of them is making a kinsman sick and must stop his invisible attacks.

Once a man dies, there are various ways of determining who did him in. Sometimes the dying man will speak the name of the *sei* in his last moments as he sees him creeping up to take his heart, or he may reveal it posthumously through a medium. If the *sei* unwittingly shows up at the funeral, the body of the dead, which is hung for viewing in the front of the hall, will contract and fluids flow from the mouth and anus. In any case, divination should be made to determine if the person identified is really the *sei* responsible. (If no one has an idea who it might be, angry relatives sometimes perform a divination for every known *sei* in the neighborhood.) In the past, once the identity of the *sei* was confirmed, a raid might have been organized against him.

The Unseen in Everyday Life

To the Kaluli, the presence of the unseen is part of everyday life. The call of a hornbill, the giant tree that dominates the crest of a ridge, a stream where one must not fish—all give daily testimony to its reality. Late at night I have been awakened by the weird triple whistle of a *sei* coming from the forest nearby. "*Wai! A sei!*" someone yells in the *aa*. Men sit up and stir their fireboxes, nervously recalling talk about *seis* in the vicinity or the recent death of someone in a nearby longhouse. Noise and talking continue for some time, a sign that the community is alert.

Most of what Kaluli know of the invisible comes from this sort of experience, from hearsay, and from participating in seances. They do not speculate about the unseen, not only because they, like most Melanesians, are not given to speculation, but also because to them matters of the unseen are matters of fact. Whenever I inquired of an ordinary man something he did not know about the invisible world, he would tell me to talk to a medium who had been there and had seen what I was asking about.

For mediums the nature of the *ane* side is a matter of direct observation. "I know when I am going to go out [to the *ane* side]," one medium said, "because when I look up at the rafters of the *aa*, it seems like I am looking up at the surface of a pool. Then suddenly like falling off an entrance ladder, I am on the ground as though fallen under the house, and there is my *ane* friend, Seyakalewɔ."

Later in the same conversation, the following exchange took place.

"When Dayame was sick, I went out and saw that a *sei* had put a stone in her throat."

"Could you see the stone right through her skin?"

"No, she was split open down the middle and the stone just put in the place of her throat."

"What did you do?"

"I took the stone out and pressed her body back together. In the morning, I told her about it, and she was all right."

"Did you tell her that you had seen her split open?"

"No, one doesn't tell people things like that, but I can tell you [an outsider]."

Mediums do not have special training or knowledge of esoteric lore but are ordinary men able to visit the *ane* side and tell what they see there. Some things, it is true, are not appropriate to tell about, but even here it is less a question of secret lore than of facts and events that would be upsetting or somehow dangerous if revealed.

Anthropologists like to talk about the "native belief system," by which they mean the native ideology about the supernatural taken as a coherent system. It is important to emphasize that the ideas most Kaluli have about the unseen are usually made up of loosely consistent hearsay, lore, and stories of personal experience that differ in their details from informant to informant. Inconsistencies, when pointed out, are as puzzling to the Kaluli as they are to the ethnographer.

Most men are not concerned with what goes on in the *ane* world in itself but rather with how events in the unseen give greater insight into events on the visible side. Much of this sort of knowledge is trivial. Several times, men spontaneously pointed out to me a windfall, an area of trees flattened by a heavy storm wind, and told me that it was in reality the reflection of a *mamul* garden. The broadleafed regrowth springing up between the trunks was the reflection of their bananas. Similarly, when it rains, I was told, the water comes from the Sili, the great river that flows invisibly through *mamul* country. The Sili has no reflection in the visible world, but every time it overflows its banks, the water comes down as rain to us. This sort of "academic knowledge" is not supposed to be secret and serves no useful purpose, but people take a certain pleasure in knowing it, even as an educated layman in our society may enjoy knowing about the evolution of man or the planets of the solar system.

At the same time, apparently innocuous occurrences may have hidden reverberations that give them portent and significance. A cicada that suddenly begins to sing in the *aa* late at night is likely to be the voice of an *ane kalu* come to announce the death of someone in the locality. Long, troubled conversations among those who have sick relatives in other longhouses or at sago camps inevitably follow.

I was once prevented from squashing a grotesque grasshopper-like creature that was crawling up the wall of my house. My cook informed me that it was likely to be a reflection of my own self (because of its light skin color and presence inside my house rather than in its natural habitat). If I killed it, I might be killing myself.[3] It is not the animal or event by itself but its peculiar features that reveal its special relation to the unseen. Not all wild pigs are reflections of invisible men: some are just ordinary pigs. Normally, my informants told me, it is impossible to tell the difference. But if a wild pig digs up and eats the sago that a man has hidden at his sago storage place, then it is probably a *mamul* or an *ane kalu* in the form of a pig. The point is that if the pig knows about sago storage places, then it cannot just be a pig. It displays acquaintance with human things and must therefore have a hidden human nature.

The Medium's View of the Unseen

In practice, the main center of Kaluli interest in the unseen revolves around the problems of illness and death, which have their locus in the relation between a man and his own underlying invisible reflection. A man may be sleeping safe and sound in his clan *aa* when his wild pig reflection sprains its leg miles away on Bosavi. The man wakes up with a sore leg. If he is prostrated with fever, it is the work of a *sei*, and it is imperative to discover in what way the sick man's body has been injured and, if possible, who in-

---

[3] I carefully carried it outside and placed it on a banana tree.

jured him. The pain and symptoms are only the visible manifestations of a hidden condition. Knowledge of the unseen aspects of the matter is available only to a medium. Ordinary men have a conventional understanding of the unseen more or less equivalent to what I have outlined so far. When a medium describes what he sees on the other side, an entirely new world is revealed that the ordinary man gets only a glimpse of. A medium's perception of the invisible side has a curious through-the-looking-glass quality. Instead of vast forest lands, the invisible world is relatively clear and covered with high grass. The sky, rather than having the appearance of a blue vault, looks like the crown foliage of a thick forest as viewed from a distance. My informant compared it to the distant, forested slopes of Mt. Bosavi.

The rivers of the Bosavi area appear in the invisible as broad roads (completely unlike the almost imperceptible forest tracks used by the Kaluli), all leading downstream to the west, one from each *aa*. Up and down these roads pass many people going to and coming from Gisaro ceremonies. A few knowledgeable older men who are not mediums know this, but they do not know where these roads lead or their significance. According to one medium, these roads are the routes of the reflections of the dead who must pass down them as soon as they have died. All converge in a single road of the dead (the Isawa River) that leads far to the west and terminates in a vast, all-consuming fire called Imɔl. There the dead are consumed before they are renewed and returned as *ane kalu*, whose visible reflections are birds in a tree or fish in a pool. The great heat of the fire, incidentally, is what is behind the swelling and blistering of the corpse when it hangs for a few days in the *aa* during the time of the funeral.

The Imɔl fire and the waters of the river Sili that provides the rains are the basis for the medium's (and the *ane*'s) ability to heal the sick. Typically, a man who is so sick that he cannot walk is discovered by the medium to have had his legs cut off by a *sei*. Most people know that the medium sticks the invisible legs back onto the sick man to cure him, but they do not know just how this is done. According to my informant, who had done it many times, the *sei* usually does not devour the legs right away but hides them for a while. When the medium discovers them, they are stinking and decomposing, but he takes them to the river Sili and washes them in its water until they come up clean and whole. Then he takes the legs down the road of the dead to Imɔl and warms them into life. They may then be pressed back onto the body of the sick man to make him well.

The medium's view of the unseen expands and completes the knowledge that an ordinary man has only piecemeal. It is in the medium's vision that the invisible takes on the appearance of a world by itself. And while the ordinary man may suspect that certain everyday events have underlying causes, it is the medium's insight that reveals their full significance in a more mythical or metaphysical framework. The river Sili, source of the rain, is revealed on a deeper level to be a kind of Water of Healing, or Water of Life. The enterprise of curing as known to the medium looks less like a practical procedure and more like a revitalization rite. The rivers of the Bosavi area are the roads of the dead. The blistering and sloughing of the skin of a dead body reflects the passage of the *ane mama* through the fire toward its regeneration in a new life. It is through insight into the unseen, whether the limited knowledge of the common man or the comprehensive understanding of the medium, that many everyday problems may be appropriately interpreted, understood, and resolved.

The Nature of Opposition

The importance of all this for our discussion is that it reveals how Kaluli think about their world or, rather, how the Kaluli world must be thought. Here, finally, we come to the fundamental significance of *alɔ bana hanan* for Kaluli experience. The world is given implicitly in relations of opposition, so that the problem of comprehending many kinds of events resolves itself into grasping the nature of the opposition that gives form to them. As a result, Kaluli tend to adopt a particular line of reasoning in relation to a problem and to accept a certain kind of solution in regard to it. For illness, the issue is clear. The body is injured, but not visibly so. The injury is comprehensible in terms of the opposition (uninjured vs. injured) brought about between those aspects of the body that are visible and those that are not. It is in the repair of the injury that the resolution of the opposition and of the problem is achieved.[4]

This way of dealing with things is not restricted to managing relations with the invisible. It is generic to the way Kaluli deal with many situations, including disputes, marriages, and prestations. The process is a typical one, and outlines a typical cultural scenario. The scenario is implicit in our discussion of the treatment of illness, but is easily identified in other contexts.

If a sick man dies, a different situation obtains from when he was ill. Again it is interpreted in terms of an opposition, but this time no longer between the sick man and his invisible reflection. Indeed, the sick man has departed and gone to the treetops in the form of a bird. Rather, the opposition exists between the relatives and supporters of the dead man who have suffered his loss and the *sei* who did him in. At this point, a new scenario opens, identical in structure to the first. A divination is made on the basis of whatever evidence is available. Traditionally, if the identity of the *sei* was confirmed, the aggrieved group might have mounted a raid to kill him as he killed their relative.

Then, when the *sei* had been murdered and his body dragged off to eat, a new opposition opened—this time between the relatives of the murdered man and the principal people who killed him. If they had made a mistake and the murdered man was not a *sei*, his relatives would not rest until they killed someone in return. If the murdered man was a *sei*, his relatives would recognize the legitimacy of the action by settling for compensation (*su*).

Each of these situations—an illness, a death, a murder—is identical in the way it is developed in the course of action and in the way it is resolved. In each, the problem is defined in terms of an

---

[4] It is important that we not misunderstand the Kaluli viewpoint from our Western perspective. Invisible events are not seen merely as explanations for visible events. They are perceived as an integral part of those events. In Kaluli perception, knowledge of the invisible gives not hypothetical explanations about possible causes but real understanding of actual relations among events and leads to a practical strategy for dealing effectively with them. A medium is capable of curing sickness and finding lost pigs because he is able to get at those invisible aspects of the situation that are at the root of the trouble.

injury or loss that sets up an opposition. The terms of the opposition are set out, and the course of the action consists of the attempt of the protagonists on one side of the opposition to make good their loss (or even up the score) in relation to the other. When the loss is made good, the opposition is resolved, though it may result in a new one (see Table 5.1).

For illness, the restoration of the damaged (invisible) body by the return of the missing parts immediately resolves the opposition and effects the cure. For a man who has died, however, or a pig that has been stolen, it is impossible to recover exactly what has been lost. Instead, the situation is resolved by taking an equivalent.

In the situation of killing the *sei*, the Kaluli say, "We took [or killed] *wel*." The term *wel* means "exact equivalent" and always implies giving or taking in return for something. When one man strikes another in a fight, someone will try to strike a return blow (*wel*) of equal severity. If a man is killed in battle, his side will immediately attempt to kill a man as *wel* from among those who killed him.

In a dispute, to take *wel* means to perpetrate on the other side an injury equivalent to that which has been sustained at their hands. In situations where it is either impossible or undesirable to return *wel* for something but where, nevertheless, people feel entitled to redress, *su* is demanded. *Su* is not the return of an identical item but a "compensation" in the form of an acceptable amount of valuables and implies settlement for a loss or injury. If another man mistakenly kills my pig, instead of killing one of his in return, my supporters and I may demand a payment in cowrie necklaces and pearl shells. If someone wounds me in a brawl that was not intended to be serious, I may likewise demand *su*.

A demand for *su* implies that those who have sustained the injury recognize either that it was inadvertent or that it was justified (as in the case of the murderer of a *sei*) and that they wish to settle peaceably. This mode of settlement is taken when people are tired of fighting or unwilling to start a fight that might lead to consequences graver than a situation warrants. *Su* thus appears in the structure of events as a kind of substitute for *wel*. *Su* and *wel*

TABLE 5.1 Structure of Opposition Scenario as Reflected in Five Types of Process

Opposition Scenario	Formation of Opposition		Terms of Opposition Set Out	Course of Action	Resolution
	Loss or Gift				Return of Equivalent
Illness	*Sei* dismembers and hides (invisible) body parts		(1) Invisible vs. visible body parts: Medium locates invisible body parts, or	Invisible treatment	Medium returns renewed body parts to body; health returns
			(2) Sick person vs. *sei*: Medium determines identity of *sei*, or	*Sei* is notified	*Sei*, notified he is discovered, desists attack; health returns
			(3) Sick person vs. wild pig reflection: Medium discovers trapped or injured (invisible) wild pig	Medium aids wild pig reflection	*Wild pig back to normal; health returns
Death	Illness, age, or accident		Relatives of deceased vs. *sei*: Relatives divine identity of *sei*	Organize raid	Relatives of deceased kill *sei* (*wel*)
	Murder		(1) Relatives of deceased vs. killers: Killers are obvious or otherwise announce themselves, or	(1) If deceased murdered as *sei* (examine heart), compensation demanded, or	Killers pay compensation (*su*) to relatives of deceased
				(2) If deceased killed in anger, or mistakenly, organize raid	Relatives of deceased kill relative of killers (same *aa* and clan if possible) in return (*wel*)
			(2) (Rarely) Relatives of deceased vs. *sei* who "ripened" him for killing: Relatives divine identity of *sei*	(1) Organize raid, or	Relatives of deceased kill *sei* (*wel*)
				(2) Demand compensation	*Sei* pays compensation to deceased's relatives (*su*)
	Killed in battle		Man's comrades in battle vs. the enemy: Enemy is obvious	Fierce attempt to kill a man in return	Man is killed on enemy side as return (*wel*) in same battle

Prestation	Gift of pork, game, grubs, or whatever	Giver and recipient: Recipient accepts and acknowledges gift	Return prestation prepared	Receiver of original gift reciprocates equivalent meat to giver (wel)
Violent thunderstorm	Loss unknown but people fear spirits are angry	Suspected antagonism: *ane mama* or *mamul* vs. men: Medium investigates spirit side	Medium discovers spirits engaged in boisterous but nonthreatening activity	*No real opposition involved—relief of anxiety
Marriage	Woman is engaged to a man	Relatives of woman who want bridewealth vs. groom and his *naesu*: Woman requested (or offered), bridewealth named	Bridewealth amount negotiated, collected, and in part transferred	**Wedding; bride brought to groom's *aa*; remaining bridewealth transferred

NOTE: Rows: process of opposition formation and resolution; columns: analogous phases of process.

*Opposition scenario incomplete since original opposition resolved by being discontinued, not closed by return of something.

**Bridewealth (*ga fud>*) is not quite the same as *su* or *wel* for the "loss" of the woman. From this perspective, marriage may be regarded as establishing an opposition that is never completely resolved, but must be continually adjusted, renewed, and rebalanced through exchange of prestations and through additional payments to wife's relatives on the appearance of children. It is partly this unresolved quality that gives affinal relations both their awkwardness and their importance.

specifically imply a resolution that brings an opposition to closure. For the Kaluli, they embody the whole process of resolution of which they are a part.

The scenario of opposition in which this resolution takes place is not restricted to conflicts and antagonisms. In its positive permutation, it is the form for one of the most important vehicles of social relationship: delayed gift exchange. *Wel* in the context of gift exchange refers, not to retaliation for injury, but to a gift given in return for another gift. Again, *wel* means an exact equivalent. If I give you a pig, and you give me a pig of the same size at a later date, that is *wel*. A return in the form of a smaller pig or a pearl shell or a net bag of smoked animals does not count as *wel*. Similarly if a man received smoked meat from a distribution at the final ceremony of a *bau aa* ceremonial hunting lodge, *wel* consisted of returning the gift with smoked meat distributed from another *bau aa*. Another kind of smoked meat would not do as *wel*.

In a dispute or conflict, the opposition is opened when one side unwillingly and involuntarily suffers a loss at the hands of the other, and it is not resolved until a satisfactory return has been extracted. In gift exchange, the opposition is opened voluntarily by one man formally giving meat (a pig, smoked animals) to another. (Such an opening gift is said to be "given *omɔb*," which means, roughly, "given freely," "not in return for something.") The opposition remains open until, at a later date, an equivalent gift is made in return (*wel*). Contributions to help a friend pay compensation or amass bridewealth are another matter. They are spoken of in terms of "giving support" to someone or as a kinship obligation. They are not gifts requiring repayment, though it would be reasonable for the giver to expect the same kind of help from his recipient in a similar situation.

The Kaluli sense of matching equivalents in resolving situations of grievance or prestation is a fine one. In this they tend to feel that *wel* is a more satisfying outcome to events than *su*. This seems to reflect a fundamental sense of proportion that emerges in Kaluli management of events. Particularly in settling disputes, they tend to resolve the action so as to settle the score on as many levels as possible in a single reciprocal act. Thus, the action may be performed so as to deliberately replicate the events of the situation it is intended to resolve. When men of Gæsumisi mistakenly killed Habo of Wabisi as a *sei*, they defiantly compounded their error by sinking Habo's body in the upstream side of a river on Wabisi land so that Wabisi people would "eat of their own brother" when they drank from the river. Wabisi, infuriated, sent so many raiding parties into Gæsumisi territory that the people of Gæsumisi abandoned their *aa* and split up among the neighboring *aas* with their various relatives. During a lull in the hostilities, a party of Wabisi men on a hunting expedition met up with a Gæsumisi man on the trail. They grabbed him and killed him and then sank his body in the upstream side of a Gæsumisi river in return for what Gæsumisi had done to them.

This kind of settlement, in which a single situation is resolved on a number of levels, parallels that in which several situations may be resolved in a single action. When Ganigi of Gæsumisi was identified as the *sei* responsible for a death at Bonɔ, the people of Bonɔ organized a raid to kill him. They surprised him at a garden house, murdered him, and were cutting into his body for the heart when a force of Gæsumisi men, alerted by the noise of fighting, arrived on the scene and chased them away. The Gæsumisi men removed Ganigi's heart themselves and found it not to be that of a *sei*. Accordingly, they determined to kill a Bonɔ man in return (as *wel*). After a period of reconnaissance, they located Dufulu, a man of clan Wabisi but a member of the Bonɔ longhouse community, staying at a sago camp and killed him there. The people of Bonɔ, who felt that their original murder was justified, were extremely irritated at this and began looking in their turn for a Gæsumisi person to kill. Both sides remained at a stand-off for several months. Then a Gæsumisi woman was identified as the *sei* responsible for the death of a child of a member of her own longhouse community. The kinsmen of the child determined to kill her but, seeing an opportunity to resolve the continuing Bonɔ-Gæsumisi confrontation as well, invited Bonɔ to do the job for them. Bonɔ did so and had the satisfaction of getting *wel* for Dufulu. The situation between themselves and Gæsumisi was considered settled.

The functional convenience of this resolution reflects more than a sense of practical efficiency. It also reveals a certain sense of form.

One suspects an esthetic element when the events of resolution are shaped with a degree of elegance that appears to go beyond the practical necessities of the situation. A man of Gæsumisi, whose wife died because of the depredations of a *sei* from Wɔsisɔ, arranged for a man from Didesa to kill the *sei* because the *sei* had previously murdered a man from Didesa. When the murder was accomplished, Gæsumisi arranged for the body of the *sei* to be distributed for eating to yet another clan, Kagabesi, since the members of the *sei's* longhouse had previously eaten a Kagabesi man. Here the retaliation was arranged not only to achieve its own ends but also to conform, on the level of sentiment, to the completion of a number of other situations, long settled, that had little relevance to the situation at hand.

For large-scale prestations, the attainment of many closures in one event is part of the purpose of the situation. The presentation of a number of gifts between many different pairs of individuals summarizes the resolution of diverse individual obligations into a closure between groups of people as a whole. This also contributes to its quality as drama, drawing the many aspects of the situation together into the same conclusion with an exciting, thorough finality. The dramatic and public context in which many new gifts are initiated at a prestation supplies an additional urgency to the obligation that each one be reciprocated. It is partly for this reason that ceremonial distributions of pork between communities tend to follow quickly upon one another until the mature pigs of the area are practically all used up and several years must elapse to build up their numbers again for another round.

Oppositions and Social Process

The process of forming and resolving oppositions is more than a mechanism for the resolution of disputes. It is the major mode of forward social motion in Kaluli society. When an opposition is brought to closure through *su* or *wel*, the result is not a return to the initial situation. This is obvious in the case of a retribution, for there is no returning a man who has been killed or a pig that has been stolen and eaten. But it is equally the case with a gift exchange. If I give someone a pig and he later gives the same pig back, that is not *wel*. It is worse than if I had never given the pig at all, for it is a refusal of the relationship that the gift was intended to affirm. If, instead, he later returns another pig, though he neutralizes the debt, he accepts and affirms the original gift and furthers the relationship. When a death or dispute or, conversely, a neglected or desired friendship is cast in the form of an opposition between two principals over a loss (or a gift) and then resolved, the situation is moved forward over the net gain or loss of the material vehicles of the opposition (the loss or gift). A certain amount of social ground is covered; a certain amount of work is accomplished. Amicable relations now newly exist despite an intervening grievous loss or injury; renewed and closer affectionate relations may now obtain over a friendship of long standing.

This creative aspect of the opposition process has its analog in the hidden processes of the unseen. The curing of sickness is itself an opposition scenario enacted between the visible and invisible sides of reality. The difference is that, when the cure involves the return of a missing (invisible) body part, it is the same part that was originally affected by the *sei*. It is not merely an equivalent part, corresponding to *wel*. The secret, however, is that the "same" part has in fact been changed and renewed. Having died and decomposed through its treatment by the *sei*, it has been cleansed, healed, and revitalized prior to being pressed back on the body of the sick man to effect a cure. Though this aspect of the healing process is known only to mediums, it confirms the creative significance of the opposition process.

As a social procedure for resolving and moving forward social relationships, the opposition scenario embodies a typical kind of Kaluli situation quite apart from the social relationships of the actors engaged in a particular opposition. The question from our point of view is not "How are the actors and their supporters related?" but "How does an issue divide people and how do they resolve it?" For any issue, for any set of actors, the scenario turns out to be the same. The actors come into opposition on the basis of an issue at hand, be it a death or a side of pork, and then work out this relationship in an ordered way.

The opposition is not primarily one built into the social structure (as, for example, one descent group versus another or a husband versus his affines), though it may also be that and though it may be brought about through obligations entailed in such relationships. It is primarily a question of the interests or grievances of particular individuals occasioned by a particular issue that brings them into opposition.

The situation entails a typical cast of characters and a typical set of roles, postures, or attitudes that they adopt. The sequence of actions and events has an internal logic of its own, independent of the particular issue of opposition. The staging of the most important scenes is often done in the same location—namely, the *aa* —and the action between opposed groups blocked out in terms of *aa biʃɔ* and *miyɔwɔ*.[5]

---

[5] The opposed groups may be referred to by more specific terms, according to relevant aspects of the issue across which they are opposed. For a man who is going to receive pork at a distribution provided by his in-laws, he comes as *miyɔwɔ* in relation to the *aa biʃɔ* (those of the house of the wife). Those who go to kill a *sei* go as *sowɔ biʃɔ* (those of the house of the dead one) to the *sei biʃɔ* (those of the house of the *sei*). These are merely forms of *aa biʃɔ* and *miyɔwɔ* named for the specific occasion in which they have come into opposition.

Chapter 6

Assertion and Appeal

Kaluli society is basically egalitarian. It consists of a number of loosely knit residence communities (longhouses) that lack important corporate groups, roles of authority, and specialized jural and political institutions. A person's sense of obligation and his appeals for assistance or support are directed primarily toward particular individuals in his own and other longhouse communities. The networks of the various individuals in a longhouse community may overlap to some extent but they are not themselves groups. Rather, they form a flexible reservoir of relationships from which temporary groups may be brought into being (whether or not across an opposition) according to the circumstances.

Within this context, it is up to the individual to take initiative in organizing his own enterprises and obtaining redress for his injuries. The man who wishes to plant a garden invites others to join him and allots them plots. The prospective groom often plays a prominent part in gathering his bridewealth. The man whose wife or brother has died is supposed to organize the raid against the *sei* responsible. His relatives and connections in his own and other longhouses will usually join or support him if he asks for it and may occasionally take action on his behalf. But basically a man is expected to look out for his interests himself. Accordingly, Kaluli men tend to project a certain assertiveness and independence in social interactions. Good-humored, affable, and gentle in normal circumstances, they soon became forceful, jumpy, and quick to anger if something in their interest is at stake. They are both importunate and generous with friends and restrained, wary, and sometimes truculent in unfamiliar situations and with people they do not know.

Kaluli Assertiveness

To a Westerner newly arrived in Bosavi, Kaluli seem pushy, intrusive, demanding. I recall awakening one morning in the government rest house near the longhouse at Wahalib when it was just barely light. Suddenly, my shelter began to shudder under the footsteps of several people climbing up the entrance ladder. I quickly scrambled into my drawers as the most influential man of the longhouse walked in the doorway, followed by his wife, three or four other men, and several children. "Here! Eat!" he shouted, thrusting some sooty cooked bananas into my hand. The others fingered my blankets, examined my pack and camera. Still reeling and groggy, virtually naked, and shivering in the morning air, I was extremely annoyed. However, I recognized the hospitality in their intrusion and managed to greet them civilly. Then I struggled into the rest of my clothes, brushed my teeth, combed my hair, and finally ate the bananas, while they all watched in fascination.

I often felt I had no privacy; people would march into my house at any time to demand or sell something or to visit. But I soon discovered that it wasn't only because I was a stranger and an object of curious attention that they treated me like this—they were the same way with one another. People seemed often to deliberately intrude their presence on each other's space. For example, once a number of people were sitting around in conversation amid a pile of old cooking stones at a gathering. One of the hosts suddenly walked into the middle of the talking, laughing group and without a word vigorously started pushing and chucking the stones around in all directions. The group rapidly withdrew while he cleared the area and began a cooking fire. In the same way, a visitor approaching a longhouse often takes gleeful pleasure in coming up quietly and then appearing suddenly with a bang of his feet in the doorway, making everyone inside jump. This kind of behavior has the effect of making one's presence explicit or of drawing attention to events. It reflects the vigorous, assertive manner of much of Kaluli's important behavior.

The pace of life is slow in Bosavi, and most days people spend their time in casual hunting or visiting, working in gardens, sitting around the *aa* or sago camp engaged in idle conversation, weaving netbags, smoking, napping, or staring off into space. But forceful, decisive reactions are never far beneath the surface. They emerge in countless minor ways in daily life: in requests phrased as demands, in the flash of rage of a man who discovers a child has dented his bushknife, in a sudden decision to marry someone glimpsed for the first time at a gathering, in the burst of exuberance that greets a plan to stage a prestation, or in the precipitous flight of a man out the back of the *aa* and into the forest when he sees enemies approaching. Kaluli are lightning fast in responding to surprise, danger, or threats to their projects. Every man acts this way some of the time, and the most forceful personalities act this way much of the time.

The tendency to quick, forceful responses contributes to the instability of any situation where feelings become aroused, especially if someone feels his interests or property are threatened or he has been injured. Thus silly minor incidents can sometimes escalate into brawls.

> Some youngsters were playing in the yard in front of the *aa* at dusk, chasing a pith ball around. Kwa (about 8 years old), running after the ball, tried to make a sharp turn by grabbing a taro plant at the edge of a garden. The plant uprooted and in the process pulled out some small pawpaw plants planted nearby. Iwalo (age 17), who owned the pawpaws, became enraged and, grabbing his bushknife, he sheared off the leaves of the offending taro plant. The taro, however, belonged not to Kwa who was too young to own anything, but to Hongowabi (about age 13). Hongowabi retaliated by pulling out Iwalo's pumpkin plant and throwing it down the side of the ridge. Iwalo, now really furious, waded into the taro garden and cut down all of the plants, most of which, however, belonged not to Hongowabi but to Madibu, a married man. Madibu, informed of this, came running out of the *aa* with his bushknife, felled a banana tree that he thought was Iwalo's but in fact belonged to Susuwo. Susuwo ran out of the house and the three of them went at each other with their

fists. Finally, after a good deal of yelling, they were separated by
bystanders and persuaded to forget it on the grounds that they
were all "brothers" in the same house group and "brothers"
shouldn't fight. (Field notes)

This kind of sudden reaction is the basis for my characterizing
the Kaluli as volatile. They find in it an attractive, dramatic, somewhat frightening quality by which a person projects himself
strongly into even commonplace events. Many times I have seen
one or two men in a garden working with a fierce vitality, wielding
the digging stick with tense and vigorous thrusts while they puffed
and stamped from one planting spot to another.

Even in nonsocial situations of physical or emotional stress,
when burdened by pain, fear, or fatigue, their responses tend to be
assertive. Once I accompanied a friend on a trip to another longhouse. He was carrying a heavy load and finding the going increasingly difficult as we progressed up a long, steep incline. Just as I
thought he would set his load down for a rest, he burst out singing
a Gisaro song. He was defying the steepness of the hill, the weight
on his back, and his own fatigue, overcoming them by projecting
himself against them in song. In the same way, people would
sometimes begin to sing as I bandaged their injuries or admin-
istered injections. More than once, late at night, when the triple
whistle of the *sei* could be heard off in the forest, I heard it
answered by some wakeful person in the longhouse, who began to
sing Gisaro.

I came to see this Kaluli assertiveness as a style of behavior, a
modality for addressing oneself to situations. It was an attitude
with which one undertook whatever task or problem was at hand.
Pondering its quality, I wrote in my field notes:

> Kaluli act in a situation as if they were "up against something,"
> like one feels alive by actively asserting himself against everything.
> The result is that everything is done as if it were part of an eternal
> indian wrestling match, where the joy of it is in the struggle not
> (so much) the win. . . .

The point here is that this consistent way of behaving suggests
certain assumptions about what human activity and exertion
mean. A man who strongly thrusts a digging stick into the ground

not only indicates to bystanders "I am working" but also reveals something about himself in relation to work.

Kaluli assertiveness is grounded in an implicit sense of personal autonomy, or independence. This sense of autonomy, together with an instinctive alertness to events and a tendency to make quick decisive responses, is geared to an existence in which the normal activities of life—sago working, garden labor, visiting, and trading—are always more or less overshadowed by anxiety about witchcraft and, especially in the past, the possibility of violence. Illness and death are always lurking in the background. Moreover, because they are always somehow brought about by others, they insinuate themselves ambiguously into all but the most familiar social relationships. *Seis*, sickness, and murder (along with pigs and bridewealth) are common topics of conversation whenever men gather around a firebox. Most Kaluli have had experience with violence and have seen a human arm or leg in the smoking rack over a firebox (if they haven't eaten human flesh themselves). Some have seen people they knew and cared for murdered in front of their eyes. In past times, men and boys always went armed with bows when traveling through the forest.

Kaluli themselves do not speak of their behavior as intrusive, assertive, or volatile. Nevertheless, they appreciate the qualities I have tried to characterize with these words. The forcefulness, vitality, and often exuberance with which they infuse their activity is part of a posture toward life, a general cultural ethos that is closely bound up with deeply felt assumptions about the nature of productive energy and of the relation between male and female.

The Vitality of Men

When speaking of Kaluli behavior, one tends to think of the behavior of men. This is partly because of the high visibility of male activity. It is the men who tend to be dramatic and flamboyant, who act publicly, who compel attention. Most of the behavior that the Kaluli themselves consider culturally important is performed in the male role. Men arrange marriages; organize hunting trips, exchanges, and ceremonies; go on trading expeditions; and carry out raids. Men perform the important acts of magic that ensure success in gardening or hunting. Almost all the significant and dramatic sociopolitical acts among the Kaluli are the prerogative of men. This does not mean that the behavior of women is unimportant. Kaluli women can be tough and insistent, too, although usually without the male flamboyance. The difference is that if a woman clashes openly with a man, it becomes a matter of appearances, and unless she has a very strong case and a few relatives around, she is bound to lose. She may be beaten by her husband and end up sitting in the *aa* yelling out her sense of injury amid angry sobs. However, as everywhere else in the world, women in Bosavi often exercise substantial influence on the course of events from behind the scenes. The husband of an intelligent woman will frequently seek her advice on important matters pertaining to pigs and bridewealth. But on the stage, where decisions ostensibly are made and action undertaken, the principal actors are men.

Kaluli see themselves as men's men; the company they keep is made up mainly of men. The qualities they discuss as desirable are those by which men measure themselves. Physical mobility, agility, and endurance are conspicuous values. Men talk proudly of traveling long distances through the forest to trade at distant *aas* or of spending a week or two hunting on the tangled, forbidding slopes of Mt. Bosavi. Hunting success depends less on skill with traps or bows than on the ability of the hunter to cover a lot of ground quickly and on sharp eyes and fast reflexes to spot animals and stop them before they can escape.

Men characterize themselves as wiry, alert, and fast, capable of considerable endurance. By contrast, they see women as heavy and slow, unable to travel quickly or far. Kaluli women, in fact, convey this impression even to an outsider, being generally bulkier in appearance than men, and carrying themselves with a certain unwieldiness that is enhanced by their swaying skirts and ample breasts. Men develop an extensive and detailed knowledge of the forest, the lay of the ridges, and the flow of the rivers over a wide area. They also have a good understanding of the habits of the animals and the kinds, uses, and general ecology of local vegetation. Women do not possess such knowledge of the forest topography, animals, or vegetation, and usually spend their time around the *aa*, gardens, and sago camps, except when escorted by men to more distant places.

The relationships between men and women among the Kaluli are unusual, by New Guinea standards, for their lack of hostility and, indeed, for their affection. Nevertheless, male and female represent two poles in a fundamental cultural-metaphysical opposition that keeps relations between them awkward and problematic.

That women are weaker and less dynamic than men, that they are slow and clumsy and know less, is part of the same general condition of debility they manifest in menstruation. And this condition is dangerous to men because it is capable of destroying their manhood. The man who spends too much time in the women's section of the *aa*, who touches his wife too often, or who eats food a woman has stepped over is likely to become emaciated, develop a cough, or lose his endurance on the trail. This baleful female influence is concentrated in the female genitalia and the menstrual discharge. It undermines growth and health and ruins the effectiveness of the instruments of productivity (particularly male productivity). Women must carefully avoid stepping over little children lest they stunt their growth, and they must not step over hunting or fighting equipment.

We have already mentioned the various restrictions on sexual intercourse (Chapter 3) that must accompany gardening and hunting activities and the fact that a husband must take up his wife's food restrictions when he marries. It struck me as a poignant irony that the person on whom a man most depends in his domestic household and whom he usually holds close in his affections is also the one most dangerous to his vitality. The danger, moreover, is located in what (at least at first) attracts him most, her sexuality, and its most dangerous vehicle is precisely the vehicle of human fellowship, namely, food. Under these circumstances, it is not surprising that relations between men and women seem somewhat restricted to the Western eye. Kaluli men warned me repeatedly against sharing the same bed with my wife and pointed to my clumsiness on the trail as the consequence of such behavior.

While the female is enervating and debilitating, the male embodies the qualities of productivity, vigor, stimulation, and energy.

This male influence is concentrated in semen. Semen has a kind of magical quality that promotes physical growth and mental understanding. A youngster going to stay in a foreign area may be fed a mixture of semen, salt, and ginger to stimulate him to learn the language quickly. By the same reasoning, frequent repeated sexual intercourse is felt to be necessary to invigorate a child in the womb. (When not looking to produce children Kaluli avoid sex, lest a man dissipate his energy.) Semen is also necessary for young boys to attain full growth to manhood. Kaluli men maintain that women attain maturity by themselves (first menses?) but that boys do not. They need a boost, as it were. When a boy is eleven or twelve years old, he is engaged for several months in homosexual intercourse with a healthy older man chosen by his father. (This is always an in-law or unrelated person, since the same notions of incestuous relations apply to little boys as to marriageable women.) Men point to the rapid growth of adolescent youths, the appearance of peachfuzz beards, and so on, as the favorable results of this child-rearing practice.

Despite its benefits, however, men's homosexual relations with boys are a vulnerable point in the male image of strength and consequently a subject of considerable embarrassment in relation to the women. Men try unsuccessfully to maintain it as a secret that women do not know. It is regarded as part of the mystery of male and female. For their part, men profess (clearly falsely) that they do not know where babies come from. "This [pederasty] is our thing," I was told uneasily by one informant. "What happens when women go to the forest and bring back a child is their secret."[1]

Notions of "productive maleness" are bound up with anything that men do but are particularly important to quintessential male concerns such as hunting, fighting, garden planting, and the beauty of ceremonies. The magic and ritual associated with these activities is carefully protected from the knowledge of women and irresponsible youngsters. For women to know about these things

[1] The subject of childbirth is delicate, being at the center of the problematic male/female opposition. The Kaluli in fact have no word for childbirth. The term they use meaning "to give birth" means literally "to put [a child] in a net bag." The term for animal parturition is never applied to human beings.

would ruin their effectiveness and bring about some sort of general disaster. By the same token, those entirely free of contact with women are felt to be most effective at male pursuits. Virgin youths and unmarried young men are the best hunters, not just because of their supposedly greater speed, stamina, and sharpness of eye, but also because animals somehow have a greater tendency to come out and appear before them. To ensure the effectiveness of their hunting and sickness-warding magic, older men sometimes arrange to have it spoken by a virgin youth who has never been exposed to the female bane.

It is in the opposition between male and female that Kaluli locate those qualities and powers that are necessary to the success or failure of their most ordinary concerns. The productivity of gardens; the strength and initiative of the individual (versus his debility, ineffectiveness); the growth and health of children; the effectiveness and luck of the hunt, of healing magic, of fighting ability—all these are affected by the potencies embodied in maleness.

In relation to femaleness, maleness encompasses the dominant Kaluli values, and the figure of a man is something of a general cultural ideal. It is the men in Kaluli society, not the women, who are seen as the primary objects of sexual attraction,[2] and men are the central performers on ceremonial occasions, while women form the audience and cheering section.[3]

When a man is dressed in full ceremonial regalia, his body painted, his head dressed in cassowary feathers, his chest criss-

---

[2] Men's descriptions of "typical" sexual encounters depict the woman as taking the initiative while the man appears shy or confused.

[3] The activity I likened to cheering here is an energetic switching, swaying, dancing step called *sosomaya*. It is performed by the women of the host group in response to and celebration of high points in the visiting men's display and dancing, or of their arrival, but not as a dance in itself. Nearly all of the women's dancing that I saw in Bosavi was of this celebratory character. It is significant that those women who individually perform *sosomaya* in the house clearing to celebrate an arrival (as opposed to those who dance on the veranda) wear special long skirts and a small version of a man's cassowary headdress tipped with red vulturine parrot feathers. Men never perform *sosomaya*, which is strictly a woman's dance, but the exuberant, flamboyant quality of the dance—projecting a vitality normally associated with maleness —requires a flamboyant outfit, hence one that resembles that worn by men.

crossed with shells and beads, oiled red cordyline leaves stuck in the belt at his back, he projects an irresistible image of beauty and splendor that (supposedly) fills women with admiration and desire. The ultimate triumph of the male image is when one or more of the unmarried girls is so smitten by the beauty of one of the visitors that she elopes by following him home after the ceremony.

Kaluli maleness had its highest expression in the *bau aa* ceremonial hunting lodge, in which the virgin youths and young unmarried men from a number of longhouses lived for periods of up to fifteen months. Seclusion from women was strictly observed. Most of the time was spent on long, grueling daily hunts ranging over wide areas of forest. In the *bau aa* the youths' special virginal hunting ability was enhanced through repeated magical and ritual actions. They gained wide knowledge of animals, forest geography, and lore and developed the manly virtues. At the same time, they accumulated an enormous pile of smoked game in the rafters of the *bau aa*. Homosexual intercourse was practiced between the older bachelors and the younger boys to make them grow, some boys and men developing specific liaisons for the time. The *bau aa* was not quite an initiation program, however. A man could attend a number of *bau aas* during his bachelor life, if he wished, or none at all. One did not attain any formal status for having attended, nor was attendance required for attainment of full manhood. Rather the *bau aa* was a celebration of productive manliness, a paradigm of the good life—and it was great fun. The virtues of a *bau aa* were felt to benefit the entire area, quieting the appetites of *seis*, warding off illness, promoting prosperity. To cap it off, a *mamul* (spirit) woman from Mt. Bosavi, in the guise of an oddly shaped stone, was married to the leader of the *bau aa* at a ceremony before the climactic distribution of smoked game to male relatives and friends from all over the plateau. The young men emerged from seclusion decked in their brightest finery, so handsome and so much grown, it is said, that their own relatives didn't recognize them. They made a tour of all the local *aas* to be admired, and in a few months, many of the bachelors got married.

Kaluli see what I have called "male vitality" (they have no

term for it) as primarily beneficial. But it also appears to have its dark side. Once when going to visit an *aa* far from my home base with some young men as my carriers, we came upon an empty (though apparently not abandoned) garden shack. The young men rushed inside and began horsing around, breaking things with their axes, tossing net bags and bits of equipment around, whooping and hollering, and wrecking the interior. I had never seen any of them behave like this at home. Fearful that our prospective hosts at the nearby *aa* would take umbrage at this treatment of their property, I managed to get my friends out of the place. None of the young men had any relative in the area, and so they felt little responsibility for their behavior.

When assertiveness becomes aggression, when desire becomes totally egocentric, overpowering, and capricious, when anger is uncontrollably violent, we are faced with the destructive aspect of strength and vitality: the characteristics of a *sei*. One does not know why a *sei* acts as he does. *Seis* are usually characterized as driven by a kind of dangerous, unreasoning willfulness or hunger that is difficult to turn aside. The direct stare of his glowing red eyes is a kind of stunning violation of a person's autonomous self that prostrates him with illness. If people ever speculate about why a particular *sei* might have attacked a person, the reasons are always trivial. It is retaliation for a theft of a pineapple, or a minor insult, or an imagined slight at a food or bridewealth distribution. Nearly all Kaluli *seis* are men. When his *sei* aspect creeps out of his body at night, it emerges as a destructive form of potency from the penis.[4] (It is for this reason that Kaluli cut the genitals from a *sei* after he has been killed.) A *sei's* impetus is thus a kind

---

[4] Kaluli describe the *sei inso*, the *sei* creature that resides in a man's heart and makes him a *sei*, as something like a leech. Leeches are like *seis* because they live by eating a living person's substance, and Kaluli sometimes refer to them as *seis*; moreover, one can become a *sei* by accidentally drinking water that has a leech in it. (This is how women are thought to become *seis*.) The characterization is curiously apt and disgusting. If one thinks of the *sei* as a kind of male potency gone destructive, then a leech waving its sucker in the air or inching along the forest path becomes like a tiny disembodied penis endlessly searching for blood. Whether the Kaluli note this particular connection I do not know. They do not specifically link *seis* with "male energy," but these images are developed within the same set of symbols, and hence bear an implicit metaphorical relationship that completes their meaning.

of male potency gone wrong. Consequently, while homosexual intercourse with a "hard" man produces proper growth and healthy life, a boy who has intercourse with a *sei* grows too quickly and dies young. Still worse, he may become a *sei* himself. (This is why a father is careful in choosing who is to provide the pederastic growth stimulus for his sons.)

However, as the image of the forceful but destructive *sei* suggests, reliance on personal force alone, in isolation, is neither good nor sufficient. A prowling *sei* appears as a kind of ugly loner on the spirit side, who uses his invisibility only to gain destructive access to his victims. By contrast, a medium enters the invisible by virtue of his connections with its inhabitants, through marriage to his spirit wife. The *sei* emerges through a man's penis as a dangerous potency. The medium leaves his body through his anus "like the door of his *aa*." It is through the amicable marriages of their mediums that Kaluli realize an effective healing relationship with the spirit side and are able to deal with the solitary destructiveness of *seis*.

Similarly, in the visible side of reality, though virgin youths are preferred as hunters and female influence is avoided when male productive capacities are particularly engaged, it is only through a relationship with a woman—that is, through marriage—that a man can develop the connections and influence that render him fully effective in his life.

Achieving Cooperation

A man by himself, however dynamic and energetic as a person, cannot make his way in life without others—kinsmen, age-mates, and affines. How is cooperation between them achieved? It is at first difficult to understand how individuals expected to embody a volatile, independent temperament and sensitive to being coerced or interfered with in their projects can cooperate so readily and peacefully with each other. One is tempted to invoke the customary "rights and obligations" between kinsmen and in-laws, but this begs the question. It is true that kinsmen and affines have mutual expectations of each other that go with their relationship.

But the question remains: how is cooperation to be solicited between people like Kaluli? We are distinguishing here between the legitimate *expectations* of cooperation between kinsmen and affines and the approach they must use to get it.

Men assume a thoroughgoing posture of equality among themselves. Any appearance of compulsion infringes on one's sense of personal autonomy and invites an angry reaction, even between children and adults. A man who dominates a particular set of events or who otherwise is a person of influence holds a position that is really first among equals. His dominance is relative to the particular pressures he can bring to bear on the situation (favors owned, appeal to kinship sentiments, presence of supporters, and so on). Appeal for cooperation must be phrased so that the participants can appear to have chosen to take part of their own free will. This is true even where kinship or affinal expectations or favors owed give them reasons for cooperating whether they wish to or not.

Under normal circumstances, it is not always clear how this is accomplished. Matter-of-fact requests between kinsmen are often phrased as demands, and Kaluli sometimes give the impression of ordering each other around, particularly in times of excitement. But demands, in the end, are only forceful requests. They carry compulsion only insofar as the circumstances of the situation or the relationship lend them weight. Their function is largely rhetorical: a demand projects a person forcefully into a situation, galvanizes others, lends motion to events. Demands may be backed up by implied threats or intimidation if a person thinks he can get away with it in the circumstances, but a person who is unwilling to comply will ignore them, make some excuse, or take off into the forest. To try to force him is asking for trouble.

Kaluli commands initiate action because they are exciting, noisy, and dramatic. In the final minutes when a fishing dam is being closed and men and youths are in a fever of activity, irritable yells fly back and forth, "More dirt here!" "Seal that crack!" "Where's more bark?" "Ax! Ax! Cut that tie!" "Go! Go! Get out of the way!" and the like. These are appeals phrased in a manly way. The people who are yelling at each other are already cooperating in the venture. The imperative mode here conveys not personal authority so much as a sense of urgency or excitement.

In a society where brothers and age-mates share most of what they have, a beloved or well-known person in need of something has a very strong appeal. No matter how their support was demanded, Kaluli never phrase their reasons for going to someone's assistance in terms of obligation or duty. Rather, they speak in terms of sympathy and compassion—"I felt sorry for him so I went"—or supportive outrage—"I was angry when those people killed his pig."

In a case of real misfortune, sympathy is immediately forthcoming. When Dasemi of Olabia died from a snake bite, Jomo of Ferisa was publicly identified as the *sei* responsible. At the funeral, women wailed over the body, while Dasemi's husband, Beli, sat forlornly in the rubbish near the back of the *aa*, his two small children playing nearby. Around him visiting men seated on the sleeping platforms shouted speeches of outraged sympathy. The children had no mother now and Beli had no one to cook for him, they yelled at me in anger and dismay. Others shouted at newcomers that Jomo had taken Beli's wife and should be made to give return. If it were not for the government, they declared, they would go right out and kill him. This was how support for the murder of Hagabulu had materialized almost of itself twelve years before.

The same kind of sympathetic assistance is also forthcoming in minor domestic emergencies. When Turinei learned that his in-laws were arriving unexpectedly the next day with a formal prestation of game (*ga sigi*), he ran to his gardens to see what he would be able to feed them. It was the season of pandanus, but few of his trees were bearing. Greatly agitated when he returned, he remarked, "Wafio! They are bringing *ga sigi* and I have no pandanus!" Within minutes the word had gotten around the house group, and three or four men departed for their gardens to get Turinei necessary food.

To some degree house group pride was involved here, since a community likes to make a good showing of hospitality to an arriving group of in-laws bearing gifts. Moreover, everyone in the house group would share the meat of the prestation. But everyone explained their assistance to Turinei as motivated by sympathy for him, not pride or anticipation of meat. These latter considerations may have been relevant at other levels, but not that of immediate feeling. Turinei and Beli were figures of pathos and that was the source of their appeal.

For legitimate and ordinary requests to kinsmen in everyday circumstances, Kaluli use a matter-of-fact or even slightly demanding manner. But the more socially distant the person, or the more unreasonable, urgent, or gratuitous the request, the more a person tries to affect a posture deserving of sympathy. Thus a man might sit down with others at the social firebox in the *aa*, take out his smoking tube, and then rummage pointedly (but unsuccessfully) in his net bag for something to smoke. Then he sighs, as if to himself, "I have no tobacco." Depending on how skillful the actor is, one may or may not be able to detect the con man underneath. People hoping to scrounge some small item from me would affect a woebegone expression and say, "I have no salt [beads, matches, soap]." Women would hold up their babies begging things on their behalf.

People who are disappointed or frustrated in their desires and feeling sorry for themselves sometimes express their feelings and try to strike a sympathetic image by breaking spontaneously into song. One day after Aebi had had another spat with his wife, I heard him singing Gisaro melody softly to himself in the longhouse, "My wife won't obey. My wife won't obey." Similarly, when Gigio's catch of fish slipped off the river bank and back into the water, he half-humorously assumed a dancer's pose, bouncing slowly and singing, "My fish have fallen into the stream. eeee-oooo." On another occasion, Wanalugo, covetously fondling a pearl shell that he had been trying to wheedle from me, began softly to sing of his desire for it.

In the extreme, when a person wants something badly that he is entitled to expect and is driven to his wits' end in the attempt to gain it, he may begin to weep. Dæba, a leading man of Wɔsisɔ, asked his wife, Masia, several times to cook him some food, but she procrastinated until he was very hungry. Instead of becoming enraged and beating her, he thought of his dead former wife, Dibe, who always cooked for him promptly, and then burst into wails. The people around regarded him with amused sympathy, but it didn't reflect well on his wife, Masia. Kaluli regard bursting into tears to express need as extreme behavior (I saw it happen only twice), but it represents only the most extreme projection of the mode of appeal that basically underlies most of their requests to one another.

In terms of face-to-face interaction, the appeal of need enables kinsmen to give and receive cooperation while maintaining a posture of personal autonomy and voluntary action. It also reflects the personal quality of Kaluli relationships.

Individuals appeal for the assistance of others along network lines. The resulting group organized to perform a task consists of a core of one or more people, often from the same longhouse, united by their mutual interest in the project, and helpers (who will also share in the proceeds of the work) recruited by each of the several core members along their separate network lines. The group takes cognizance of itself according to the task to be performed, not the social relationships involved. The result, in most group activity, is visible in the posture of autonomy preserved by each man engaged in the common project.

When several men decide to work together at something, like building a fishing dam or clearing the stump of a large tree from the houseyard, they do not really function as a coordinated team but divide the job into a number of separate but parallel jobs. To remove a stump, for example, each man chooses a single root to work on and works at his own speed with ax or digging stick, resting when he feels like it, regardless of what others are doing. Though the job gets done effectively, the performance does not project a coordinated effort. Even when there is a truly combined effort, as when men must pull together on a rope to rip the stump out and pull it over, there is no unified heave-ho. Everyone grabs the rope, and, whooping and stamping, pulls more or less together until the stump goes over. Unity of effort is effected through numbers more than teamwork and roughly synchronized through rhythmic stamping and mutual exuberance.

A sense of unified effort is often brought about ceremonially in just this way. Kaluli often begin (and sometimes conclude) a project with a noisy, dramatic, climactic display that they call *ulab*.

Ulab. Men arriving at a wedding run, intoning and stamping into a circle.
(Photo by B. Schieffelin.)

As people are standing around waiting to do something, a few men, sensing the moment, suddenly jump up, shouting "Bruh! Bruh!" in deep-throated tones and begin stamping and bouncing up and down together in place. Others immediately run to join the circle, everyone bouncing vigorously, waving axes over their heads, twanging their bowstrings. Shouts of "Bruh! Bruh!" give way to a low note "ɔɔɔɔ," which increases in intensity until the stamping, pressing men in the circle suddenly bring their waving axes and bows down together and end their motion abruptly with a single unified shout: "*UUUU!*" Then all rush off to do what they were about to do. The noise and motion of *ulab* projects an atmosphere of vitality and exuberant spirit. The stamping and shouting not only synchronize their noise and motion but are a real exertion. The men pound the earth dancing themselves into tune with each other, working each other up into a mutually vigorous and wonderful state.

Ulab is performed to initiate a garden planting or to announce a successful murder of someone in the forest by a raiding party. It announces the approach of visitors in the forest bringing gifts and concludes an arrival display in front of an *aa*. Through *ulab* a group unifies itself, projects its energy, and declares itself as a force to be reckoned with. It is a means by which male energy can be visibly mobilized in cooperative social action.

Chapter 7

Anger, Reciprocity, and the Rhythms of Experience

Kaluli refrain from courses of action that presume too much on another's generosity, frustrate his legitimate expectations, or trespass on his interests. This is because they fear his anger.[1] An act of lashing out in anger among the Kaluli has a directly reciprocal meaning. In the West, we tend to view a strike in anger in its punitive aspect: a negative reward for an undesirable action. If we ask why A struck B, the answer is usually "Because B did such and such." A Kaluli, however, would reply, "Because A was angry." His act is viewed primarily as a satisfaction for his feelings through return of the injury[2] rather than as a punishment or deterrent to an offender. (Of course, it also acts as a deterrent, but the implication is one of direct personal retaliation rather than approved sanction for misconduct.)

[1] Kaluli sometimes take some trouble to avoid frustrating others. If, for some reason, a wedding is called off at the last moment, those who are responsible will not only return all of the bridewealth, but give a few extra items of wealth to the disappointed groom "so that he won't be angry." Similarly, a man who is reluctant to give something that is forcefully requested by a man to whom he owes favors will try to deflect his friend's importuning and disappointment by offering him something else.

[2] Occasionally, the purpose of retaliation is not to return an injury but to arouse anger. Thus, in one case, A was furious because B had killed his pig as a provocation, so A tried to kill B's brother "to make him angry" in return.

Anger and a Sense of Proportion

Kaluli never hold a grudge. They always direct anger immediately outward and express it vigorously if circumstances permit. While an angry man is implicitly someone who has been injured or suffered loss and thus a figure of sympathy, at the same time, he is not necessarily in full control of his feelings and actions. People tend to stand clear of his stamping and yelling until they find out what is wrong. Then support or recriminations are forthcoming, and eventually action may be taken.

Anger is part of one's "masculine vitality": it is an indication of productive strength for a man to become angry and strike back if he has been sufficiently provoked. Kaluli do not speak of this in so many words, but they are aware that a person who does not react angrily in appropriate circumstances displays a social weakness and may be taken advantage of by more assertive individuals. Parents and relatives try to teach their children to react aggressively if they are picked on in play.[3] This, however, is more than merely a question of learning an aggressive retaliatory response. An angry act (unless rage is wholly uncontrollable) must be constrained in proportion to the particular social relationships, the sense of injury involved, and the nature of the circumstances:

---

[3] The connection between assertiveness and growth here is implicitly recognized. Since Beli's mother was dead, he had been sent by his father to live with his mother's brother's family until he was able to walk. His uncle, however, did not give him the attention due to a true son, and, at about three years of age, Beli was often teased by his little cross-cousins, Dauwa and Dibe (about six and nine years old). Though not fretful by nature, he was often provoked to tears. He spent more time than the average child crying unhappily on the veranda of the *aa*. When he was about three and a half, his father came to take him home to another longhouse. Three months later, they returned for a visit. I was astonished to see how much Beli seemed to have grown and changed. He appeared to be an inch taller, filled out, and much more confident. His mother's brother explained to me that he had eaten much meat at his father's *aa* and so had grown. Dibe, however, one of the children who had been playing with (and tormenting) him, told me that when he was living at Bonɔ he had been hit a lot by the other children (and thus stayed small). At his father's place, with his brothers, he wasn't picked on so much and so he grew. The Kaluli association of social assertiveness and physical growth was perfectly clear to my nine-year-old informant, who saw Beli not from the perspective of a neglectful uncle but as a peer.

Gurambo was clearly worried about his sick wife, Gania, and cooked her a meal of pandanus. Gania, however, refused to eat. Gurambo persisted in pressing her until, in a flash of anger, she cursed him and told him to take the stuff away. Others in the small *aa* flinched, as her curse was the kind that causes men to die and gardens to wither (*ililæ siyɔ*). Furious, Gurambo leaped up, grabbed an ax, and laid into his side of the *aa*, sending splintered partitions, sleeping platforms, and pieces of fireboxes flying in all directions. Then he cut through all of the houseposts (except one that kept the roof from collapsing) and finally rushed outside to kill one of his half-grown pigs. It was all over in less than two minutes.

Gurambo had been insensitive in urging the food on his sick wife, but Gania had overreacted in laying a curse on him that endangered his life. Gurambo, though understandably enraged, did not wish to injure her, so he wrecked their place of domesticity instead (a not uncommon response of a man seriously angry with his wife). Killing the pig forestalled the possibility that he himself would die from the curse, and the commotion brought sympathetic attention from others. (Field notes)

Social circumstances, personal sentiment, and obligations outstanding determine how far a person may be pushed, taken for granted, or exposed to minor slights and frustrations—and also how he may modulate his anger in response. It is clearly possible in a flash of rage to overreact, to retaliate with a large injury over a small matter. (This is a characteristic attributed to *seis*.)

The key to the controlling sense of proportion here lies in the frankly retaliatory character of an angry outburst and the fact that Kaluli frequently refer to an angry act as *wel* for an injury or loss. Anger is a matter of reciprocity, even if only for hurt feelings, and it is the sense of reciprocity that provides the limitations for anger. Moreover, it modulates Kaluli behavior on all levels of interaction, whether between men in battle or between children playing in the houseyard.

Kaluli learn reciprocity very young since it provides the limitations that prevent children from being unduly bullied by their peers. Older children have a finely developed sense of this and encourage small fry to fight back when they lose their nerve or change sides to support those who are getting the worst of an altercation.

Deyæ (a boy, about four), Dauwa (a girl, about six), and Baidæ (a boy, about four) were walking together in the house-yard. Deyæ threw a stick at the other two. Dauwa turned and smacked him on the back and he began to cry. At this, Baidæ, supporting Deyæ, smacked Dauwa, who promptly returned the blow, and he too began to cry. At this point, Gigio (a boy, about thirteen) came up yelling at Dauwa, "What are you trying to do, anyway!" and hushed up the two crying little boys. Then he gave one of them a stick to chase Dauwa with while she ran away laughing.

Such interventions, which were quite common, seem aimed more at allowing the interaction to conclude properly than with scolding or punishing an offender. On another occasion, when Ayaka, an older boy (about sixteen), provoked Dauwa, she seized a banana stem from the rubbish and went after him. Ayaka did not grab the stem out of her hand, or hit back, using his superior strength, but simply ran away. He could not lose face by being chased by someone obviously not his equal, so he concluded the interaction appropriately by running away, as any adult would do if someone armed came after him.

For the Kaluli, the sense of reciprocity, embodied in the notions of *su* and *wel* carried out in the action of the opposition scenario, provide the measure and context by which a person exercises his powers and learns his limits; they shape his social space and the rhythms of his actions throughout his life.

Deyæ (about four), is more of a whiner and crybaby than are other children his age. I have seen him, big as he is, occasionally carried by his mother in a net bag like a baby. He is generally fretful, weak, and nonassertive, a less formed personality than his peers.

Today, while it was still raining and the yard in front of the *aa* was quite muddy, Hingulu (age ten), Kogowe (age eight), and Deyæ came out to fool around. Hingulu and Kogowe engaged Deyæ's wrath in some way, and as they were walking over toward my cook house Deyæ came running up behind them angrily holding a tin of water to throw. Gigio, at the door of the cook house, laughingly shouted a warning. "Deyæ's going to get back at you, better look out, he's right behind you." Hingulu and Kogowe turned around and jumped aside just in time to miss most of the water. They immediately scooped up some mud and began to chase Deyæ with it while he ran back fretful and frustrated, beginning to show signs of tears. Hingulu and Kogowe splattered him with mud and he began running away and jumping up and down with rage and frustration, not knowing what to do. Gigio immediately ran out yelling, "Deyæ, Deyæ, here. Gather up mud like this." He pushed up some mud in a pile with his foot. "Put it in the tin." Deyæ, as much distracted from his fret as given a way to act in the situation, immediately began gathering up mud in his hands under Gigio's direction, looking with fear and fret in the direction of Hingulu and Kogowe, who were also gathering up mud. He seemed to be afraid that they would gather up theirs first and throw it at him before he had his ready. However, when they had their mud together they just stood there ready to throw waiting to see what he would do. Deyæ filled his can and started forward toward them, Gigio hallooing and jumping up and down in the background to whoop up the fray. Deyæ's face as he hesitantly approached the two other boys showed a flickering change of fear and anger, loss of nerve, edge of weeping, and the determination to throw his can of mud. Kogowe and Hingulu watched him calmly, a little amused, it seemed, not so much at his pitiful figure as at the game that was going on. Gigio, in the background, continued to whoop and holler and when Deyæ hesitated, urged him, "Throw it! Throw it!" Finally, Deyæ ran a few steps forward, awkwardly heaved his can of mud, and then wheeled and ran, his momentary look of angry determination giving way to fear and fret. Hingulu and Kogowe, who were not struck by anything Deyæ had thrown, stepped forward a few paces and threw their charges of mud at him from a distance (they did not take the kind of advantage of his weakness that I have seen kids do in the West, namely, wait until the less experienced party has thrown his charge, and then run up on him and give him a heavy, humiliating barrage at close range).

It was evident that everyone except Deyæ had some distance on the situation. Gigio was maintaining an atmosphere of excitement by whooping and laughing and jumping up and down. Hingulu and Kogowe seemed mildly diverted finding their situation at the same time a little ridiculous, but I had the feeling that they both felt they had to keep it up as long as Deyæ took it seriously, lest they appear to be laughing at him. But they were willing to enjoy it too. Deyæ alone was totally engaged, wrestling in this game with his own inadequacies.

Deyæ ran back to where Gigio was standing. He was obviously not at all sure whether he would be allowed to gather up more mud before being reattacked, but Kogowe and Hingulu, after gathering more mud for themselves, waited for him again. Deyæ finally advanced again to where they were standing, but they waited no matter how close he got, until he had thrown at them first. They then threw in return at him. Deyæ came up again uncertainly, but with increasing confidence, and had another shot, retreating immediately but in better order. The remainder of the game became more and more noisy as Deyæ, gaining confidence, began to enjoy it. He realized that he would be allowed his throws before suffering a barrage of mud himself. Hingulu and Kogowe seemed to be throwing according to how effective Deyæ's throw had been. A bad shot got a desultory response. A good one got a more calculated response. For all there was a certain excitement and danger. Deyæ was permitted to take an equal part in the interaction according to his ability. He understood he would get response according to what he gave. (Field notes)

Here the sense of reciprocity provided the context and maintained the order of interaction among naked little boys throwing mudballs. The situation is clearly more than a game. It is a social and psychological struggle set and resolved within deeply sensed cultural forms. The "rules of the game" (the feeling for *wel*) furnished sufficient balance to the situation for the weaker member to keep his feet. As a result, his self-confidence and ability to handle this kind of situation visibly improved. Reciprocity not only links men together, but it also structures their expectations and regulates their conduct in social situations. Self-confidence, assertiveness, generosity, and friendship are all developed and given proportion in its context.

Where *wel* and *su* provide sense of balance to interactions, events unfold in the shape of reciprocity scenarios (what we have called opposition scenarios). Even when little boys are throwing mud, it isn't a continuous all-out battle but a series of exchanges— analogous in adult terms to a murder in return for a death or a pig in return for a pig.

Reciprocity and the Sense of Time and Events

Reciprocity is bound up, moreover, with the Kaluli perception of time and events, which is somewhat different from ours. In the West, we tend to think of time in terms of a linear progression of events, one situation developing out of another. We measure this progression in intervals: days, weeks, months. Hence, we have a cycle of seasons, a year, and a cumulative sense of history. Kaluli recognize three seasons, not by counting months (*ili*, moons) or by noting changes in the weather, but by marking changes in the forest vegetation. The "season" of *dona* is when the *dona* trees are in fruit; *imɔ* (literally "tree base") is when the leaves fall around the base of the trees; and *tan* is characterized by pandanus coming into fruit.

However, this sense of season does not imply a strong sense of cyclicity.[4] For Kaluli, the *dona* trees do not come into fruit because it is the season of *dona*; rather it is the season of *dona* because the *dona* trees have come into fruit. Thus, while they recognize that these seasons repeat themselves, they do not associate them with an abstract cycle. In fact, my informants experienced difficulty in trying to recall for me which season followed which. They knew which season it was at the moment, but there was considerable discussion between men and youths as to which one was supposed to precede it and which was likely to follow. Kaluli experienced similar difficulties when trying to recall the historical sequence of events in the past.

For the Kaluli, the perception of time seems to be constructed around events, rather than events being primarily related to each other in time. This perception is enhanced by certain properties of the Kaluli language. Words that denote time at various removes from the present (comparable to "later" or "a while ago" in English) distinguish, not between past and future, but only distance in time. The words for "tomorrow," "two days from now," and "in three days time" (*ali, inali, æmæ inali*) also mean "yesterday," "day before yesterday," and "three days ago," respectively. The word for "a long, long time ago" (*mɔlu*) also can refer to the distant future. The tendency is to group events concentrically around the present (or a particular event of the past) and to mute the sense that the event in question is part of a larger sequence. It is as if an event stands, not in a temporal continuum, but in

4 The same is true for the people of Lake Kutubu (see Williams, 1940); this feature of temporal perception may be widespread throughout New Guinea.

isolation, and other events at various temporal distances are referred to it. This is not merely a property of the language but appears to be an aspect of the way events are actually thought of and perceived.

All this is not to say that Kaluli cannot think "historically" about their past in some way comparable to the Western mode, but it is not their tendency to do so. Their perception of events is not governed by notions of causal or developmental sequences. Rather, it is strongly bound up with the way events are related in the opposition scenario. If one man kills another's pig, that act is resolved by the retaliatory killing of his pig (or payment of compensation). With that, the incident is closed. That it may be but one incident in the escalation of a long-standing hostility did not immediately emerge from my informants. To them, an incident and its resolution forms a closed sequence more than a part of a larger situation of hostility, and they do not see any necessity to proceed beyond that sequence in explaining it.

"Why did Bonɔ attack Muluma's *aa* and kill Walaga?"
"Hali of Bonɔ was angry because Aube of Muluma had girdled his sago trees, so he killed his brother, Walaga."
"Why then, did Aube girdle Hali's sago trees?"
"Well, when Sogusuwɔ of Kɔlɔdɔ had come as a *sei* and caused the death of Aube's brother, Hæmindæ, Aube asked Hali to go to Kɔlɔdɔ and hold him to be killed. Instead, Hali warned Sogusuwɔ and Kɔlɔdɔ drove off the attackers, so Aube was angry and girdled Hali's sago trees."
"Why did Hali warn Sogusuwɔ if he was a *sei?*"
"Someone had stolen some sago from Hali's storage place, and Hali thought it was a Muluma man so he was angry with [anyone from] Muluma."

And so on. To me, it was like pulling teeth, even with interested and willing informants.[5]

Unexpected or important events tend to be perceived (or dressed up) as sudden and dramatic, calling for an instantaneous

[5] To be certain of the proper order in my inquiries, I had to get people to refer to the location of their longhouses at the time and which gardens were currently being planted. The sequence of these things seemed always to be clear because one lived at a given house site for about two years and was familiar with the exact stage of growth of all of his gardens at any time.

and vigorous response. If an event is powerful but there is no "vigorous" way to react, Kaluli have difficulty dealing with it. For example, Kaluli are deeply disturbed by thunderstorms. Everyone in the *aa* becomes tense with apprehension as the rain pours down. Grown men startle and curse when the thunder suddenly booms. Some chew magical bark, snap their fingers, and mutter spells to make the noise go away. In my own house, my thirteen-year-old cook and his assistant would dive under the table. Other youths would respond assertively by whooping and stamping around in the yard or in the hall of the *aa*. While everyone knows that thunder is the stamping and shouting of the *mamul* people from Mt. Bosavi, it is not because of that that people are so disturbed. Rather, they told me, it is the sudden tremendous *noise* of the thunder that frightens them. The crack and roll of the thunder are invisible blows that galvanize one's reflexes but to which there is no meaningful way to respond.

The "appropriate" response, of course, would have to be reciprocation for one's fright. During a moment of excitement in a conversation with a Kaluli friend, I once banged my hand loudly on the table for emphasis. My companion jumped into the air, fear and astonishment flashing across his face. The conversation stopped as he recovered himself: "Whsssh! Bage! My soul [*mama*] has jumped to Bosavi!" Recovering from my own surprise at his reaction, I stammered, "Did your soul really jump to Bosavi?" "No," he answered, "but that's what one says." Then, half teasing me, he said, "Wa! Give me matches! Give me soap!" He was asking for compensation. His metaphor of his soul's flight to Bosavi and his demand for *su* suggest that he experienced his fright as a momentary loss of something.

On other occasions such a "loss" is treated as quite real. Once a visitor arrived at Sululib with an eight-foot python as a gift to his affines. It was still alive and wriggling as the people gleefully unwrapped it from the bundle. At this point, the government medical orderly and his assistant walked into the *aa* to see what the excitement was about. One man proudly thrust the serpent forward for their inspection. In seconds the medical orderlies were down the hall, off the veranda, and halfway across the yard. They were Papuans from the coast and had never seen a snake that size before. When the Kaluli themselves had recovered from their surprise, Wanalugo and one or two older men ran out after them, begging them to stop and saying that no harm was intended. Two large packets of crayfish were immediately brought forward from someone's catch and offered to the still-trembling orderlies, "in order," it was explained to me later, "that they not be angry." These were government men; the Kaluli were not sure how they would take this fright and so compensated them immediately to forestall any trouble.[6]

Whether shock and loss are material (through death or accident) or psychological (through surprise or fright), compensation may appropriately be offered by those responsible to forestall an angry reaction. In ambiguous situations, the impact of the precipitating event, the force of tension and anger, and the need for finding a satisfying resolution can clearly affect the cognitive appreciation of what is going on.

In November 1967 my wife and I accompanied a group of people from the longhouses of Sululib and Doba to build a fish dam across the Isawa River. About thirty men and boys worked all one day and part of the next to build it while we took notes and photographed the proceedings. Finally, late in the morning great strips of bark were laid over the structure to seal it, and the water began to rise. The people drew back onto the shore and waited intently to see if it would hold. The river rose a few minutes and then, with a cracking of timbers and a roar of water, the dam gave and was washed away. The men whooped and hollered and danced

---

[6] Kaluli sometimes use this form of startling and then compensating a person in a prankish manner—for example, when announcing to a young man that he is about to be married. The preliminaries of selecting the bride and collecting the bridewealth are usually arranged by the older men in the house group without the knowledge of the prospective groom. By the time they are ready to announce it to him, he is the only one not to know. A quiet time is chosen, as in the evening. One of his buddies, who is in on the secret, saunters up the hall of the *aa* and then lands with a bang in front of him yelling, "Your wife, Wadeo!" (or whatever her name), as he thrusts a pearl shell under his nose. The startled groom is then pressed with other objects of bridewealth from all sides. The show of support for him incidentally neutralizes whatever shock he may have experienced in the sudden realization of his new status in life.

up and down in the excitement and drama of the moment. Then, as the water subsided, they seemed not to know how to react. The general mood shortly turned to anger and dismay as people looked out over the settling water.

Everyone was highly wrought up; some were downcast and unhappy; others seemed scared. Wanalugo, whose dam it was, was furious. He came striding up to me and yelled that before the government or I had come to Bosavi their dams had never broken. One other day we had come with our cameras and photographed a fishing dam and it had broken. Now this one had broken as well, and we should get out of there. Some of the uncertain people seconded him. Sogobaye, an important visitor, looked very angry and grave in the background. Another man took a conciliatory, tactful tone, saying that he was going back to the *aa* and wouldn't I like to go with him? The Kaluli, having felt rather self-conscious with all my photography, seized on this as the reason for the disaster. Wanalugo looked so angry as he came up to me that I reflected that if this were ten years before and there were no government officer, the situation might have been resolved reciprocally then and there with an ax.

I responded with a yelling, angry speech of my own. I declared that the dam broke, not because my wife and I took pictures, but because they hadn't fixed the supports properly against the bottom of the river. I demonstrated this with a stick. Several doubtful people immediately brightened up and broke into smiles as if to say, "Hey, yeah, that's why it happened." One urged me to stay. Others, however, still looked uncertain when, to my surprise, Sogobaye climbed up on a stump and made a speech in which he recalled that the day before I had told him that the mission was lying when they said that all Bosavi was going to be consumed by fire (the UFM mission was a Fundamentalist church). He elaborated, saying I had told him everyone would be all right and eat well. The thrust was that I wished no harm to Kaluli people. This rallied the confidence of at least some of the others. I then made a speech saying that a camera could not hurt the dams since all one did was look through it. I offered it to anyone who wished to examine it, so that they could see for themselves. At this, the atmosphere cleared and shortly afterward, hallooing and hollering and waving axes, all the men leaped into the stream to rebuild the dam.

The dam was a big project, and a lot of effort had gone into it. At the crucial moment of its completion, the whole thing was dramatically destroyed. Everyone was angry, bewildered, frustrated, and the situation was left hanging without a resolution. As far as the builders were concerned, they had made the dam in the same way as all the others they had ever made, and those hadn't broken. A dramatic event such as this needed an explanation and a resolution.

One direction in which to move was obviously into the opposition scenario. An unusual event such as this could not have happened without cause: My wife and I and our cameras were incongruous elements in the situation; the fact that a dam had broken previously in the presence of our cameras was the clincher. In these terms the situation became intelligible, not so much through discovery of a cause as by formulation of a response: anger and our expulsion. They were looking for a well-ordered and familiar course of action. Its dramatic pull was obviously very powerful, even in the face of its trumped-up nature. In order to counter it, I had to provide an alternative but mundane explanation. In addition, the situation required a speech by a favorable character witness and the examination of the camera by those present to demonstrate its harmlessness. In effect, I was providing an emotionally and dramatically much less satisfying alternative, something whose ordinary nature fitted rather uncomfortably with the Kaluli sense of the unusual quality of the event. It could be accepted, however, and implied its own sort of response: the dam was faulty; it should be rebuilt more carefully.

The Kaluli sense of the immediacy of the present, the precipitous shifts of emotional experience, and the quickness of reflexes in responding to situations combine within the dramatic rhythm of the opposition process to give events a compelling force quite apart from their logical or cognitive qualities. The sense of this rhythm contributes to the "sense" of the situation that enables one to decide if an explanation is plausible or a course of action rightly conceived.

A person who has been wronged, insulted, or suffered loss does not withdraw into depression; he reacts angrily. His anger is justified and given proportion within the sense of reciprocity shared by all Kaluli, and he is a figure of sympathy. At the same time, there is meaning and direction to the thrust of his feelings, and impetus to action, since within the notions of *wel* and *su* there is a way to resolve them. The scheme of action outlined in the opposition scenario is already implicit in the loss itself. Grief and anger gain focus and purpose through the implication that there is a way they may be meaningfully resolved. In this way, the opposition scenario, energized by the urgency of a man's anger, affects the notions of causality of the events that bring it about. Serious events have proportionally serious causes.

So it is with death. For us, a person dies, and there is no way to resolve or make up his loss. For the Kaluli, there is the *sei*. So devastating an event as death cannot be fortuitous; it must have a cause or it is unintelligible[7] because there is no way to react. One's grief is only helplessness; there is no object for one's anger, no source of resolution or compensation for one's feelings. Hence, if the *sei* did not exist, it would be necessary to invent him. From this perspective, the *sei* is not so much a belief (for the Kaluli it is an experience) as a requirement for making cognitive and emotional sense out of a situation so that it can be brought to meaningful closure.

[7] Kaluli friends once asked me if there were *seis* in my country. I said that there were not. "Then you don't die?" they exclaimed. "No," I told them, "people get old and die." "Oh, then you have *seis* after all!"

Chapter 8

The Perception of
a Human Condition

Kaluli themselves do not talk about reciprocity or "opposition scenarios" as such. These are my own constructs intended to clarify the implications and significance of Kaluli behavior. Now it is time to examine how they themselves perceive their lives and express the concerns important to them.

Kaluli are not prone to slip into a philosophical mood and reflect systematically on the human condition. Nevertheless, it seems to me that they have a pervading sense of the quality of their life and a set of dominant attitudes toward it. These things are articulated piecemeal—whether in the self-projective vitality of hard work, the pathos of a ceremony, a thought shared, or a simple remark.

Warmth and Sentimentality

Kaluli have a deep sense of nostalgia and a love for their forest homelands that they feel especially when in a peaceful mood. Often a person sitting on the longhouse veranda will sigh, "Ah, my Bosavi," as he gazes raptly across the rolling forest to the slopes of the mountain. After a rain, people would call me as I pounded on the typewriter, "Wa! Bage! See the waterfalls!" and point to the silvery threads on the distant mountainside. Everyone would pause to watch them for a while.

My wife and I sometimes liked to sit with people and watch the sunset when it was particularly spectacular. "Whsssh! Isn't that nice?" a friend remarked to us once. "Doesn't it make you homesick?" Puzzled, I said, "No, why?" "Ah, if a Bosavi man is in a distant land and sees a sky like that, it makes him miss his home." "Oh, my Sululib," he added as example. Then he turned to the others and remarked that, since we didn't miss our homeland, we would never leave Bosavi.

There is no mistaking the feeling of affection and warmth when two or three men burst into song on arriving back at their own territory after an absence of a few days at another longhouse. Singing is appropriate not only because it projects the feeling of the singer but also because it is something to be *heard*—of a piece with the sounds of the forest itself. Sound images are much more evocative than visual ones for the Kaluli. The Ilib Kuwɔ dancers who drum up and down the hall of the *aa* during the afternoon before a ceremony spend a great deal of time tightening and adjusting their drum heads to produce just the right tone. It is not the rhythm of the drumming that is important here (indeed, with more than one drummer, the result is anything but rhythmic); rather, it is the quality of the drum sound itself. The object is not to produce a solid Dom! Dom! Dom! with every blow of the hand, but rather a two-syllable Dowo! Dowo! Dowo! "Ah, Bage, do you hear?" one man said to me, while listening raptly to two dancers who were banging away at either end of the *aa*. "The drum says 'Father! Father! Father!' [*dowo*]. It is a little child calling for its father." People who had lost children, he told me, sometimes wept when they heard the Ilib Kuwɔ.

The drum, then, is not only stimulating and exciting but, to one in the right mood, it is a call of need, of hunger, of someone who is absent. People who are absent play a large part in Kaluli feelings, even in everyday circumstances. Several months after Turinei, a well-liked young man of Sululib had gone away on a two-year labor contract, Dalabiæ, a leading man of Wahalib, came to Bonɔ to visit. The houseyard was deserted when he arrived. After wandering around for a few minutes, he went up into the *aa*. There he saw Turinei's two wives sitting by themselves in the women's section with their babies. The pathos of the sight and all it evoked about Turinei's absence was too much for him. He flung himself out the door against a housepost on the veranda and burst into loud wails and sobs for his absent friend.

The nostalgia for one who is absent and the appeal of a hungry child calling for its father cut to the heart of Kaluli sentimentality. It is bound up with their feeling of the need people have of one another. Most of the important things in a man's life—his wife (through bridewealth), his safety (through hospitality), his gardens (through labor assistance), and even his protein intake (through meat prestations)—he owes in large part to others. As human relationships are actualized and mediated through gifts of food and material wealth, so these things come to stand for what is deeply felt in human relationships. A man will say, "He helped me with my bridewealth, and I give him beads and salt," in commenting on a friendship. Another expresses his grief at the death of his young son by saying, "He would have helped me cutting trees." Bemoaning the death of his wife, another man exclaims, "Who will cook my food? Who will beat my sago?"

As I was about to leave the field, my friends told me they would be sad because there would be no more soap, salt, or tobacco. Everyone would have to go back to scrubbing themselves with leaves and eating tasteless sago as before. Later, when I was pondering this statement with some disappointment, Seli, a shrewd young man of rising influence in the community, came into my house and told me to give him my lantern when I left. He was willing to pay for it but hoped I would give it to him for nothing. When I was gone, he added, and he couldn't see me anymore, he would look at the lamp and be reminded of me.

Where human relationships are stated so strongly in terms of material reciprocity, material gain and personal affection are not so morally dissociated as they are in the West. Consequently, material concerns are also sentimental ones, and to state one's desires in terms of sentiment is not the hypocrisy it would be for us.

To be without food, wealth, assistance, and hospitality means in effect that a man has no human relationships at all. This possibility, which is unlikely in real life, has great reality to the Kaluli imagination. A man without human companionship is more than lonely; he is also isolated and vulnerable. He dreads being alone in a foreign *aa* where he has no acquaintances and is given only minimal hospitality. This situation is at once pitiable and frightening. The danger is not so much of being physically attacked by one's strange hosts as of being exposed to the hidden depredations of those among them who are *seis*. The absence of human relationships' here becomes equated with the presence of death.[1] It is for this reason that people visit in groups at long-houses where they are not well known.

It is difficult to convey the atmosphere of uneasiness that anxiety about *seis* casts over Kaluli activities. Under normal circumstances, people usually push it to the back of their minds. But when sickness is around, they become subdued and cautious, avoid sleeping alone, and travel through the forest in twos and threes even on their own house group lands. If someone is seriously ill in the longhouse, everyone becomes jumpy and apprehensive, and the atmosphere is sometimes positively spooky.

> Fomesa, a woman who had come to visit relatives, was very sick, lying in the women's section weak with fever, unable to sit up. As darkness came, the people gathered about their fireboxes. The fires were all roaring and lit the whole interior with shifting light. There was a great deal of loud talking. I went over to Seli's firebox as I came in, and he announced to me that they were talking *sei* talk. The atmosphere was one of tension among a good-humored people, and some of the talk evoked nervous laughter.
>
> Baseo, sitting at a firebox across the hall, his eyes wide with fear, exclaimed, "Damned long-peckered *sei*," and everyone chuckled, half at him and half at themselves and each other's discomfort. Seli was talking about Okaba, a man from Muluma, who could go out into the invisible world in his dreams and see *seis* creeping about on their deadly business. Okaba had recently seen a man named Ola in the *sei* aspect take the body of old Sando, a woman who had died a week or so before, out of its grave, carry it to one of the carrier sheds,[2] lay it on a piece of cloth, and start

---

[1] For a person to wish to be alone means that he is either antisocial or ashamed. The word for doing something off by oneself means "stealth" and connotes activities that are either embarrassing or intended to be clandestine. Those who need privacy for such activities as sexual intercourse take advantage of those times when they are off by themselves, working sago or weeding their gardens. Private activities are carried on in such a way that the real intentions of the excursion to a place of privacy is masked by an apparently legitimate pretext.

[2] An outbuilding built to house the men who carry for a government patrol when it passes through.

cutting it up with a small knife. Okaba had said, "What are you doing here?" and Ola had grabbed up the body and run off crouching toward his house in the forest.

Wanalugo made a speech to everyone saying that if anyone here was the *sei* responsible for Fomesa's illness, he should forget about it and let her be. "Tie the *sei*. Tie the *sei*," he said (so that it wouldn't go out and finish Fomesa off).

The people seemed to be frightening each other more and more. Every small night sound made them start and look up. Suddenly there was a loud "Huurruf!" almost directly under where we were sitting. "Wafi! Long pecker. . . . That sounds like a pig!" Everyone looked at each other. If it was really a pig, it was in the fence and would get into the sweet potato gardens. On the other hand, it might be something that only sounded like a pig. . . . Each one looked at the other as if to say, "Shall we go and check?" Wanalugo looked at everyone's reluctance and broke into his "isn't that just typical!" chuckle. Finally, he and Aebi got up and went. Others followed, lighting their way by waving glowing embers. A thorough search under and around the house revealed there was no pig to be found, but a hole was discovered in the fence where it might have gotten through. After looking a while longer, people once more retired inside.

For some time afterward people shouted "Wao!" from the *aa* at the slight sounds of the night and called out admonishing each other not to sleep, especially those who were sick.

Late at night I was awakened by someone singing a Gisaro song to let any nearby *sei* know that people were awake and watching. (Field notes)

Nothing warms the Kaluli heart like a house full of friendly people. Noise and movement mean the presence of others, assistance, support, familiar faces, and safety from the depredations of *seis*. In a quiet way, this is the atmosphere on everyday occasions, in the *aa* or at a sago camp in the forest, when people are engaged in their usual domestic tasks in a familiar place. When visitors arrive, especially if they are carrying presents of meat, the tone becomes exuberant. The small prestation between the people of Bonɔ and Wabisi referred to in Chapter 4 serves as a typical case. At dawn of the appropriate day, a boy from Sululib (clan Bonɔ) arrived at the Wabisi longhouse at Doba with the news that they were about to receive visitors. Preparations were barely completed when, about noon, there was a terrific *ulab* off in the forest heralding their arrival. As soon as the people could be seen filing through the trees, the men of Doba held their own *ulab* in the hall of the *aa*, an exuberant stamping tumult that made the house echo like a drum. They then retreated to the sides of the hall as the people of Bonɔ entered. The Bonɔ men stamped importantly up the hall and threw their bags of smoked animals on the floor in front of those of Wabisi for whom they were intended, shouting, "Here, this is for you!" Immediately a leading man of Wabisi appeared with hot pitpit for the guests.

All the men sat crowded around the social firebox at the head of the hall and engaged in a noisy, happy conversation about recent events, each yelling his comments at the others at the top of his voice. Everyone was talking at once. The conversation continued until the late afternoon when the smoked meat was recooked and passed out by those who received it to their housemates, while the visitors finished a meal of pandanus. A man with meat would stamp up to each of his housemates, yelling "Wao!" and thrust the meat in his face. Each person took his share sheepishly and dropped out of the conversation to eat in silence. The conversation gradually died down as it got later and men stretched out on the sleeping platforms. Each Bonɔ man slept huddled next to his closest Wabisi relative. In the women's section, their wives did the same.

The next morning, in the course of conversation, a Wabisi man remarked that he didn't have long to live. His wife had come into her period the day before and had cooked him some food, thus exposing him to her menstrual debility and endangering his life. His Bonɔ relative was outraged to hear this, and immediately began to stamp up and down the hall of the *aa* yelling for wealth compensation for the imminent loss of his relative. The others of clan Wabisi stood around looking embarrassed, while other Bonɔ men joined in yelling comments in support of their angry kinsman.

Presently a senior woman of Wabisi came out of the women's section to harangue the guilty woman, who by now was wailing at her sleeping place at the other side of the house. Finally, amid general recriminations, the woman's husband climbed over the partition and, to the increased weeping of his unfortunate wife, removed her shell necklace and gave it to his angry relative from

Bonɔ. That being settled, everyone from Bonɔ stamped importantly out of the house to return home.

The volatile, intrusive, self-projective behavior accompanying the prestation here is really a forceful display of manly affection. A man who throws down a bag of smoked animals shouting, "Here, this is for you!" is pledging mutual good faith. "In the past you have given me meat, brother-in-law. Now I have brought you some in return!" The man who demanded compensation was really expressing his concern and affection for his relative, who might suffer from his wife's carelessness. (It was making the statement that was important. He later returned the shell necklace.)

Exuberance and Violence

In general, Kaluli social events are characterized by a high level of exuberance, crowding, and noise. Presences, interactions, and feelings are rendered explicit, projected into the open. On important occasions of celebration, it is usual to have three or four Ilib Kuwɔ dancers pounding drums up and down the hall of the *aa* from dawn to dusk to keep the place filled with noise and commotion. This projects an appropriately dramatic atmosphere even if the house is nearly empty and the conversation subdued. The exuberant spirit of Kaluli gatherings and the pleasure of company, food, and important events unite people in a mutual euphoria, tempered, as we shall see, with a certain exciting, expectant tension if a ceremony is to be performed that night.

The same manly energy that invigorates a gathering at a prestation, also moves the crowd of angry men who, with their bows drawn, stamping and yelling, burst into a dark and sleeping house, grab a man from among the terrified inhabitants, smash his skull, and drag the corpse out the door to dismember it at the edge of the clearing.

The Kaluli themselves are aware of these features of their life. Wanalugo told me a story about it.

Long ago, Newelæsu was living on Wilip [a hill in the Bosavi area], and Dosæli with his sister Towa was living nearby. Dosæli had a wife but Newelæsu had none. Newelæsu asked Dosæli for

Towa to be his wife, but Towa was unwilling and Dosæli refused. Newelæsu was angry and so he went and killed a cuscus [an arboreal marsupial with a somewhat human appearance and manner of movement] and put its heart up on a pole. "Everyone gather!" he called out, and everyone from the surrounding *aas* gathered. "This is the heart of a *sei* I have killed," so some angrily demanded wealth compensation and others going to Newelæsu's side helped him to pay it. And that is how it has been ever since.[3] (Field notes)

I asked if this was the story of the origin of the *sei*. Wanalugo said no; *seis* had originated before that. This was the story of how they first came to be killed. "Before, people were just sad when somebody died," said Wanalugo, "but they didn't do anything." After Newelæsu had put up the cuscus's heart, however, they killed *seis*.

This, then, is the myth of the origin of retaliatory murder and the payment of compensation. In a larger sense, it could stand as the origin myth of the opposition scenario. The result was the underlying danger of violence and the consequent tension that permeated Kaluli society before outside contact, a situation the Kaluli did not like but had to live with. "Newelæsu did a bad thing," Wanalugo said about the story. "The government was right to stop the killing of *seis*." This didn't mean that *seis* weren't bad, he said. He was afraid of them, it was bad to die, but the violence and subsequent tension of precontact times did not appeal to him either.

Kaluli, in any case, do not seem to have been great warriors and fighters; they were pushy, quick to anger, and aggressive in response, but they were not warlike. Most Kaluli, asked if they would like to return to precontact conditions, said that they would be afraid. Informants never reminisced nostalgically about fighting. There was no boastful pride in fighting prowess. One got the idea that fighting was a tremendously exciting but dangerous and

3 Dosæli and Newelæsu are the principal characters in a series of Kaluli folk tales and myths. Dosæli is the straight man, good looking, moderate in his appetites, competent in what he performs. Newelæsu is a clown or trickster, a weedy little man who bungles most of what he does because he cannot control his appetites. He is often cast as Dosæli's cross-cousin.

serious business, and men fought not because they enjoyed it but because they were angry.[4]

After the government outlawed killing, the general consensus among the people seemed to be one of relief from the tension, volatility, and danger of the old days. They agreed that murderers should be jailed. The fear of the power of the government officer and of the inhumanity of incarceration in exile served very well to cool tempers in heated arguments that threatened to get out of hand while I was there.

With the intervention of the administration, however, there was no way to alleviate the tension and possibility of violence brought about by death. From the Kaluli perspective, death, inevitably caused by a *sei*, was as good as a murder—it was the attack of one person on another. To not retaliate when one was deeply bereaved and angry, and to continue to deal in friendship with the man (or his group) who was responsible for the death of one's own relative, was to accept one's loss lying down. Moreover, Wanalugo pointed out, without fear of retaliation, *seis* would not be afraid to go out and take people whenever they liked. So, much as Kaluli feared and deplored the tension of precontact times and were grateful for the presence of the government, the basic problem was not resolved. The government had prohibited killing *seis* but had not provided an alternative way to deal with death. It had not succeeded in invalidating the traditional system of retaliation, but simply rendered it too risky and expensive to carry out.

---

[4] The Kaluli seem to have been horrified as much as excited and gratified by a murder. Informants who mimed a killing often seemed to register distaste as they relived the experience. Their vigorous motions with an imaginary ax to the neck, shoulders, hips, and knees seemed directed to getting the body to stop twitching and struggling, as much as to killing. Wanalugo said that the first thing after a body had been dragged out of the *aa* was to cut open the chest and throw the heart out onto the ground. Then all the nearby warriors jumped aside while the heart moved around in the dirt until the *sei* creature inside it was able to escape and make its way off invisibly into the forest. The same sort of ambivalence was expressed about cannibalism. Although most older men had tasted human flesh, some men were frankly uneasy about it and did so only rarely. Others would eat it only if it didn't come from a *sei*. Those who were known to favor human flesh and from time to time had had an arm or a leg in the smoking rack above their fireboxes appear to have been in the minority.

Kaluli have tried to bring the situation to completion by demanding compensation from the *sei* who is positively identified (by pig heart divination) as responsible for a given death. This is rarely successful, however, since the *sei* usually refuses to pay and there is no way to compel him. He will be sharply told that he is no longer welcome at the longhouse of the death, but after a few months the anger peters out and relations are normalized again. Only once while I was in the field, at the death of a prominent man with many friends and relatives, was sizable compensation extracted from a *sei*. Yet without successful retaliation or compensation, the situation of death remains essentially unresolved until, eventually, feeling about it dies away.

To return to the story of Newelæsu and the cuscus for a moment, we recall that the practice of retaliation against the *sei* was not, in fact, brought about by a death but rather by a refusal of marriage. This places the story in an interesting light. In the broadest terms, it contrasts the integrative aspects of society, embodied in marriage and reciprocity, with the destructive aspects manifested in death and retaliation. Regarded in terms of the oppositions within the story itself, if the refusal of marriage results in the retaliation for a death, the state of being without a wife is equated with the state of bereavement.

Newelæsu's killing a phony *sei* in response to a refusal of marriage was rather overdoing it from the Kaluli point of view (a characteristic typical of Newelæsu in Kaluli stories). Nevertheless, Newelæsu, as symbolic bachelor, is a sympathetic figure because he outlines a situation poignant to Kaluli imagination: the denial of human relationships. It is in this that death as providing the ultimate devastating loneliness has its major significance. When Kaluli speak of death, they speak less of the fear of dying and more of the sorrow and anxiety of losing someone and being left alone. This awareness animates the pathos they perceive in their lives. Missing people and places form the basis of their nostalgia.

Reactions to Death

In gloomier moments, Kaluli often imagine themselves becoming fewer and fewer, dying out (*danili*), their *aas* standing empty, and

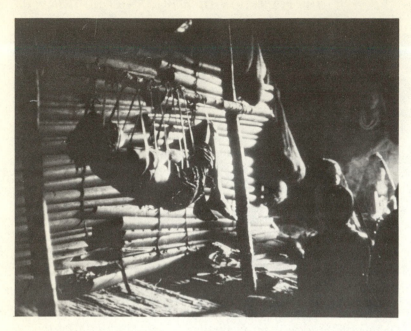

Funeral. An old woman hangs in cane loops among mourning women near the front of the *aa*.

their gardens abandoned to weeds. One time, at a funeral, I was with a group of men sitting around the social firebox discussing the patrol officer's recent edict that they were to bury their dead and fence the cemetery. "Better make it a small cemetery," Sialo remarked with black humor. "Then only one man will die. If you make it big, many will die and you will be used up, finished." Death, not for the dead, but more for the living, drains the substance out of life. It is the end of a woman passing a man his packet of cooked sago over the partition in the *aa*; it is the end of throwing down a bag of dried meat saying, "Here, this is for you." It is the end of men whooping and stamping together in *ulab*. The noisy shouting and laughing around the firebox reverts to silence as the people one by one disappear and the house becomes abandoned.

Formerly when a person died, the closest relatives were supposed to strip the body completely of ornaments and clothes and, covering the pubic area, suspend the body in cane loops from a pole that was hung near the front of the house by the women's section. A smoky fire was lit at the head and foot, "to keep down the stink," and a shallow bark basin was put under the suspended body in case it dripped. During the following days, friends and relatives from other house groups would come to mourn and view it. After about a week, the corpse was carried out of the house and placed in a raised structure called a *kalu ɔidɔ* a short distance from the house, where it was left to decompose. When the bones were dry, they were put in a net bag and hung up under the eaves of the *aa* over the front veranda as mementos.[5]

Individual gestures of sentiment were often made at the time the body was placed in the *kalu ɔidɔ*. A man's bow and arrows might be hung there. The necklace he normally wore might be broken up and thrown in also, along with perhaps a dance head-dress, a new net bag, or other possessions that were not given to his wife, children, or close age-mates.

These goods were not placed for use in the afterlife. Indeed, the idea would appear ridiculous to the Kaluli, for a man who goes as a bird to the treetops has no need of a bow or a necklace. Rather, the objects that the deceased liked to use or had intended to use before he died were thrown into the *ɔidɔ* so that others could not use them. It was an attempt to preserve the integrity of the dead through the preservation of the integrity of the objects he normally used. The more grief-stricken and angry the next of kin, I was told, the more of the dead man's possessions he would throw into the *ɔidɔ* that others might not use them. In a more poignant gesture, the father or spouse of the deceased might put out a little food near the *ɔidɔ* once or twice to feed the dead, should he come near in animal form.

After a death, the surviving spouse and/or children observe a number of compulsory mourning taboos (*dabušo*) on various kinds of foods. But, in addition to this, any grieving relative may voluntarily taboo himself some other particular food in memory of the dead. One man told me he had given up eating breadfruit

---

[5] The Australian colonial government required bodies to be buried after August 1968.

when his brother died because breadfruit had been his brother's favorite food. Similarly, a person may give up the food with which he shared a *wi aledo* with the deceased. More commonly, however, a person will taboo himself the food that the deceased had intended to eat just prior to his or her death. If a man's wife brought some pandanus home from the garden before she died, the grieving husband often cannot bring himself to eat it. "She brought it home to eat with me," one said. "Now I would have to eat it alone." He gives it to others in the longhouse and thenceforth gives up eating that kind of pandanus. In a similar manner, a husband may give up eating food from a garden he had recently planted with his wife, because they had intended to share it.

These taboos are entirely voluntary and sentimental. They are customarily continued until the *sei* responsible is dead, or at least until the pain of the death has receded from memory. By refusing to eat food he intended to share with the deceased, by saying, in effect, "If I can't eat it with so-and-so, then I won't eat it with anyone," a person reserves that food as a memorial to his relationship with the one who has died.

When someone dies, Kaluli once again confront their fear of loneliness. This does not lead, however, to a tragic view of life in the Western sense. The Kaluli reaction in confrontation with death and loss is to strike back. Even if grieving and frightened, Kaluli traditionally attempted to resolve the matter in retaliatory violence against the person who was responsible in his aspect as a *sei*. In this way, through the opposition scenario, life, in its vitality, forced death to pay its due. This was not a happy state of affairs, but it had its own dignity, and the Kaluli lived with it.

Chapter 9

Ceremonial Occasions
and Preparations

Kaluli stage their ceremonies most often to celebrate occasions when they formally create or affirm friendly relations with people in other longhouse communities: typically, marriages or major prestations of meat. Big prestations, where pigs are killed or huge packages of sago grubs are exchanged for smoked game, take some months to prepare. Each stage in the preparations may be celebrated with formal visiting and ceremonies before the climactic distribution itself.

Table 9.1 outlines the various stages of one such prestation made by the people of the longhouse community at Muluma. Succulent grubs, a gourmet delicacy to the Kaluli, were exchanged for smoked game and fresh crayfish. Grubs take several months to incubate in sago and *wayo* palms felled especially for the purpose; thus, preparations for the prestation, which was to take place in February, began in October of the previous year.

There were five opportunities appropriate for holding ceremonies, but Muluma decided to invite visitors for only three. Each of these was significant, however, for formally communicating information about the coming prestation between donors and recipients. Sometimes Kaluli choose one of these ceremonial occasions as an appropriate time to hold a wedding, if bride, groom, and payment are available.

With each succeeding phase in the process, there is a tendency

**TABLE 9.1   List of Occasions of Celebration During Preparation for a
Fele Noa Presented by Muluma Longhouse Community,
October 1966–February 1967**

Event Celebrated	Ceremony Performed	Stage of Preparation	Related Activity
Commencement of preparations for *Fele Noa*	None (Muluma people gathered in aa to get organized; one *ilib kuwɔ* dancer to celebrate; no invited guests)	"*Wayo*-cutting month" (October–November 1966)	Following celebration: *Wayo* palms felled for grub incubation; sexual intercourse prohibited for duration of preparations; Muluma people issue invitations for visitors to attend celebration for next stage
"Palm heart" celebration	Sæbio	"Sago-cutting month" (November–December 1966)	At celebration, hearts of palm from newly felled sago trees are presented to visitors who are later to receive prestations; amount of palm heart indicates proportional quantity of grubs to be expected; following celebration, remaining sago palms are felled for grub incubation
"Soul of the grubs" celebration	None	"Grub incubation month" (December 1966–January 1967)	People of Muluma made a painted plaque ("soul of the grubs") from a ritually important variety of sago and set it up in the aa to magically encourage growth of grubs; potential recipients from other aas catch crayfish, trap and smoke game for reciprocation
"Pulling out the grubs" celebration	Gisaro	Ten-day period required for recovery of grubs (Late January 1967)	Grubs removed from sago felled ritually in third stage are recovered, wrapped in packets, and set up near "soul" plaque; number of packets indicates general abundance of grubs to be expected; following ceremony, grubs are taken from rest of sago and *wayo* palms, packaged, and cooked for prestation
"*Fele Noa*" prestation	Heyalo (Ceremony altered: hosts and guests dance together; no weeping)	Conclusion of process (First week in February 1967)	Packets of grubs given to visitors in return for quantities of fresh crayfish and smoked game

for the ceremonies to become bigger and more elaborate (for example, first Sæbio and then Gisaro) except that the final ceremony, on the eve of the prestation itself, is usually altered so that it is dramatic and exciting but not deeply moving. A noisy, energetic dance such as Heyalo[1] is staged (twenty men dancing at one time with drums), but hosts and guests dance together and deliberately sing songs that everyone has heard before so that no one is moved to tears. The distribution of meat on the morning following the ceremony is supposed to be the climactic event of the occasion; thus, a mood of mutually exuberant celebration is appropriate, and a deeply affecting and violent ceremony would overshadow the prestation. Kaluli told me that people were unwilling to be burned before receiving pork or grubs. If, as occasionally happened, a really powerful ceremony was planned for the day of a prestation, the prestation would be made in the afternoon, and the ceremony held afterward.

Moving and violent performances increase the tension and excitement among those involved in the occasion to be celebrated. A really effective performance that causes a lot of grief for the hosts (*aa biśɔ*) not only requires that they be given compensation (*su*) but motivates them to return the same (*wel*) to their guests. This is often what is behind the feeling of urgency to arrange a quick response to an occasion. Prestations are usually preceded by sufficient ceremonies to satisfy return of *wel* (see Chapter 11). But a powerful ceremony at a wedding may encourage the groom's longhouse community to incorporate his first gift to his affines (*ga læsu*) in a larger prestation (with accompanying ceremony) of their own.[2]

Under great emotional stress, a return ceremony may be performed simply for its own sake. I once was present at a Sæbio dance performed by the youths of Sululib longhouse at Wahalib at the request of members of that community who were performing

---

[1] Gisaro is paced too slowly to be performed as mere entertainment; it would be a terrible bore. Even with an active dance such as Heyalo, when it serves merely as entertainment most of the members of the audience fall asleep late in the night because the songs do not move them.

[2] In this case, they would make a large expedition to their recipient's *aa*, present smoked game in the afternoon, and perform the ceremony that night.

sickness-warding magic. Sæbio is usually a minor dance sometimes performed before a larger ceremony, but the young men of Sululib stretched it out for the whole night and sang so beautifully that many people wept. The senior men at Wahalib felt rather foolish at unexpectedly being moved so much to tears. As soon as the dancers had left, they called in affines and relatives from other longhouses and two days later came to Sululib to stage a Kɔluba that caused nearly everyone there to weep.

Ceremonies are themselves reciprocal transactions in a scheme of emotional and esthetic reciprocity, which makes them to some degree independent of the occasions they are staged to celebrate. Indeed, most people feel that they have a special efficacy of their own. They perform them by themselves in times of regional anxiety (for example, when sickness is moving from longhouse to longhouse) or at the appearance of fearful portents (for example, the arrival—in 1936—of the first aircraft over Bosavi). Which ceremony is to be performed is the choice of those making the major offering on the occasion: the donors in the case of a forthcoming prestation; the bride's family in the case of a wedding. Once this has been decided, it is up to the guests (miyɔwɔ) to recruit dancers and prepare the performance.[3]

The dancers are recruited by sending out requests for volunteers. The principal men among the miyɔwɔ (those primarily involved in the wedding, prestation, and so on) may decide among themselves that they would like dancers from each of their supporting clans. The request goes out phrased in a general way: "We want one dancer from Gæsumisi, one from Bonɔ," and so on. Nearly always there are several people who wish to dance. The dancers are not necessarily significantly related to the principal figures of aa bišɔ or miyɔwɔ, and they need not have any stake in the events being celebrated. The only restriction is that a man must not dance at his wife's father's aa (or his children will die).[4] Dancers may

---

[3] The discussion that follows will be restricted to Gisaro, though preparations for the other ceremonies are very similar.

[4] This is an affinal taboo, on a par with the prohibition on speaking an in-law's name. The taboo is directed symbolically against the wife's father's place of residence as a whole. A man may dance before his father-in-law if the latter is a member of the hosting group in another longhouse, but may not dance be-

have mild-mannered or flamboyant personalities in ordinary life, and most older men have danced in several ceremonies.

Gisaro, for the dancer, is an extremely painful and wearing ordeal, and it is difficult for a Westerner to fathom why people would wish to do it. The Kaluli themselves are not very articulate on the matter. They never cite prestige, proof of manliness, or even duty to relatives or affines among their motivations. Sometimes a man will evoke an appeal to sentiment: "My father intended to dance Gisaro at that longhouse before he died," one man told me, "but it was called off. Now [years later] I, the son, will do it." Another man, whom I pressed hard to explain his motivation for dancing on one occasion, said doubtfully after considerable thought, "Well, those people of Wabisi were among the ones who danced Kɔluba here and made our old men cry a lot. So I thought I would Gisaro at Wabisi and make them cry just as much." Most men simply say, "They asked for Gisaro dancers, so I said to myself, 'I'll be one.'" Or as another man put it, "I am hungry to Gisaro." (Shortly afterward, when the ceremony was called off, this man immediately volunteered to dance in another.)

The reason for this "hunger to dance" becomes clear during the days immediately preceding the ceremony. The enthusiasm with which the performance is discussed and prepared for gives the impression that Kaluli think Gisaro to be one of the most wonderful things in the world. In the midst of it, the dancer will play the central role, at once a figure of pathos and magnificence, sorrow and desire, which moves people to the bottom of their hearts. Such a tremendously exciting role, for all its cost in pain and compensation payments, has a compelling appeal.

Howæ told me he had volunteered to dance Gisaro at Wabimisæn longhouse when he was only fourteen years old. "My father's mother was a Wabimisæn woman. I thought, when they see me they will think, 'Alas, our cross-cousin's child,' and be reminded of my father who was dead. They will feel sorry for me and weep." "At the performance," he continued, "Dæba [a leading

---

fore his wife's father's longhouse community at their *aa* even after his father-in-law is dead. The issue seems to be that the presumptuous intimacy of the ceremony is disruptive to a man's formal relations with his in-law's community (see Chapter 10).

man at Wabimisæn] said, 'Alas, a child. Hey! This is a child, don't burn him!' " Howæ's considerations for dancing Gisaro were that his status as a youngster and remote relative would be unique assets to his appeal as a performer. He was right; they burned him severely.

The impact of Gisaro, or any other ceremonial performance, depends on taking the *aa bišɔ* by surprise. To this end, if it is up to them, the *miyɔwɔ* will try to keep secret even the kind of ceremony they are going to perform. Even if the *aa bišɔ* know this, it is important that they not learn the identity of the dancers until the day they actually arrive. Moreover, the dancers themselves should not be men who visit frequently at the longhouse where they are to perform. The audience would not take a dancer's performance seriously if they knew him too well as a person. They would be unimpressed with his withdrawn and oblivious demeanor, try to joke with him, and not pay attention to his songs. Under these circumstances, the dancer would fail to be moving.

Finally, since the greatest impact of the ceremony lies in the songs, it is crucial that people who will be *aa bišɔ* not hear them. The force of a song depends heavily on its being unexpected. If one has heard it sung before, it will not be moving. Gisaro takes longer to prepare than other ceremonies because its songs are long and elaborate.[5] New ones must be composed and carefully practiced for each ceremony. Each dancer must learn at least twelve by heart, and those in the chorus must try to learn most of them. Considerable time is usually spent by dancers and chorus, practic-

---

[5] The Sæbio ceremony requires the least preparation of all, since all that is needed is for one person to know the conventional song lines, and eight or ten to be willing to dance. There is no special costume. For an Ilib Kuwɔ dance, there are no songs to learn. All it requires is an elaborate costume and a drum, which may be gotten together if the need is urgent in an afternoon. For Kɔluba and Heyalo, about fifteen to twenty dancers must be gotten together, each supplying his own costume, which is virtually identical to that of the Ilib Kuwɔ. Kɔluba songs appear to consist of standard frames into which ground names or food names may be inserted and are not difficult to learn. Heyalo songs, on the other hand, must be composed anew for each ceremony and then memorized. The songs are simple, however, and a few days of practice is usually sufficient for most people to learn the words and melodies. The major difficulty is in getting all the people together for a long enough time to learn them.

ing together to develop just the right atmosphere and sonority. (In my observation, Kaluli have spent as long as three weeks in practicing Gisaro songs, and as little as five days.)

As the time for a ceremony approaches, the general hustle and bustle of preparations at the longhouses of the *miyɔwɔ* increases. By day, people are weaving armbands, burying bark belts in the mud to blacken, and making expeditions to borrow regalia from relatives. By night, the *aa* resounds with mournful practice singing, occasionally punctuated by the wails of married-in women who are moved to tears by the songs that are intended for their relatives in the *aa bišɔ*.

On the day before the ceremony, the people who are going to be *miyɔwɔ* gather in the *aa* that will serve as the departure point. Here, the four dancers have the *mise æsu* tied into their hair. *Mise æsu* are the mark of the Gisaro dancer. They are frames of ropes made from fire-resistant bark that hang down over the dancer's neck and back to his waist, affording some protection against the torch. They are heavy enough to be uncomfortable, and the dancers walk bent slightly forward, as if carrying a burden, a posture that has considerable appeal in the performance of the dance.

The last evening is spent in practicing the songs for the last time and in loud exuberant conversation among people from different *aas* who have not seen each other in some time.

The following day, as the people depart for the place where the ceremony will be held, the women are sent ahead, while the youths and men search through the trees along the side of the trail for magical substances to enhance the performance. All Kaluli ceremonies have some magical practices associated with them, but Gisaro has the most elaborate. The substances collected and applied are aimed at strengthening the endurance of dancers and chorus, riveting the attention of the audience on them, making listeners restless and disturbed, predisposing them to burst into weeping. Wanalugo likened the *aa bišɔ* under the influence of an effective Gisaro to fish stunned by poison and rising to the surface of the water. Preoccupied with the songs, they forget to seat people properly, forget to feed the chorus, and generally neglect the generous, solicitous behavior hosts should observe toward their guests. In a good Gisaro, he declared, the hosts act as if they had lost their understanding and do not regain their senses until day-break when, at the end of the performance, they are compensated.

The journey from one *aa* to another for a ceremonial occasion takes much longer than it does under normal circumstances. People wash, paint, and decorate themselves along the trail just out of sight of their destination so that their regalia will be new and fresh, not smeared or disarrayed by passage through the forest. When all is ready, the *miyɔwɔ* give an *ulab* to notify the *aa bišɔ*, and when an answering *ulab* is heard, the entrance procession be-gins.

The clearing of the houseyard is dominated by the looming presence of the *aa*. Women and girls are swaying, stamping, and cheering on the veranda. The arrival becomes a dramatic, tumul-tuous spectacle as the Ilib Kuwɔ dancers lead the procession out of the forest with their drums, followed by the arriving women trudging along in bright red headcapes and shining shell necklaces. As they line up along one side of the houseyard, painted men burst out the door of the *aa* waving axes and bows and stream down the entrance ladder to circle into a rousing *ulab*. Then, as they move to the side of the houseyard, the arriving men come running out of the forest and tear by them at top speed, throwing the magical leaves and stems they have collected in the forest at their chests while the dancers splash them with fish poison.

After the arrival, the Ilib Kuwɔ dancers and the women go into the *aa*, and the older men of the hosts and guests sit down in the sun to converse. The Gisaro dancers withdraw to one side of the houseyard. There they sit by themselves, facing away from the others, withdrawn and silent. Nearby, also withdrawn and facing away from the *aa*, sit the youths and younger men who intend to sing in the chorus.[6] This behavior is to conserve their voices, al-ready hoarse from nights of singing practice, and to maintain esthetic distance from the *aa bišɔ* so the performance will not be

---

[6] Gisaro is the only Kaluli ceremony where magical substances are thrown at the hosts during the arrival and where dancers and chorus sit conspicuously apart. For Heyalo or Kɔluba, the people who will dance sneak off during the afternoon to the forest, where they prepare their costumes, and do not reap-pear until the ceremony is about to begin.

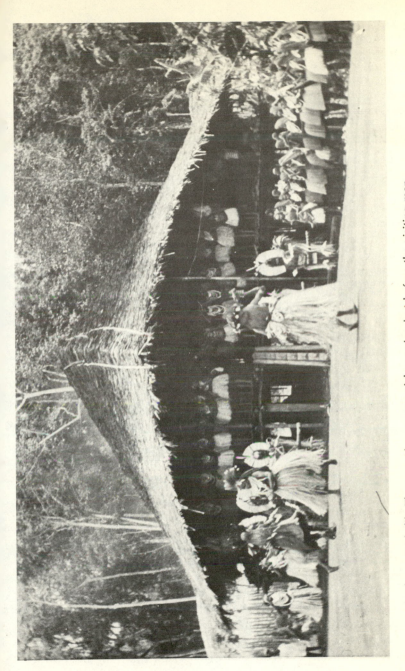

Welcome display at Wahalib. The scene is a ceremonial occasion just before the visiting men enter the houseyard. Hosting women stand on the veranda. Those wearing headdresses and long skirts dance sosomaya in the yard. Visiting women, who have just arrived, line up at the right, while Ilib Kuwɔ dancers flank the longhouse entrance ladder. (Photo by B. Schieffelin.)

vitiated with too much familiarity. At the same time, such a conspicuous group of silent people lends a certain tension to the air.
The *aa bišɔ* for their part attempt to break it down by trying to
make them laugh. They usually concentrate most of their efforts on
the dancers.

Amid the general spectacle of feather headdresses, painted faces,
shell necklaces, and bright sprays of cordyline leaves, the dancers
present a sorry sight. With their stringy *mise æsu* hanging down
their backs, their belts wrapped in old pandanus rubbish, their
armbands and even the "bone" through their nasal septums made
from wilted leaves, they look naked and scruffy. Youths and young
men of the *aa bišɔ* come over to crack ribald jokes to break their
withdrawal. "Wa!" says one, grabbing his companion and point-
ing to a dancer sitting on the ground, "What a big man! If he
screwed you, you'd get as big as this banana tree!" "I've got to
piss," says another, aiming a rolled up banana leaf from his crotch
at another dancer's back. "This one is really going to get the
torch," says another man. "Let's see if he is afraid." He leaves for
a moment and comes striding back with a huge ember log from
some nearby fire, which he throws dramatically down next to the
dancers. Another man comes bumping and grinding right up to a
dancer's face. "Hey! you're looking pretty skinny. I'm going to
give you a screw!"

Joshing in this vein continues intermittently throughout the
afternoon, while the dancers struggle not to notice. If they laughed,
I was told, the ceremony would come out badly; but the dancers
never laughed. This foolery seemed to me largely prankish in intent, a good-humored test that everyone, even the *aa bišɔ*, hoped
and knew the dancers would pass.

The sexual reference in this joking, while directed at an embarrassing male secret, no doubt partly reflects another excitement in
the air. Ceremonial occasions when many men and women are
gathered all night in the longhouse or its smaller outbuildings
provide both the temptation and the opportunity for clandestine
rendezvous. With their straitlaced attitude toward sex, Kaluli do
not characterize their ceremonies as times of sexual license and
would deplore anyone's thinking so. Nevertheless, everyone knows
it and it is in the air. I several times saw a man thrashing his wife

on the morning after for having disappeared with someone during the night. For youths and marriageable girls, these gatherings provide the best chance for looking each other over surreptitiously or for catching one another's attention, through looks or by little bits of food tossed or given in the darkness. For girls particularly this is almost their only opportunity to control the choice of their husbands. If a girl loses her heart to a man at a gathering (or sees one there she has already developed a liking for), she may take the occasion to elope by following him home after the ceremony. Elopements following a ceremony are a sensation and general social coup.[7]

In any case, these sexual implications in the air add an extra, spicy expectation to the already excited ambiance of opposition marked by the withdrawn performers as the dancers are led away in the afternoon by their mates to be decorated and prepared for the ceremony.

[7] The elopement is subject to veto by the girl's father or other principal relatives, but if the young man wishes to keep her, her relatives usually agree and appropriate bridewealth is arranged.

Chapter 10

The Gisaro

As evening falls, torches are lit in the *aa*. When word is received that the Gisaro dancers are ready, the Ilib Kuwɔ, who have been dancing with drums in the *aa* all afternoon, cease and dismantle their costumes. With the end of their constant drumming, an awkward, restless quiet pervades the *aa*. By now the interior is crowded with people (*aa biʃɔ* and those *miyɔwɔ* not in the performance). Five to twelve young men holding torches stand about in the central hall. They do not participate much in the actual burning of the dancers but supply the torches to older men and women who do. Older men stand or sit by the sidelines along the row of houseposts on either side, eating bananas and conversing, their painted faces, feather headdresses, and shell ornaments reflecting the firelight. Behind them, women sit crowded together on the sleeping platforms, while further back in the recessed darkness other young men perch on the partition to the women's section.

Expectant tension fills the air. To feel more at ease, men seated on opposite sides of the hall laugh and shout jokes at each other. Presently, to the shouts of women on the outside veranda, the men of the Gisaro chorus quietly enter the front door. A hush falls over the longhouse as they move quietly up the hall and divide into two groups facing each other across a space of about twenty-five feet (Figure 10.1). After a moment of silence, all whisper, "Sssshhh!" and sink to the floor, seeming to vanish from sight and leaving one dancer standing dramatically alone. He is bouncing slowly up and down in place, humming and singing softly, accompanied by the soft clash of a mussel-shell rattle, suspended by a string from his hand, against the floor.

The nondescript figure of earlier in the afternoon is now totally transformed. His face and body are covered with red ocher; his eyes are outlined in a black mask carefully edged with white. Bands of red and yellow beads and braids of brown fiber crisscross his chest. His wrists are bound with seed bracelets; red bird of paradise plumes spray from armbands woven in black and yellow. His hips are decorated with a looped garment of yellow string above a new red pubic cloth, while his waist is cinched in a black bark band woven with cane designs. His head is crowned with waving black cassowary plumes with a single weighted white dancing feather bobbing back and forth in the middle. His whole figure is outlined with shiny yellow stripped palm leaf streamers, which shoot up to shoulder height from his waistband in back and fall rustling away to the floor. The dancer bounces slowly in place, his feathers and streamers waving and bobbing around him. A pungent, spicy aroma fills the air—the scent of Gisaro. The dancer is anointed with fermented vegetable resins.

The *aa biঃ*, who have paused in their noisy conversation to watch the dancer appear, now take up where they left off, more loudly than ever. Their shouting and laughing has a nervous edge. "They act like that," an informant told me, "so they won't cry too soon."

Presently the dancer sways forward and progresses slowly toward the other end of the dancing space. Under the noise of the audience, the chorus (mostly youths and younger visiting men, eight to eighteen in number) softly begins to sing. Eventually the dancer returns to his original position and sits down; the second rises to take his place. As the singing becomes louder and the words of the songs more audible, so does the hosts' ribaldry and distraction.

An old man puts on a peculiar hat and goes about twitching and staring like a lunatic. Youths seated on the partition to the women's section stick their rear ends out over the visiting women seated below and make loud, raucous, grunting noises as if about to defecate on their heads. At one performance, a man appeared with a huge penis carved from a banana stem hanging over his pubic covering. He waddled among the visitors, sticking it over the women's shoulders and rubbing it against the mouths of the chorus. It required considerable effort on the part of the performers not to laugh at this and destroy the elaborately maintained mood. As the third dancer follows the second, the singing swells to fill the whole house, its stately pace and mournful mood reaching the point where the *aa bišɔ* can no longer distract themselves and the atmosphere of the performance perceptibly begins to change. An old woman was the first to weep at one Gisaro. A senior man threw an arm around her shoulder and exclaimed, "This one I'll take!" (in marriage). Soon after, as the singing became still louder, another man burst into tears. "Oh!" yelled someone, "Dæba is ripe and taken [that is, by a *sei*]. Clan Wɔsisɔ! On the alert! Throw the weepers into the Kulu [River]!" As others begin to cry, "The fish are rising to the surface," new wails are greeted by shouts of "Bruh! Bruh!" from the young men of the *aa bišɔ*, who begin stamping and yelling around in the dancing space. An old woman comes angrily out from the sidelines, takes a torch, and puts it out on the dancer's shoulder. The clowning is over. Tension rapidly rises and the mood of the *aa bišɔ* becomes serious and grim.

FIGURE 10.1   The Arrangement of Performers and Audience During the Ceremony

The diagram on the opposite page shows the usual arrangement of audience and performers in a longhouse just after one Gisaro dancer has stood up and turned around to sing. The men's sleeping platforms are occupied mostly by visiting women (*miyɔwɔ*), who, together with a few aa *bišɔ* friends, have been there since they entered the *aa* after the arrival procession. The choruses sit on the floor at each end of the dancing space. Torchbearers stand along the sides of the hall or group around the dancer. Other young men sit on the partitions to the women's section. Older and married men of the aa *bišɔ* sit along the sidelines of the dancing space, behind the chorus in the front of the hall, or stand in the women's socializing area (*ga kudɔ*). Aa *bišɔ* women stay in the women's sleeping areas of the house (*gælæ suluke*), in the ga *kudɔ*. Unmarried girls and younger married women dance *sosomaya* as a kind of cheering section behind the chorus at the front of the house. Other people, both aa *bišɔ* and *miyɔwɔ*, spend part of the night outside the *aa* sitting around fires in the yard or in small shelters listening to the singers from there.

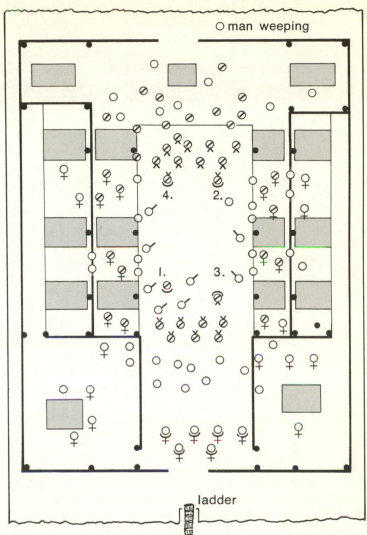

man weeping

4.

2.

1.

3.

ladder

Numbers record order of dancers

⚱ ⊘ *miyɔwɔ*

♀ ○ *aa bišɔ*

⚲ *sosomaya* dancer

♂ torchbearer

⚲ seated chorus member

⚲ ⚲ Gisaro dancers seated/standing

Men holding torches along the sides of the hall now lower them, narrowing the space around the dancer with their flames. Torches held above the dancer's head shower his shoulders with drops of burning resin. Others are held uncomfortably near his face. People told me that this was to better light the dancer so that his beauty might be seen, but it seemed also directed toward threatening and intimidating him.

Through it all the dancer seems oblivious. He remains downcast and sad, singing of ridgetops and sago places. Despite the flamboyant splendor of his bobbing feathers and streamers, he seems curiously remote. He does not address those around him. He bounces in place, rhythmically bending his knees, his body bent slightly forward, arms held at his sides, eyes on the floor. He is withdrawn, unnoticing, absorbed in his singing. Surrounded by torch fires, he seems to inhabit a kind of terrifying solitude, which draws and fascinates the audience. In the motion of the dance, Kaluli may perceive a reflection of themselves. When Kaluli youths amuse themselves by mimicking people from other areas, they can skillfully mime the rolling gait of a Huli from the highlands or the strut of a patrol officer. But to express Kaluli, they adopt a downcast posture with arms held at the sides and the step of a Gisaro dancer crossing the dancing space. Indeed, Kaluli men tend to walk with a characteristic slight bounding movement. This up-and-down movement in other contexts expresses particular moments of experience. Men jump vigorously up and down, legs apart, when they are keyed up and alert, intoning *ulab*. This becomes a rapid series of side-to-side leaps when one approaches an enemy, fires arrows in a fight, or bounds up the hall of the *aa* to announce exciting news. In the Gisaro, the feet are held together (legs apart is bad form), and the motion is graceful and controlled, self-consciously beautiful throughout the ceremony.

The appeal of the dance lies in more than the motion of the man himself; it is in the whole bobbing and flowing motion of his regalia. The split palm leaf streamers at his back move with a waving, falling motion, reminiscent to Kaluli of forest waterfalls. Other feathers and leaves bob and beckon with motions familiar in the forest: the waving of the sago fronds or banana trees the dancers often sing about. The movement has an abstract appeal that some-times leads people to bob a blade of grass or a weighted feather, in idle moments, just to watch it move.

The four dancers are painted and costumed exactly alike, so that as one sits down and another stands up, throughout the course of the night, the figure moving in the middle of the longhouse remains the same. Dancers are coached to "be like a wild pig"— that is, anonymous, like a person from a distant area whom nobody knows. As their individuality is submerged, so their image is ele-vated to an abstraction. The effect is magnified by the dancer's isolation. Moving in the firelight, the dancer seems to be the only living thing in the vast, motionless interior. When he suddenly leans forward and approaches along the torchlit dancing space, he seems larger than life amid his waving plumes and streamers. Coming through the avenue of lowered torches, he seems remote, archetypal, a figure emerging from an infinite distance, another time and place.[1] His single voice sounds far away. But then, as the chorus breaks in, the sound swells to fill the whole house, surrounding him with song. The effect is powerful. A person is startled, Kaluli say, when the dancer approaches because in his masklike face he recognizes his dead brother (or other relative) who danced in Gisaros in times past. Only when the dancer has come close does one recognize him. When recognition comes, the figure has an immensely lonely quality that exerts a many-sided appeal to Kaluli nostalgia. Members of the audience are drawn to think of sorrows this person has suffered, or that they share with him, or even how much his knees must ache and his

---

[1] The appearance of fascinating isolation and the "emergent" quality of the dancer is important to the effect of the performance and is largely a result of the kind of lighting provided by the torches. Twice I attempted to light Kaluli ceremonies (not Gisaro) with a 500-candlepower pressure lamp in order to take pictures. The change in the atmosphere was palpable. Every member of the audience and every dark corner of the longhouse was brightly lit, revealing and encouraging a colorful but distracting profusion of activity. People talked among themselves and seemed to pay little attention to the dancers. Soon miyɔwɔ people begged me to turn off the light as no one would weep, while aa biśɔ urged me to keep it on. When I did turn it off, the change was im-mediate. Dancers suddenly emerged out of the darkness as the audience vanished into it, talking ceased, and within minutes people began to weep.

burns pain him. The dancer reflects, in one image, one's self and one's sorrows, one's beloved dead and those one cared for in the midst of need. At the same time, his rhythmic motion at the center of the house, reflecting the motion of man, of waterfalls, and of the forest, unites the three things and provides the pace and measure for the performance.

The motion of the dancer, communicated through the rattle, becomes the rhythm of the songs. The melodies of Gisaro songs have a plaintive, mournful quality. The music wails, descends, and drones. When sung with the chorus, it fills the *aa* with measured stately sound. The dancer sings with a high, thin voice that rides on a resonant central tone, regularly renewed, into which the melody resolves itself at the end of each line. This tone produces a finely tuned, compelling unity of effort among the chorus. The result is a tremendously intense, resolute musical order that visibly renews the courage of the dancer and gives the ceremony its relentless movement.

The Songs

Of all the elements that contribute to an effective Gisaro, Kaluli emphasize the songs. It is the songs, they say, that move a person to tears. A Gisaro ceremony contains twenty-four to twenty-eight songs. Each is sung four times by a dancer and makes up one of his turns dancing before the torches (about fifteen to twenty minutes). Every song is composed of two parts, one called the trunk (*mɔ*) and the other the branches (*dun*), which he sings with the chorus. They are separated by lines (*talum*) that the dancer sings as he is about to progress from one end of the dancing space to the other (*sagulu*). The songs are long, containing between twenty-five and thirty-five lines, each of which is repeated twice in the singing (see Figure 10.2). The songs are not sung in Kaluli but in another related language said to be that of the Sonia people west of the Bosavis, the direction from which Gisaro is supposed to have originated. Whether or not this is so, everybody understands the songs, and their peculiar language gives them a certain exoticism that adds to their appeal.

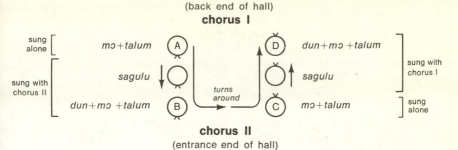

FIGURE 10.2 The Progression of the Dancer

The turn begins as the previous dancer finishes his song and sits down. The dancer, who has been seated facing the chorus at his end, rises (*dasi-taki*), takes a step backward, and turns around to face across the dancing space toward the opposite chorus. He sings the *mɔ* and *talum* by himself, bouncing in place. At the *sagulu*, he leans forward and starts his progression across the dancing space. The opposite chorus now answers him in the mode of overlapping call and response. When he arrives at the opposite end of the dancing space, the dancer sings the *dun* of his song, and then the *mɔ* again with the chorus, facing it. At the *talum*, he turns around, facing back toward the original end of the dancing space, and repeats the *mɔ* and *talum*—this time alone. At the *sagulu*, he moves back across the dancing space and sings the *dun*, followed by *mɔ*, *talum*, and *dun* again with the chorus. Then he sits down (*asitaki*). If the song was a particularly good or moving one, the aa *bišɔ* may request the dancer to sing it over again, and he does a repeat performance without sitting down.

The songs refer to places and landmarks in various surrounding localities familiar to the listeners in a poignant, nostalgic way:

Mɔ	A *kalo* bird at Dubia Ridge is calling juu . . . juu.
	The *kalo* calling there is calling you.
	Go see the Walægomono pool,
	Go see the fruited *gala* sago.
	A *kalo* bird at Dubia Ridge is calling juu . . . juu.
	The *kalo* calling there is calling you.
	Go to the mouth of the Alim stream.
	Look at the fruited *safu* sago there.
	A *kalo* bird at Dubia Ridge is calling juu . . . juu.
	The *kalo* calling there is calling you.
Talum	Go look at the Masemonodugu pool,
	See the *bobolɔk* tree there.

Sagulu   Oooo-eeee.

Dun   Do you see? Do you see the Galinti pool?
Do you see the crocodile?
The *uf* tree up there at Wasisawel, will it break?
Will the *uf* tree break?

Do you see the Galinti pool?
Do you see the crocodile?
The *mɔl* sago at Wasidugu, will it break?
Will the *mɔl* sago break?

Do you see the Galinti pool?
Do you see the crocodile?
The *beulin* tree up on top there at Gunisawel, will it break?

Do you see the Galinti pool?
Do you see the crocodile?
The base of the stone at Waimɔk, will it pull out?
Will the stone pull out?

Alas, the hill that is up there.
Alas, Balesawel that is up there.
The water pool,
The Gigidin water pool.

Oooo-eeee.

(Composed and danced by Hawe of Bonɔ at Wabisi Gisiro, April
17, 1968. In the original every line is repeated twice.)

All of the places mentioned—Dubia, Wasidugu, Balesawel, with
their various trees, streams, and ridges—are real localities on the
territory of the Sululib longhouse along the Isawa River.

The mood of the song is nostalgic. The voice of the *kalo* is a
familiar, lonely sound of the forest and evokes such things as
lost children. Fruited sago (which is no longer fit to eat) evokes
the ruin and waste of food. The familiar *uf* and *beulin* trees on
Dubia Ridge are seen as racked back and forth in the violent winds
of a storm; the rock at Waimɔk is ready to uproot. The entire
beloved landscape seems about to be destroyed. The image of
desolation is completed with the reference to Balesawel, an
abandoned house site on the opposite ridge. The composer told
me he had made up the song one day on the way to his breadfruit
garden by incorporating the names of various places he passed into
song lines as he went along. Naturally the sago he sang about had

not fruited, nor were trees cracking in the wind; he heard no *kalo* call, nor saw a crocodile. (A crocodile in a pool is another possible spirit image.) He had sung it as he did for effect. His metaphors of solitude, waste, and destruction are in fact entirely conventional metaphors and images and are aimed at awakening a sense of the passing of familiar things.

The sound of a woman beating sago at an isolated camp in the forest is a familiar sign of human presence and domestic activity. It carries some distance through the trees to the ears of passers-by. People often pause on the trail to wonder who it might be. In Gisaro this is transformed into an image of hunger and loneliness.

> Mother, beat my sago
> At the Gisæ mouth, beat *kalɔk*.
> The Feleyowe hill hears it, the hill hears it.
>
> At Amalagalodo beat, beat the sago there.
> Iwalo hill hears it, the *bæ* tree hears it.

(Part of a song composed by Jubi of clan Bonɔ at Sululib.)

"A woman must work sago for her child," the composer explained, "but at the mouth of the Gisæ stream there is no sago or anything else to eat. She beats *kalɔk* [an inedible cane][2] in her sago trough. The sound of her working carries through the forest, but no one is there. Only the hill hears it." Next she works at Amalagalodo, where sago is abundant, but there is still no human presence. The passage clearly has a special poignancy for people whose personal affection is expressed in hospitality and gifts of food.

Framed in sentiments of loneliness or abandonment, the mention of particular trees, hills, and other details of the locality evoke for the listeners particular times and circumstances. The dancer continues:

> He has gone from the spring of the Waido stream,
> He has gone from his house by the Waido.
> I will sleep under the *dona* trees.
>
> Has he gone to the Hɔnsilen stream?
> Has he gone beneath the sago there? . . .

[2] This is a poetic image. In reality no one would do this.

"A man [played by the dancer] has gone to visit his relative," my informant told me, "only to discover that he is not home and the house is closed up." He realizes he has no place to stay and must sleep the night in the forest by himself. He wonders where his relative may be. Perhaps he is at another stream, looking at the sago he owns there. The house and places named in the song, and the people alluded to, were all familiar to the audience, and those who heard the song knew where and who they were. The people who owned the house felt sorry for their relative and wept for their abandoned house.

Each person knows the streams and landmarks of his longhouse territory, and these recall the people he worked and shared with there. This growth of young trees, that patch of weeds with a burned housepost, the huge *ilaha* tree that dominates the crest of a ridge reflect the contexts and personalities of his life. Here is an old garden planted by one's mother before she died; there is the site of a former *aa* where they killed many pigs. A stream recalls the fishing dam built there with one's affines some time ago. A swampy place littered with rotting sago trunks and broken-down processing troughs evokes a forgotten scene of domesticity.

Kaluli can discuss quite explicitly who or what they mourn for in regard to any particular place named in a song, though these persons and events are not obvious from the composition itself. When these names of particular places are projected in images of melancholy, hunger, and forsakenness, they evoke unbearable sorrow and nostalgia. One man wept at the song about the *kalo*, although it didn't concern his lands, because his brothers-in-law had invited him to pick pandanus from their garden at the Alim stream when he had none himself. The garden was now exhausted and left to weeds, but he wept because, I was told, "He used to go there, but doesn't anymore."

The deepest and most violent sorrow evoked by Gisaro songs is that evoked over death. About two months after Beli had lost his wife, Dasemi, at the small longhouse at Mundameyo, a Gisaro dancer rose and sang:

[At] Mundameyo [one has] disappeared.
A little *okari* tree disappeared.

I have no brother. Where shall I go?
A *jubɔlɔ* [bird] calls [from a leafless *malaf* tree]
Come see the mouth of the Bibu stream.
Come see the *okari* there.

I have no brother. Where shall I go?
I have no cross-cousin. Where shall I go?
A *kalo* bird calls [in] a leafless *haido* tree.
Come see the Sæluwæ stream.
Come see the sago there.

I have no brother. I'm hungry.
A *muni* bird calls from a leafless *obora* tree. . . .

(Composed by Gaso and sung at Muluma Gisaro, February 1967. All lines are repeated twice in the original.)

The pathos of these lines needs little elaboration: Who is to work the sago at the Sæluwæ? Who is to share it? Beli and others drove torches into the dancer's shoulder. These things are unbearable because they are a poetic formulation of something that is real. Sometimes a composer knows an area well and makes up his songs with a particular person in mind, as above, but it is also common to find that several different men have each contributed a few locality names when no single one of them knows the area well enough to compose a song alone. They may have no idea who is associated with those localities, but if there are people from these places present at the ceremony, the song will ferret them out and cause them to weep. It is as though the place names (when appropriately framed in the melancholy images of the songs) are effective by themselves. The references to localities are anonymous, like the figures of the dancers, and the people in the audience see different things in them, each his own particular memories and sorrows (or those of dear friends). For a given song, some in the audience pay little attention, and others listen raptly. To an observer, it seems as if each listener thinks the dancer sings only to him. Sitting half-hidden in the shadows at the sidelines of the dancing space, each one seems to turn inward, lost in his own mood and thoughts.

As it refers first to one place and then to another, a Gisaro song represents a progression across some area of land. That is, the song traces an actual path, as if one were to travel that way across the ground. It is possible with any song to construct a map of the region concerned, including hills, streams, gardens, sago stands, and other resources, and from the allusions and associations of the sites trace a history of the area going back ten or fifteen years.

Kaluli develop the intensity of the ceremony and work the mood of the audience to the appropriate pitch by managing the order of the songs. Those sung early in the evening, as the dancers are newly arrived in the longhouse, do not usually concern the lands of the hosts but rather the guests' and dancers' home territories. The isolated bursts of wailing that occur at these times come mostly from women who married into the hosts' longhouse from the longhouse(s) of the guests or from in-laws of the guests who are familiar with these places through visiting. As the evening progresses, the songs gradually concern localities closer and closer to those belonging to the hosts, until finally (after five or six songs) they cross over into the hosts' lands themselves, and the weeping and violence begin in earnest. From this point on, the songs move back and forth across the hosts' lands, evoking enormous anguish in the audience until the morning comes and the ceremony ends.

The degree of subtlety and complexity in the interweaving of geography and personal allusion in some of the songs may be illustrated by a song composed by Seli of clan Bonɔ at Sululib. Seli intended his song for a Wabisi woman named Iše, whom he knew well. Iše was the widow of his mother's brother, Deina, who had died about four years previously. The "track" of the song leads from Deina's old garden house on Bonɔ ground to the place on Wabisi land where he died. It represents an imaginary journey such as Iše might take in returning with her children from Bonɔ to Wabisi after she had been widowed.

Mɔ   *Kalo* bird at the Alim waterfall; juu, father, juu.
Do you hear father calling from the bank behind the Afo spring?
Perched singing in a *dona* tree, do I hear my father?

Kalo bird at the Alim waterfall; juu, father, juu.
Do you hear father calling from the bank behind the Išen spring?
Perched singing in the *ilaha* tree, do I hear my father?

Kalo bird at the Alim waterfall; juu, father, juu.
Do you hear father calling from the bank of the Bɔlu?
Perched singing in the *ilaha* tree, do I hear my father?

Kalo bird at the Alim waterfall; juu, father, juu.
Do you hear father calling from the Bišan stream?
Perched singing in the *til* tree, do I hear my father?

Talum   Eeeeee-oooooo.

Sagulu   I cross, I alone cross, I cross at the mouth of the Bišan stream.

Dun   At the Dædæ stream the trees stand out against the sunset.
Ti sago at the Dædæ stream, the *ti* sago at the Dædæ stream has fruited; will a *howen* bird eat it?

At the Dædæ stream the trees stand out against the sunset.
Ti sago at the Anu spring, the *ti* sago at the Anu spring has fruited; will a *bolo* bird eat it?

At the Dædæ stream the trees stand out against the sunset.
The *wayo* palm at the Bala spring is all dried out; will an *olɔn* bird eat it?

(Fɔs)   A waterfall roars, the Dulu waterfall roars.
Gather at a high place! Gather at Baladagom hill.

(Composed by Seli and sung by Jubi at Wabisi longhouse, April 1967. Each line is repeated twice in the original.)

The track followed by this song does not follow an existing trail (though in some songs it does), but is rather a logical progression from landmark to landmark along the ground. The relevant area (from a map drawn by the composer) is given in Map 10.1.

The first part of the song (the *mɔ*) refers to a place on the Alim stream where two small waters run together as they go over a waterfall and down into a gorge. Between them, above the waterfall, Deina and Seli had built a small house and planted a pandanus garden together.[3] The call of the *kalo*, Seli told me, evoked the image of a child who is hungry and calling for his father, and made people think of Deina's small son Kogowe, who now doesn't have a father. At the same time, he said, it could be taken as the spirit of Deina himself singing in the trees near where

---

[3] Deina was a member of a lineage of clan Wɔsisɔ living with Seli's clan (Bonɔ) in the same longhouse (at Sululib).

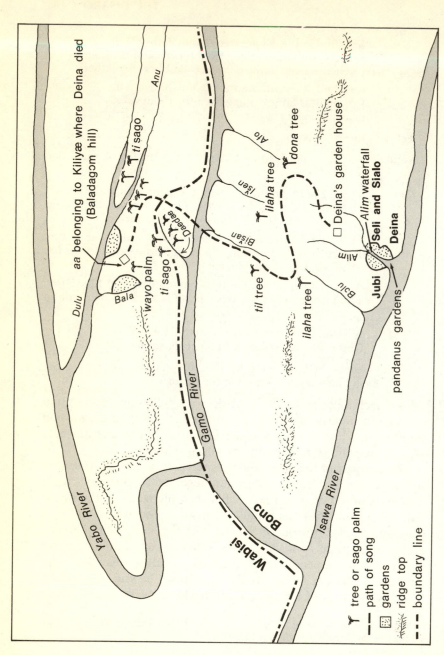

MAP 10.1 Sketch Map of the Area of Seli's Song for Iše

he used to live. Both images would be poignant to Iše (Kogowe's mother, Deina's widow), who had shared the house at the Alim. The image is repeated three times, each for a different stream and tree, moving from place to place along the ground. At the *talum* and *sagulu*, the reference is to a place on the Gamo River, which forms the border of Bonɔ and Wabisi land. The image evoked is of Iše crossing the Gamo alone, returning home to her relatives now that her husband is dead. The transition thus works on several levels: moving from the first part (*mɔ*) to the second part (*dun*) of the song, from Bonɔ to Wabisi ground, and marking the movement of the dancer across the dancing space.

The first lines of the *dun* complete the image. Iše arrives on her own clan lands in the gathering dusk, through dark trees standing out against a red and yellow sky (Seli's description). Here the song reference becomes more complex. The area referred to near the Dædæ belongs to people of Bonɔ (through a complicated history of gift and inheritance) but is on "Wabisi ground" (that is, the Wabisi side of the river) and the sago palms mentioned belong to a prominent Wabisi man, Yayabo. Thus the verses are, for the first time, aimed at someone besides Iše at Wabisi, namely, Yayabo.

The song continues with mention of sago and *wayo* palms at two other places deeper in Wabisi land. (Seli knew where they were, but not who owned them.) The *wayo* palm is near a place where the Bala stream runs into the Dulu, isolating a toe of the ridge. A person standing there can hear the waterfall nearby. It was at this spot that Iše's brother Kiliyæ had built a small *aa* (now burned down) and it was there that Deina had died. The image is that of people being called together to build a house.

Iše was not the only person to weep at this song. Suaga, Seli's sister, who was married to Kiliyæ, also grieved, though the song was not aimed at her. She wept for her former husband Dægili (also of Wabisi), who had died shortly after Deina and was associated by coincidence with some of the same lands in the song.

Seli commented that the song track went along a "marriage road" between Bonɔ and Wabisi. The song ended at the site of a house owned by Kiliyæ and other prominent Wabisi men so as to open the way for subsequent songs to be aimed at them. The various levels of allusion in the song; the self-conscious structural analogies between the land, the transitions in the ceremony, and the "marriage road"; and the transitional ending intended to open the way for new songs aimed at other people is unusual for the general run of Gisaro songs and reflects the gifted character of the composer. (Seli was a man of fast-rising prominence in the Bonɔ community at Sululib.)

Gisaro songs rarely attain this level of deliberate complexity. Less inspired composers, and those who do not know their hosts' lands well, manage nearly as effectively by fitting place names into conventional poetic images. The persons and events that people weep for are then organized, not by the intent of the composer, but in terms of the natural conformation of the land described in the song.

Conventional images (the call of the *kalo*, trees in the sunset, and so on) and appeals ("Sister, I am hungry, what shall I do?") indicate *types* of situations that become specific only in terms of a particular named location. Repetition and variation of the same poetic line diffuse the concrete place and event back into an abstract *type*.

The *kalo* calls from first one spring and then another, each time singing from a different tree. The song plays repeatedly on the image of a woman crossing a stream at sunset near ruined sago palms. The point is particularly clear in the following lines (also composed by Seli):

I will beat fish poison in the Ɔidɔmin River pool.
A *wagi* fish has turned belly up,
Oh, father, won't you look at your child?
Is the Auladugu cliff hanging in front of your eyes?

I will beat fish poison in the Ɔidɔmin River pool.
A *mobalo* fish has turned belly up,
Oh, brother, won't you look at your child?
Is the Isikaluɔ Ridge in front of your eyes?

I will beat fish poison in the Ɔidɔmin River pool.
A *halo* fish has turned belly up,
Oh, cousin, won't you look at your child?
Is the Olo swamp in front of your eyes?

(Each line sung twice in the original.)

The song was aimed at a man whose son had died some time before and was believed to have gone to live in a river in the form of a *wagi* fish. It refers specifically to a time during a fishing trip when someone had caught a *wagi* and the boy's grief-stricken father had been unable to look at it.

Here the same allusion is repeated over and over, each time describing a different fish (all of which can be souls of the dead), appealing to a different kinsman, and naming a different place of "hiding the eyes." The lines are not addressed specifically to the father, for whom the song was composed, nor do they seem necessarily to concern only the one boy whose soul became a *wagi* fish. The lines use the actual incident as a basis on which to construct a number of poetic variations, changing the type of fish and the kind of kin feelings involved by the appeal to different relatives. Variations on the known incident open out a tragic type of Kaluli situation. Repetition brings abstractness to the event, rendering the particular people involved indistinct, and poetically elevates the incident from a concrete occurrence to a form. In this way, events referred to in Gisaro songs become embodiments of a general human condition.

The Violence

In the West, an audience maintains an attitude of essentially passive contemplation in relation to the action. The possibility of strong feeling is brought about by the suspension of disbelief. It is up to the audience to maintain esthetic distance from the performance. A man who is deeply moved remains in his seat. If he believes the action is real and rushes onto the stage, he ruins the show and becomes an object of contempt.

With the Kaluli, the situation is reversed. The maintenance of esthetic distance is primarily up to the performers. They create a distance from the audience by withdrawal into unresponsive obliviousness, which is unaffected by anything the audience might do. The dancer (or chorus member) who cries at his own songs, laughs at the clowning of the *aa bišɔ*, or runs from the torch ruins the mood and is the object of annoyance and disappointment.

We recall that Kaluli aggressively yell their own place names as war cries (*kamo salab*) at attacking enemies (who are primarily strangers) in order to intensify the antagonism, to frighten and confuse them, and to scatter them into retreat. Such place names are called "our *kamo*" by the people who use them. Indeed, during the violence in Gisaro, the youths who leap into the dancing space and the women shrieking in the back of the *aa* are yelling *kamo* much of the time.

In the singing of Gisaro, this relationship is reversed. Here it is not the *aa biŝɔ* aggressively yelling their place names to confuse enemy strangers. It is friends (but strangers in their anonymous dance regalia) beautifully singing the same *kamo* names back at their hosts. Instead of the aggravation of fighting hostility, there is the intensification of excruciating intimacy. The *aa biŝɔ* project themselves in battle by yelling the places with which they most deeply associate themselves. When the same names are sung back at them in Gisaro, they are thrown back into themselves upon all that those places mean to them. The grief evoked by the songs becomes in this way something of an intrusion. "When the dancer sings about Alimsɔk," one informant said, "I am reminded of my dead wife, Yano, who planted pandanus and breadfruit there with me. He [the dancer] is saying, 'Now you go alone to pick from the gardens you planted with your wife. Now there is only you.' I feel, 'Why do you sing about my gardens? Why do you say I am alone? What do you mean? Kadaaa!'" (He plunges the torch.) Another informant said, "Who is he to speak of my sorrow? He doesn't belong here!"

This painful tension between grief, anger, intimacy, and violence becomes visible when someone from the audience angrily thrusts the torch out on the dancer's shoulder and then throws his arms around him, hugging him affectionately and wailing uncontrollably.

As people get more wrought up, they visibly jump or startle when they hear the names of their lands sung, as though dealt an invisible blow. Wails of anguish are punctuated by shouts of "Bruh! Bruh!" As men stride into the dancing space to stamp out their torches on the dancer, the youths and youngsters leap in from the sidelines stamping and banging, waving axes, celebrating their kinsmen's retaliation in a fierce, triumphant, and rather frightening pandemonium. Those who remain listening by the sidelines gaze at the dancer with utter absorption.

The shiny red stalk of cordyline leaves bobbing back and forth amid the streamers of the dancer's costume beckons to some listeners like someone who is absent or dead saying, "Brother, come here." Choked up and enraged, men will stride up and rip the offending cordyline off the dancer's costume in the midst of the performance. Others thrust their torches amid the plumes of his costume, ruining his cassowary headdress and bird of paradise sprays. The dancers become increasingly bedraggled and disarrayed. As song followed song late into the night, I would sometimes get a feeling of a kind of desperation coming from the *aa bišɔ*.

In the smoke and dust, the streaming sparks, wailing, war cries, stamping, and banging of the men and youths, the dancer is sometimes lost from sight. Occasionally all the torches are put out on him at once and the *aa* is plunged into darkness.

> The dancer stands and has barely begun to sing when the men who were dropping sparks on his predecessor, suddenly turn and jam five torches into his back. A bystander holding a spray of cordyline leaves thrusts them in with the torches trying to provide him some protection. Water is called for, poured, and spat over his back, which is smoking. The dancer hasn't changed his expression or faltered a note in his song. Youths and young men are relighting their torches, stamping and yelling, dropping sparks of burning resin over him.
>
> Again he is suddenly descended on by the torches. The men and boys stamping and yelling, the man with the cordyline thrusting it in wherever he can, water being poured on from bamboo tubes, incredible pandemonium and stamping, some people waving axes. Others run to relight their torches to jam them again in the dancer's back. During this time he hasn't faltered or flinched, although he is sometimes shoved forward by the force of the torches in his back, and one grinning man holds a torch to his face to watch his reaction.
>
> Finally, the dancer turns back to his original spot. There is a smell of resin, smoke, and burned meat. Another torch is put out on his back. An older man throws his arms around him, bursts into wailing, and then runs out the back door to wail on the veranda. Finally, the dancer reaches the end of his song and sits down. (Field notes)

Dancer is burned while some *aa bišɔ* try to protect him with cordyline.

In the midst of all this, the clash of the rattle continues relentlessly, a thread of order amid the chaos. The greater the noise and
disruption, the more sonorous and unified the singing and the
more determined the whole performance becomes. Chorus and
dancer answer each other, overlapping call and response, with a
kind of passionate and triumphal concentration that defies disruption. The rattle and the melody reach beyond the pandemonium
to maintain an overarching unity and order. Within it, hosts and
guests, sorrow and anger, beauty and violence constantly strive
against each other in precarious balance. The violence of the
audience does not disrupt the performance because it is absorbed
and contained within it.

When the ceremony reaches its highest pitch of excitement, the overwrought *aa biʃɔ* may start weeping chain reactions. As one person begins to wail, others break down also, group by group along the sidelines. In the midst of all this sorrow, even the chorus and visitors are moved to tears at the sight of their hosts' suffering. They must not weep openly lest they ruin their own performance, but one may see older men of the visitors sitting back in the shadows with tears running quietly down their cheeks.

At this point in the ceremony, not only the dancers but also members of the chorus suffer from the torches. Chorus members who sing particularly strongly, or who seem to know a song better than the dancer, are assumed to be the composers and are burned by the *aa biʃɔ*.

An attack with a torch is not considered a serious injury and is not actively resented by the victim. Only those injuries that disable a man or draw his blood are real offenses requiring redress. Since a burn with a torch does not fall into either of these categories, Kaluli regard it primarily as a retaliatory infliction of pain. It does not serve to compensate the hurt feelings of the hosts but only to release them for the moment. Appropriate compensation must wait until later.

The chorus and dancers make no attempt to defend themselves against the attack of their hosts.[4] Nevertheless, it is possible for a member of the *aa biʃɔ* to go too far. If he attacks the dancer by clubbing him with a log, or burns him "badly" (too severely, too repeatedly, or on a place other than the shoulders and back), the dancer may bolt and the ceremony breaks up. When that happens, there is usually a brawl between *aa biʃɔ* and *miyɔwɔ*, compensation is refused for those who caused it, and general bad feeling prevails. Even then, however, the dancer or chorus must make the move that ends the performance.

Most of the time, fortunately, the *aa biʃɔ* are able to keep the violence somewhat under control. Those among the hosts whose ground names are not presently being sung, and who are not

---

[4] Ray Kelly (1970) reports that among the Etoro people (to the north of the Kaluli on the plateau), he has seen a dancer in the Kɔsa ceremony (the Etoro version of Gisaro) gesture with a small knife in his hand in such a way as to keep the hosts from approaching him too closely on one side. I never observed this among the Bosavi people.

moved to tears at a particular time, are aware of the dancer's suffering.[5] Especially later in the night, when most of the dancers have been repeatedly burned, these people try to give them some protection from excessive attacks from their infuriated brethren. They do not attempt to restrain those who are grieving and angry since that would provoke them further. Rather, they try to ward off their attacks by shielding the dancer's shoulders with cordyline leaves or pouring water over the torches.

The wailing and violence continue all night long. The Gisaro performance does not build to any single climax. Once the songs have crossed over onto the territory of the *aa bišɔ*, it consists of a series of climaxes of weeping and anger, continued relentlessly and without resolution throughout the night. The tension accumulates from song to song as people get more and more wrought up, until at some point the dancers may sing a few songs about other places to give themselves some respite from the ordeal. Toward morning, the tension usually begins to ease a little as the people become exhausted. The performance ends abruptly at dawn. When the first birds begin to sing and the dancer comes to the end of his song, the choruses rise to their feet with a shout of "Buu-wɔɔɔ!" and all immediately troop out of the *aa* for home.

Denouement

As the performers leave the house or pass out of the yard, they give small items of compensation to those of their hosts whom they have made cry. A mirror, a box of paint, a small knife, a shell necklace—these soothe the feelings and terminate the anger of the *aa bišɔ* and establish reassurance of the mutual spirit of closeness between the two sides. A few minutes later, loud wails can be heard from the forest as members of the *miyɔwɔ* release their sorrow and weep for the pain the *aa bišɔ* had suffered during the night.

Other items of compensation are given during the following few

---

[5] People usually phrase this as concern for the dancer's children. They need their father to hunt for meat and bring food from the gardens, which he is not able to do for some time if he is incapacitated from burns.

days as members of the *aa bišɔ* ask for them. Sometimes the recipient will give another small item of wealth in return, carrying the significance of compensation over into a particular sign of mutual friendship.

If the performance was a good one and many people wept, dancers and chorus exclaim in appreciation as they depart, "It looks like your souls will stay with you; you won't be dying!" Then the *aa bišɔ* try to calculate when they will be able to stage a Gisaro performance and make their guests weep in return.

Aftermath

The dancers' burns usually take three to four weeks to heal completely. During the day prior to the ceremony, they are extensively anointed on the shoulders and upper arms with a mixture of plant juices and resins known as *giliso* "to keep the burns from hurting." *Giliso* also provides the pungent aroma of the ceremony, acting like a perfume. The torches (*æsɔn*) with which they are burned are made from tree resin wrapped in leaves and baked to congeal. It seemed to me that the torch flames had a very low temperature; it is difficult to light straws or other tinder from them, and Kaluli always use embers from a firebox to light things. They didn't bother to extinguish drops of flaming resin that fell on or under the bark floor of the *aa*; indeed, flaming resin sparks often could be seen falling outside through the floor under the *aa* during attacks on the dancers. My own experience of having flaming resin occasionally drop onto my hand or leg was that it stung fiercely for a while but rarely raised a blister. This may be one reason the dancers are able to withstand such an onslaught. The burns inflicted during the ceremony are usually extensive over the shoulder blades and backs of the upper arms. Sometimes the skin blisters and sloughs off entirely during the performance. Otherwise, it sloughs off within a day or two, leaving raw, exposed, fleshy-looking surfaces. Doctors I have spoken with estimate that the burns are largely second-degree.

The dancers spend much of the first ten days or so after the performance convalescing from their ordeal, sitting with their burns exposed to the sun in the houseyard, waving stalks of leaves to keep the flies away. The burns always heal to dark skin in about three or four weeks. Kaluli can remember only one person who died soon after dancing Gisaro, and it wasn't clear from the description that his burns were really the cause.

Chapter 11

Gisaro and the
Opposition Scenario

What, then, is Gisaro all about? The songs project the members of the audience back along their lives, through images of places they have known in the past. As a visiting government interpreter once remarked to me, "It is their memory." Tragic situations are renewed, allowing people to take account of them once more and settle them in their hearts and minds. It is not the nostalgic content of the songs, however, but the angered and anguished *taking of account* in Gisaro that is most striking to an outsider, and it is the taking of account, I believe, that to the Kaluli gives the ceremony its special character. The listeners' feelings and reactions are not merely a response to the performance; they are integral to its structure and significance. The dancing and singing by the performers and the weeping and burning by the audience stimulate and aggravate one another. If the *aa biʃɔ* fail to respond to the songs, even enthusiastic performers soon lose interest, and the ceremony falls apart before the night is over. On the other hand, if the *aa biʃɔ* weep and burn the dancers even desultory performers rapidly pull themselves together and assert a determined momentum. The movement of Gisaro is ultimately to be understood in terms of the opposition scenario.

A Drama of Opposition

Gisaro is a drama of opposition initiated by the dancers but played out by everyone. Within a structure of reciprocity, the action of the performers and the feelings of the audience are brought into a relation with each other that allows intelligibility and resolution. But at the same time, *aa bišɔ* and *miyɔwɔ* confront each other in an interaction of such tension that it not infrequently blows the performance apart. If an enraged host treats a dancer too harshly, or a minor dispute among the gathering escalates, or some other event occurs, people may jump angrily to their feet shouting recriminations, and the ceremony ends abruptly.

On one occasion described to me, an *aa bišɔ* youth began banging on a drum. This was probably part of the clowning the hosts perform during the first part of the ceremony, but it had the effect of drowning out the songs. Unfortunately, the dancer at the time was a man of strong temperament, who became enraged, left the dancing space, smashed the drum, and threw the youth bodily out of the *aa* longhouse. With that, the *miyɔwɔ* jumped to their feet, grabbed axes, and wrecked the interior of the *aa*. A few *aa bišɔ* squared off in token defense, but most fled outside appalled at what was happening and how their young man had behaved.

In social anthropology, when violence and antagonism are expressed ceremonially between two groups, it is customary to assume that they represent underlying stresses between the groups and thus to search for a deeper content to the opposition in the underlying tensions of social relationships. The *aa bišɔ* and *miyɔwɔ* involved in any occasion of celebration (or dispute) are not opposed as residential or descent units but as action groups, of temporary and heterogeneous composition, in which members of the same lineage or residential unit may be on either side. There are no clear-cut or lasting lines across which *structurally* engendered tensions might develop. The oppositions invoked on ceremonial occasions are circumstantial and pertain to the particular *issues* involved.

The question then is: Are the particular issues of the occasion the basis for an antagonism expressed in the ceremony? Kaluli ceremonies are usually connected with weddings and prestations. At a wedding, when a woman is brought to her husband's *aa*, the *aa bišɔ/miyɔwɔ* opposition is roughly between those who are giving bridewealth (the hosts) and those who are to receive it (the guests). For a prestation, the division is roughly between those who are making the prestation and those who are receiving it. Since about 60 percent of the meat on these occasions is given to people classed as affines, we might suppose that the *aa biʃɔ* and *miyɔwɔ* on ceremonial occasions are opposed principally across lines of affinal connection.

While the principal donors are often *aa biʃɔ* for celebrations of preparation, some future recipients act together with them as hosts for one ceremony and come as guests for the next, or vice versa. Often this is done in a kind of rotation, so that, in effect, everyone gets a chance to be *aa biʃɔ* and *miyɔwɔ*. The only time when the line between *aa biʃɔ* and *miyɔwɔ* really approximates that between donors and recipients is on the day of the distribution itself, when hosts and guests dance *together* and there is no weeping or burning. Because *aa biʃɔ* and *miyɔwɔ* divide and switch around in this manner, it is difficult to say exactly what these oppositions really mean for a Gisaro in terms of the opposing groups and affinal exchange.

A wedding presents a more clear-cut opposition. The social division is drawn between those who support the groom and those who come with the bride. The question is whether the Gisaro ceremony performed for the occasion can be taken as fundamentally expressive of a temporary antagonism between the two sides. The issue is difficult to resolve clearly. The locus of tension is associated with the bridewealth negotiations and focuses on those people involved in them. However, the principal figures in the Gisaro ceremony—for example, the dancers—are more often than not peripheral to the bridewealth issues (if they are involved at all) and bear no close network relation to the negotiators.

Figure 11.1 outlines the relationships between dancers and those receiving the major bridewealth payments in a representative wedding. Although everyone on the list knew all the others, none of the dancers volunteered out of close kin or affinal connection with the bride's family or important participation in the bridewealth. Similarly, those who composed the songs for the ceremony (not shown) did so because they had some knowledge of the groom's clan lands and those of other *aa biʃɔ*, not because of network connections to the family of the bride. In other words, the

FIGURE 11.1 Relation of Dancers to Principal Bridewealth Recipients

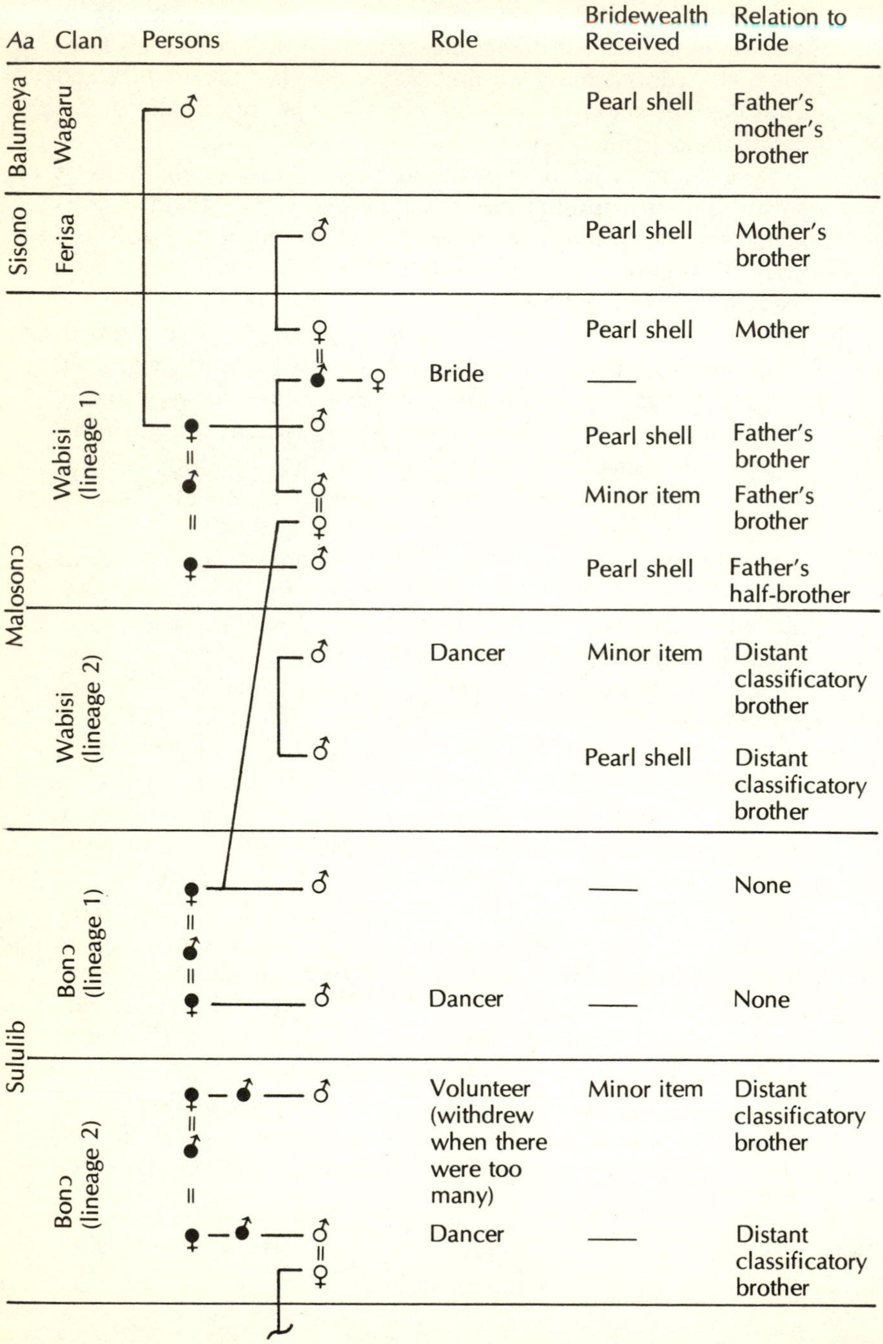

Aa	Clan	Persons	Role	Bridewealth Received	Relation to Bride
Balumeya	Wagaru	♂		Pearl shell	Father's mother's brother
Sisono	Ferisa	♂		Pearl shell	Mother's brother
Malosonɔ	Wabisi (lineage 1)	♀		Pearl shell	Mother
		♀ Bride	Bride	—	
		♂		Pearl shell	Father's brother
		♂		Minor item	Father's brother
		♂		Pearl shell	Father's half-brother
	Wabisi (lineage 2)	♂	Dancer	Minor item	Distant classificatory brother
		♂		Pearl shell	Distant classificatory brother
Sululib	Bonɔ (lineage 1)	♂		—	None
		♂	Dancer	—	None
	Bonɔ (lineage 2)	♂	Volunteer (withdrew when there were too many)	Minor item	Distant classificatory brother
		♂	Dancer	—	Distant classificatory brother

Aa	Clan	Persons	Role	Bridewealth Received	Relation to Bride
Kolodɔ	Gæsumisi	♀ ‖ ● ‖ ♀ — ♂ (♂)		Pearl shell	Distant classificatory cross-cousin (nosɔk)
Wahalib	Tæmæsi	— ♂	Dancer	—	Husband of distant classificatory sister
	Gæsumisi	— ♂		Pearl shell	Classificatory cross-cousin

NOTE: The major items of bridewealth (mother-of-pearl shells, axes) customarily go to the closest relatives of the bride—her father, mother, and mother's brothers—and perhaps one or two other people of particular influence. In the above case, however, the bride's father was dead and his function was taken over by his brothers and relatives. Certain irregularities in the marriage and inflation of the local wealth situation due to European contact resulted in this bride price being unusually high. The diagram omits numerous smaller items of bridewealth (shell necklaces, bush-knives, beaded chest bands) made to peripheral people. All major items of bridewealth were paid before the wedding.

♂ ♀ = dead; ♂ ♀ = living

principal figures in the Gisaro performance are not themselves set up in opposition to the *aa bišɔ* on the same basis as those involved in the bridewealth negotiations. In any case, the grief and violence involved in the ceremony seem far out of proportion to whatever actual tension and difficulties are involved in the particular occasion. The antagonism evoked in the ceremony may indeed parallel, and perhaps dramatize, those concrete social tensions that do underlie the occasion, but it is not primarily founded on them.

Now undoubtedly a certain amount of personal pique between particular individuals on the *aa bišɔ* and *miyɔwɔ* may be worked off through the medium of the songs and the torch. However, only once did I hear someone speak of using ceremonial violence to express outside grievances. In a heated conversation in the longhouse, I overheard a man complain about a dispute with his brother-in-law over rights to a fishing spot. "Just wait until they Gisaro," he yelled. "I will really plunge the torch on that man!" Those who have serious grievances against someone at a ceremony either settle them publicly before the ceremony or refuse to attend. If hostility exists between two groups who show up at a ceremonial occasion, it will usually erupt before the ceremony begins. Kaluli are not good at masking their anger or keeping their feelings to themselves. On one occasion that is well remembered, some members of the *aa bišɔ* and *miyɔwɔ* who had only recently reached a settlement over a murder become enraged with each other over a trivial incident during the afternoon. Men leaped up, bows were drawn, and those not involved had to rush between the groups and push them apart. They were then segregated in separate houses near the *aa*, and the ceremony was held without them.

From the Kaluli point of view, the fear that people will fight, attack the dancers too severely, or refuse to pay compensation is not the reason why they do not Gisaro when they are on bad terms. Rather, the reason is that the *aa bišɔ* would be "hard," no one would weep, and the ceremony would go off badly.

Thus, though there is room in Gisaro for expression of displaced antagonism between people, it would be a mistake to emphasize this kind of factor in the significance of the ceremony. Whatever social tensions may be present on a Gisaro occasion, they are better understood in terms of a displacement of antagonism *into* a violence that already exists in the ceremony, rather than as the hidden basis for the violence.

We have already discussed (Chapter 5) the fact that Kaluli social processes proceed through the formation of oppositions and that these have implications of their own apart from the particular circumstances that bring them about. Whenever two groups, however temporary in composition, stand against one another in opposition over a transaction, there is a certain awkwardness to the situation. This is reflected in the formal message customarily conveyed in the fact that *aa bišɔ* and *miyɔwɔ* do not share food. If a ceremony is to be performed, especially if withdrawn dancers and chorus are present, the atmosphere of tension is thereby increased. *Aa bišɔ* and *miyɔwɔ* are placed implicitly in a posture of assertion against each other.

Kaluli do not regard their ceremonies as expressing hostility. They see them as grand and exciting, deeply affecting, beautiful and sad, but not antagonistic. The songs are presented, not as taunts or mockery of the listeners, but in the same spirit of sympathy with which the guests themselves weep at the end of the ceremony for their friends and relatives among the hosts who have suffered. Indeed, composers and dancers sometimes share with their listeners the sorrows their songs are about (see Seli's song for Iše). The ceremony is much too moving to be accepted in an atmosphere of animosity. It is for this reason that hostile listeners would not let themselves be open to it—would be "hard"—and instead of the dancers being attacked with increased savagery, the ceremony would fail altogether. The anger expressed in Gisaro thus has more to do with mutual understanding between friends than hostility between enemies.

We have already spoken of the assertiveness, the posture of independence, the pride in physical endurance that are traits of Kaluli character and style. This is intensified in the image of the Gisaro dancer: beautiful and strong but sorrowful; self-sufficient but lonely. He is at once desirable and touching, magnificent and enraging. His song is a gentle but relentless imposition on the *aa bišɔ*—calling to them, appealing to them, inflicting on them their own grief and pain. At the same time that the songs provoke anger in the listeners, they are a resolute source of strength to the dancer. As a man sings out against his own pain or fatigue or fear, so do the dancer and chorus assert themselves resolutely against the attacks of the *aa bišɔ*.

An outsider gets the impression that the more the hosts attack the dancers, the more the dancers dare them to do their worst. The more anger is generated and energy expended, the more intense and powerful the performance becomes. The music drones and swells, filling the house and permeating everything with a resolute and majestic order.

The hosts, for their part, respond to the evocation of loss and sorrow by retaliation. The swift and decisive reaction in the ceremony has a dramatic magnificence that inspires the Kaluli imagination. It asserts and embodies a person's inviolability and integrity, the fundamental aspect of a person that we call human dignity. There are recognized limits to which the violence can go in the ceremony, but to deny a person permission to attack the dancer is an assault on his fundamental self-image and the intelligibility of his life.

A Sense of Proportion

While I was in the field, the local administrative officer decided to prohibit the burning of dancers in Kaluli ceremonies because of the dangers that he felt would result from infection of burn injuries. Kaluli could still hold ceremonies, he said, but they were not to burn anyone. This edict was received with general consternation. It was widely feared that, if people could not retaliate for their grief, they would refuse to grieve. There would be no weeping and the ceremonies would come to nothing. To preserve the ceremonies, the Kaluli hit upon the idea that the *aa bišɔ* could attack the dancers, but only thrust the torch into the *mise æsu* (protective coverings), so as not to actually hurt them. They also adjusted the mode of compensation so that, instead of paying a single item of wealth to a host who had cried (but retaliated), the *miyɔwɔ* would pay each host an item of wealth for each time he had wept. The local village constables put on their uniforms to supervise the proceedings.

The result was that the violence, rather than being more controlled, got completely out of hand. In two Gisaros that I saw, the pattern was the same. At first, the *aa bišɔ* thrust their torches into the *mise œsu*, but later, as they became increasingly furious, their frustration at not being able to give real retaliation to the dancers led them to seek new ways to attack them.

Men began throwing huge ember logs at the backs of the dancers; they showered them with burning coals and pounded them on the *mise œsu* with their fists. The torches were painful, but blows with ember logs and fists promised to be dangerous. The first Gisaro under the new regime broke up early in the night when a dancer was burned with a misdirected torch. The second broke up when a furious member of the *aa bišɔ* clubbed a dancer on the head with a log. On that occasion, a brawl was only narrowly averted.

To move a person deeply with the songs and then deny him the right to retaliate is to make him suffer helplessly, unable to return his pain. Kaluli reactions are immediate. The grief and anger generate a tension between dancers and audience during the performance that requires some sort of periodic release if the ceremony is not to blow up. This cannot be accomplished by stamping a torch out on the *mise œsu*, no matter how forcefully. "If one plunges the torch only into the *mise œsu*," one informant told me, "he comes away [still] angry. But after burning the dancer on the skin, he is only a little angry." For listeners to wait until the end of the ceremony was more than the urgency of their grief and rage could sustain. In the ceremony that followed these two disastrous Gisaros, the Kaluli went back to burning the dancers.[1]

This does not reflect a Kaluli inability to control their violence but rather a return to their proper sense of proportion. The burning of the dancers allows a balance to be maintained between the audience, whose feelings are anguished, and the performance, which continually aggravates them. The prohibition of the burning

---

[1] This was facilitated by the fact that the government-appointed Papuan medical orderly, who had been living in the area, departed at this time for his leave, so that there were no outsiders remaining nearby who the Kaluli thought would inform the patrol officer.

by the government officer interfered directly with the way this balance was maintained, with results both disastrous to the ceremony and producing ill feeling in the community.

Payment of Compensation

The sorrow and the violence coming to terms with each other show that people may suffer grief and loss without being helpless. As the listeners strive against the dancers, they return pain for anguish, transform their sorrow by releasing it in anger, and turn their vulnerability into strength and positive action.

However, retaliation on the dancers releases only the listeners' anguish of the moment and allows them to assume a posture of strength. It does not finally reconcile their feelings or give satisfactory closure to the event. This comes with payment of compensation (*su*) at the end of the ceremony, which completes Gisaro dramatically and emotionally by asserting that one will receive return for the things in his life he has lost, as sympathy and/or conciliation from those who are responsible. Without *su* one suffers in lonely, angry humiliation, deprived of acknowledgment or release from the pain of his situation. "A person is not unwilling to weep," one man said in reference to Gisaro, "since he knows he will receive compensation. If he thought he were not going to receive it, then he would be unwilling." If people are not compensated at the end of the performance, they feel hurt, insulted, and angry. It is this that animates the discussion in the longhouse after every ceremony when the dancers have left. Those who feel slighted in compensation go off to ask for more. If no compensation is forthcoming, as sometimes happens, bad feeling arises, which is then carried over for expression and resolution into the context of the next ceremony. This was the motivation for almost every comment I heard people make about intending to burn someone at a forthcoming ceremony. One well-remembered incident occurred about 1964:

> The people of clan Didesa (Wanagesa longhouse) performed Gisaro on two occasions at Olabia without paying adequate compensation. The people of Olabia were so angry that later, when people of clan Ferisa (Sisono longhouse) planned to perform

Gisaro at Olabia for a wedding, Olabia requested them not to have any D‡desa men as dancers. When the bridal party arrived, however, there was Wano of D‡desa with *mise æsu* tied into his hair. The people of Olabia were extremely annoyed but said nothing.

However, one man, Tæluwa, had been so incensed at the refusal of D‡desa to pay compensation previously that he had made preparations in case a D‡desa man should show up to dance. He had made a huge torch, said to have been as big around as a man's leg, which he hid in the Olabia *aa*. After about the third cycle of the ceremony, Wano stood up and began singing Olabia grounds. Tæluwa burst into tears and, lighting his huge torch, rammed it into Wano's shoulder. The pain was such that Wano immediately sat down. His brother Kulu, who was sitting in the chorus, said to him "Stand up. . . . You said you wished to dance when other Ferisa men wished to do so. Now you should dance." And Wano got back up. Tæluwa yelled, "What! Is he still alive?" And put the huge torch out again on his other shoulder. Kulu enraged, yelled at him from the chorus, "When you eat pig, do you not give some to us?" (that is, What? Are you not our brother? What are you doing that for?) and Tæluwa answered, "You should not sing our ground names if you don't pay compensation," and smacked Kulu over the head with the torch. The Gisaro broke up in a brawl. (Field notes)

The acts of compensation at the end of a ceremony formally convey a certain intimacy of feeling. The dancers, chorus members, and other guests make an effort to see that everyone who wept receives something but also tend to pass it out to those who are the most important and/or beloved figures in their networks of personal relationships. Figure 11.2 gives a list of payments made by people of one longhouse community for the same Gisaro at Wabisi mentioned in Figure 11.1. The list covers only the contribution of the dancers and chorus members from Sululib *aa*. It encompasses some of the same relationships involved in the meat prestation (described in Figure 4.2), which occurred about seven months later. Comparing the two lists reveals that several of the men who later gave gifts of meat to people of Wabisi had compensated them or their wives for the sorrow they had suffered in the Gisaro, whether or not they had anything to do with producing the performance. Composers tended to compensate the people their songs were aimed at (often relatives or close network friends).

FIGURE 11.2 Compensation Payments Made by People of Clan Bonɔ (Sululib Longhouse) for Weeping at a Gisaro at Wabisi

Giver (G)	Role in Ceremony	Recipient (R)	Item	Relationship (G and R)
♀–♂–♂ ‖	Miyɔwɔ (chorus member)	♂ ♂	Shell necklace Shell necklace	Rs are G's first wife's classificatory brothers, but not important network connections
♂ ‖				G's more important connections at Wabisi (through second wife); were later given prestation of meat
♂–♂ ♀	Dancer	♂ ♂	Shell necklace Shell necklace	Rs are G's classificatory cross-cousins and old friends; important figures in his network before he married
		♂ ‖	Beaded chest band	R was husband of G's father's brother's daughter and an influential man at Wabisi, but not a primary figure in G's network
		♀	Mirror	*R is G's father's brother's daughter, termed sister
♂–♂	Composer of songs	♀	Blanket	*G's true sister, subject of meat prestations; R's husband is an important connection

Bonɔ (lineage 1)

Giver (G)	Role in Ceremony	Recipient (R)	Item	Relationship (G and R)
♀ =		♂	Beads	R is an influential man, husband of G's distant classificatory sister
♂–♂└♂	Miyɔwɔ (chorus member)	=	Small knife	G is R's wife's younger unmarried brother (age about 14)
♀–♂	Miyɔwɔ	=	Cloth	*R is married to G's classificatory daughter; they exchange meat; important connection
♀–♂	Dancer	=	Beaded chest band	G gave compensation to R "because he cried a lot"; no meat exchange or close network connection
♂	Miyɔwɔ	=	Cloth	*G exchanges meat with R over R's wife, G's classificatory daughter; important connection
♂	Miyɔwɔ (chorus member)	♂	Shell necklace	Rs are G's wife's classificatory brothers from clan Gæsumisi at Kæsi aa who came as aa bĩsɔ; no information on network status
		♂	Shell necklace	

Bonɔ (lineage 2)

NOTE: Genealogies show how people are related by descent, but do not indicate groups.

♂ ♀ = dead; ♂ ♀ = living

*These people also passed gifts of meat (G to R) in the prestation referred to in Figure 4.2.

Others simply compensated those they felt close to or particularly sorry for.

In any case, Gisaro achieves a closeness of feeling and energizes (slightly rivalrous) goodwill between *aa bišɔ* and *miyɔwɔ* through the playing out of a deliberately evoked and staged opposition scenario. These sentiments are achieved, however, in a manner inverse to the way similar ones are effected by a wedding or a gift of pork, and the mood of the ceremony is the reverse of that of the occasion it celebrates.

The Significance of Gisaro

Kaluli social occasions are characterized by exuberant fellowship and conversation among familiar friends and relatives; people turn outward toward each other. Gisaro is marked by agonized intimacy forced on one by an attractive but oblivious stranger (the dancer); people turn inward and confront themselves and their sorrows. Prestation celebrates closeness achieved between friends through gifts of food or a marriage. Gisaro represents the closeness achieved between reconciled enemies through (sometimes mutual) sorrow, retaliation, and payment of compensation. Both affirm faith in the reciprocity of human relationships, though in different ways, and both assume a continued relationship through predication of a return of the occasion (whether it be prestation, bride, or ceremony). In the end, the two are complementary but inverse statements of the same reality. Appropriately enough, therefore, weddings and prestations take place in the day, whereas Gisaro is performed at night.

From the point of view of traditional social-functional analysis, the songs make present to the *aa bišɔ* the most deeply unmanageable concerns of their lives. In this Gisaro can serve as a vehicle for the expression of social ambivalences and minor hostilities between *aa bišɔ* and *miyɔwɔ*, and it certainly evokes those centrifugal forces of antagonism that would seem frequently to threaten to tear Kaluli society apart. The ceremony, then, attempts to weave these back into sociality by symbolically allowing their resolution and reiterating the orderly form of social processes.

The intelligibility and indeed practicability of human life depends precisely on well-understood, even beloved, processes in which the values of the society are actualized to bring about those results in life that every person desires and in some sense stands for. As action and value arc adjusted in events, esthetic considerations of form and proportion play a prominent part. For Kaluli to view the opposition process esthetically is not merely to celebrate or embellish it but to render it into more perfect form, hence increasing its acceptability, its intelligibility, and its efficiency. Though the tensions of Gisaro derive from sorrow for the dead and times past, the songs and response are cast in a processual framework generic to the way all losses and conflicts are handled in Kaluli society. In doing this, the ceremony generates, in the abstract, the movement of Kaluli social life itself. For it is the formation of oppositions and the progression toward their resolution, whether over death and dispute or weddings and prestations, that provides the motion of social and political events.

However, to anyone who has seen Gisaro, the ceremony is clearly more than a continually reiterated statement about the nature of life and social relationships. It is a way of constantly reflecting on and reworking these things. Gisaro is not really concerned with how conflicts are resolved but rather with how conflict resolution is integral to human relationships and life. It does not state the problems Kaluli society has, with its centrifugal tendencies; it embodies the way these centrifugal tendencies energize the human actions. Oppositions and their resolutions are seen, not as problems or strategies for affecting life, but the very stuff of it. An outsider is tempted in these circumstances to endow the opposition scenario with a metaphysical significance.

Kaluli do not come to understand their lives by explicating them in a rationalized system of ideas. Rather, they play out and resolve the issues of their lives in a passionate and dramatic ceremonial performance that shakes the participants profoundly and calls upon their deepest emotional resources. Gisaro puts events of life, death, and the passing of time into intelligible relationship without at the same time putting them at a reflective distance. Thus, they may be resolved emotionally and accepted concretely in committed real action. Gisaro is therefore more than a statement concerning life. It is a thrusting oneself on it. It is not so much a reflection on death as it is an assertion against it.

This assertion to the Kaluli is quite real. We recall that Kaluli ceremonies, and particularly Gisaro, are felt to have a death-averting or sickness-halting power. My informants were not able to explain why this was so, beyond saying that one danced during times of sickness to "keep back the dying out" (*danili*). In other contexts, they would remark that a *sei* usually will not attack people at a ceremony. This was not because everyone was noisy and wakeful but because even the *sei* himself is charmed by the performance. He loses his rage on seeing the dancers and is caught up in the prevailing mood of pathos and nostalgia. At the same time, Kaluli do not seem to connect the charming of *seis* with the sickness-averting power of the ceremony (though that might seem to us a contributing factor). Rather they feel that both of these are the result of the generally life-enhancing power of the performance itself that derives from something they cannot easily articulate about its significance.

There is, then, apparently a dimension of significance to Gisaro that we have not yet been able to reach. To look for it, we may turn, as Kaluli often do in times of puzzlement, to see how Gisaro appears in relation to the unseen.

Gisaro and the Unseen

At first sight, Gisaro performances would seem to have very little to do with the invisible side of reality. Ceremonies are not performed in relation to invisible people or for their special benefit. *Ane mama* are believed to sometimes come and watch ceremonies invisibly from the rafters of the *aa*. (They are said to be called by the *miyɔwɔ* before they leave their longhouse for the ceremony, though I never saw this done.) A moth or other insect flying around the dancer is an indication of their presence. Occasionally an *ane* person will contribute a song or a bit of magic to a dancer through a medium, and these things are supposed to have special potency to move the *aa bišɔ*. But the actual concern about the presence or participation of *ane* people at the Kaluli ceremonies I witnessed was at best a very minor one.

However, other contexts and traditional lore reveal that Gisaro provides an important link between the two aspects of reality. During a seance, when an *ane mama* enters the body of a medium in the fully darkened *aa*, he first addresses the assembled audience by singing a Gisaro song. The listeners answer him in chorus. Soon, singing of river pools and forested hills, they attain a unity of melodic purpose and attention and settle into an intimate, expectant, nostalgic mood that provides the atmosphere in which dead and living may converse. Here Gisaro not only recalls to Kaluli their sorrows and their dead but establishes a solidarity between them. Singing Gisaro with one's dead brother at a seance is one way, for a short while, of being with him again.

Kaluli informants generally agree that Gisaro was originally given to men by the *ane* people, though they differ about exactly how. Some say that *ane mama* originally taught people Gisaro by coming up and singing through a medium. One version describes how a medium went out into the invisible to investigate the origin of a thunderstorm and discovered *ane mama* coming together for Gisaro. He attended the ceremony and found it good. Later, the *ane* invited him to dance himself. *Ane mama* came up through his body and sang Gisaro songs to the people of his *aa* all night. When morning came and lit the *aa*, he was seen to be decorated as a dancer. Then he showed everyone how to do Gisaro.

A quite different version comes across rather like a myth:

A man went hunting and was going through the forest when he heard Gisaro singing. "What's this?" he said. He searched and searched the ground, the trees. "What is this?" Then lo! by a waterfall there was a man: a beautiful headdress, *mise æsu*, bird of paradise plumes, woven black and yellow armbands, a beautiful *olɔ sæsælɔ* (striped cane), a beautiful shell rattle! The man was dancing by the waterfall. The man who had come to see him stayed hidden and watched and listened to the songs, learning them. When the Gisaro man was finished singing and started to leave the waterfall, the other man grabbed him and asked for the magic of this thing he was doing. The Gisaro man told him, whereupon the other man threw him into the river pool and shot him with his bow when he emerged to the surface. Then he grabbed the *olɔ sæsælɔ* and the rattle, and took off the armbands and the bird of paradise feathers and the bark belt and the fiber streamers and the headdress, and took them back to his *aa*. (Field notes)

The story continues to the effect that the man returned to his *aa* and taught other people to do Gisaro. They first sang and wept among themselves (as today with practice singing); then they decided to perform it at another *aa* when they brought a bride to be married. To their astonishment and gratification, a woman was so moved that she followed a dancer home; ever since, people have performed Gisaro at other *aas*.

There are various differences of opinion about the first part of the story. Some people say the man at the waterfall was not killed but merely passed on his knowledge and costume. Some say he was a *kalu hungɔ* or an *ane* person; others insist he was an ordinary man who lived alone. His appearance in full regalia singing alone by a waterfall (often the home of *ane* or *hungɔ* people) has a definitely preternatural quality.

It was from this man by the waterfall that the hunter obtained the first *olɔ sæsælɔ*—the key contribution of the *ane mama* to the Gisaro ceremony. The *olɔ sæsælɔ* is a piece of arrow-making cane about one-quarter inch in diameter and about three inches long, carefully decorated with incised lines (one of the few decorated objects I saw in Bosavi) and containing a piece of rock crystal (*Gisaro i*, "Gisaro wood"). This object can come only as a gift from a soul of the dead to one of his relatives who is living. It is presented to a chosen person from the chest of a medium. The *olɔ sæsælɔ* is the magical object that rivets the attention of the *aa biŝɔ* and enables the dancers (who suck on their *olɔ sæsælɔ* when they are practicing) to be graceful and remember all their songs. In performance, dancers use it as the handle by which to hold the string to the mussel-shell rattle. Thus, it performs the mediating juncture between the dancing motion and the music. *Olɔ sæsælɔ* are carefully preserved and passed from father to son or brother to brother, and everyone who dances must obtain one somehow, or no one will weep for his singing.

The relation between Gisaro and the unseen is crucial. People of the unseen are responsible not only for the origin of Gisaro among men but also (through infrequent gifts of *olɔ sæsælɔ*) for its continued efficacy. What part, then, does Gisaro play in the unseen itself? Is there something important about the ceremony that has its manifestation in the visible world but whose true significance is invisible?

Descriptions of the invisible by knowledgeable men always characterize what are rivers in this world as broad roads leading to the west (downstream), which people pass up and down on their way to Gisaro ceremonies. My friends remarked that they themselves performed Gisaro infrequently and only on the celebration of big occasions, whereas *ane mama* went from house to house to Gisaro all the time, without need of special reason. This was a situation Kaluli clearly found enviable by comparison with their own. The full significance of these invisible Gisaro ceremonies, however, was known only to mediums and perhaps to a very few senior men.

Most people know that when a person dies his soul goes to the treetops in the form of a bird; they don't know the process by which this happens. According to a medium who has seen it:

> When a man dies, his soul doesn't go out the door of the *aa* and down the entrance ladder. Rather he finds himself suddenly under the house as if he had fallen there. As he picks himself up and takes his small bag of possessions, dogs of the house gather round him barking (because he didn't give them much food in life) and chase him off to the Isawa River. The Isawa appears not as a river but as a wide, white road. The dogs chase the soul far downstream. As he gets toward the end, they call out, "Blow on the fire!" and *ane mama* gathered there blow on the dormant embers of a huge fire called Imɔl, which is built in the water, and it bursts into enormous flame. The dogs chase the soul into the fire, where it is burned to a crisp.
>
> Meanwhile, among the *ane* people who have been watching is a young woman, who, seeing the man running, has taken a fancy to him and wants him for a husband. *Ane* people may enter the fire without harm, and so she takes the burnt remains of the soul, wraps them in soft yellow leaves, and puts them in a little net bag. Then she carries him back up the Isawa, stopping at each (spirit) *aa* on the way to attend a Gisaro. At each performance *ane* men dance while those *ane* women who have dead souls' ashes in their net bags sit among the chorus near the front of the house and chorus the dancer (something that is never done in a real

ceremony). These Gisaro ceremonies are intended to make the burnt remains of the souls grow up into a man again. Finally, after attending many Gisaros they reach the man's homeland and say: "Enough. This is your home. Be here." And the *aa biŝɔ* of the place say: "All right. Now go as a wild pig. Come back. Go as a cassowary. Come back. Go as a *kalo*," and so on. And so forth for all of the various manifestations a dead soul can assume. The soul is then washed with water drawn from the Sili, so that he cannot be seen by living men, and his tongue is cut so that he cannot speak with human voice but only as a *kalo*, *hi*, or some other bird. He is then married to the woman who brought him in the net bag and lives thereafter in the *ane* house. (Field notes)

In this account, Gisaro appears in a new light. It clearly plays an important part on a whole other (though hidden) level of Kaluli experience—in an invisible journey of the dead. There seems to be no clear counterpart to these events in the visible realm; thus, to understand what they mean, it seems reasonable to examine them in relation to other events that we know take place in the unseen. The most conspicuous of these are those involved in the curing process. (See Table 11.1.)

We recall that a medium cures illness by restoring the missing pieces of a man's invisible body, which have been dismembered by a *sei*. He does this by first locating the missing parts, cleansing them of decay in the invisible river Sili, and then warming them back to life in the Imɔl fire before sticking them back on the body. The journey of the dead involves the opposite transformation (to death, not health). A man is first chased from his home and destroyed by the Imɔl fire; then he is rescued by an *ane* woman who carries his remains in a net bag (like an infant) back to (near) his original home, where he is finally washed in water from the Sili to complete his transformation into an *ane mama* and is married to the woman who saved him.[2] The figure of the woman here appears to have the significance of both mother and bride. My informant (a medium), however, spoke of her entirely as "wife" or "woman" (*ga*), not as "mother" (*nɔ*), and seemed to see her recovery of the

---

[2] The description of what happens to the dead was given to me entirely in terms of what happens to men. When I asked about women, my informant said vaguely that "it was the same," but that it was a man who rescued the female soul from the fire, and so on.

soul from the fire as analogous to the recovery of invisible body parts in the cure. (Certainly, rescue of the soul from the fire is motivated by conjugal rather than maternal sentiments.) Such a curative rescue by a spirit sweetheart had its counterpart in my informant's own curing experience. Once when he was very ill, he heard a noise and, looking up expecting to see a *sei* approach, he found instead his *ane* wife beside him with a net bag full of his dismembered body parts, which she had brought back to put together. What mediums do for ordinary people—returning the invisible body parts of the sick—is sometimes done for the medium himself by his spirit wife.

If we examine these two sets of events closely, we see that the differences between them match the opposite significance of the events themselves: cure and return to life versus death and permanent removal from life. The major symbolic elements of water and fire are reversed: the fire that warms the body parts back to life in the last stages of the cure destroys the soul at the first stage of death. The water of the Sili that cleanses the body parts of death (decay) in the first part of the cure irrevocably separates the soul from life (confers final invisibility) in the final stages of death. Moreover, the treatments by fire and water no longer occur between the "recovery" of the damaged body and their "return," as they do in the cure, but precede and follow them, respectively. This, in turn, changes the significance of the mediating figure (the medium for the cure, the spirit fiancée for death). The medium restores a situation to what it was before (health to health); the spirit woman transforms it into something quite different (transition to permanent spirit condition).

The narrative "gap" left in the journey of the dead—where, in the curing scenario, fire and water are used to heal and revitalize— is filled by Gisaro ceremonies. The woman carrying her destroyed love from Gisaro to Gisaro to grow him back to manhood corresponds to both of the crucial transitional treatments performed by the medium in the cure: cleansing of decay and revitalization to life. This is consistent with the Kaluli feeling that Gisaro has a death-averting, healing power.

If we examine the Gisaro ceremony itself in relation to the curing sequence (see Table 11.1), we find the same symbolism present

TABLE 11.1 Comparison of Journey of the Dead, Curing Process, and Gisaro Within Framework of Opposition Scenario

Opposition Scenario	Formation of Opposition		
	Loss		Terms of Opposition Set Out
Journey of the dead	Death: soul chased from home by dogs	Soul consumed by fire	Burnt soul recovered by *ane* woman
Curing (1) For medium (occasionally)	*Sei* dismembers, scatters, and hides invisible body parts, causing illness	(Body parts begin to decompose)	*Body parts located by medium's *ane* wife
(2) For ordinary man	(As above)	(As above)	Medium locates body parts
Gisaro	Dancer brings pain, grief, consciousness of loss (doesn't cause real loss)		Hidden sorrows of the aa *bišɔ* located (in poetic allusion)

Course of Action		Resolution	(Further Events)	
Ane woman takes soul in net bag to Gisaro ceremonies and soul grows to manhood		Soul returns full grown with *ane* woman to home area	Soul washed in Sili by *ane mama* of home area to render it invisible to living	Soul marries *ane* woman, moves into *ane aa;* full status as dead
Ane wife washes body parts in Sili	*Ane* wife warms body parts in fire (Imɔl)	*Ane* wife returns renewed body parts to body; health returns		
Medium washes body parts in Sili	Medium warms body parts in fire (Imɔl)	Medium returns renewed body parts to body; health returns		
Aa biš ɔ weep	*Aa biš ɔ* burn dancer with torch	Dancer returns compensation		

NOTE: Rows: process of opposition formation and resolution; columns: analogous phases of process.

*The soul's marriage to an *ane* woman after death corresponds to the medium's marriage to an *ane* woman before death; both are linked by marriage to the spirit side.

in both. Fire and water in Gisaro are manifested not in the Sili and Imɔl but in the weeping and the torches. The *aa biʃɔ* plays the role analogous to the broken spirit body. A complicating difference between the ceremony and the cure is that there are two figures of mediation in the latter but only one in the former. In illness a *sei* opens the scenario by dismembering the invisible body. A medium then treats it with water and fire and returns it to wholeness. In Gisaro the mediating figure is the dancer, but he corresponds to neither the *sei* nor the medium alone but to both at once. He causes sorrow and distress, not by acting like a *sei*, but by acting rather like a medium, not by taking apart and hiding a person's invisible pieces, but by revealing and putting together scattered images of a person's past life. In Gisaro the *aa biʃɔ* understandably retaliate for the pain they suffer. But as the dancer acted like a medium in order to *cause* pain, so, in a matching reversal, the sufferers apply the fire and water to him in the passage toward catharsis. The dancer, like the medium, brings back wholeness to the proceedings but by paying compensation rather than by returning exactly what was lost. Here clearly Kaluli express their awareness of reciprocity as a healing, life-restoring process.

We have called the scheme in which reciprocity takes place an "opposition scenario" because the original gift (or loss, or whatever) sets up an opposition, a certain tension, between the two sides—defining them against each other. The "healing" aspect of reciprocity comes at the point where reciprocation of *su* or *wel* is completed and this opposition is resolved (just as the return of the rejuvenated body parts effects the cure). But what about the nature of the opposition itself before reciprocity is completed?

In real life the awareness of a live opposition provides an urgency, a kind of energizing tension to the activities of the participants that motivates their preparations for resolution. At the same time, resolution through reciprocation embodies a certain element of transformation. The object given or taken as *wel* must be *different from*, though equivalent to, the original one; otherwise resolution does not take place and there is no social movement. The meaning of *wel* here is revealed metaphorically in the scenario of the cure: the "same" body parts are returned, but they have been rejuvenated. Here rejuvenation is analogous to "differentness." The change takes place while the opposition is in force and is absolutely necessary for its resolution.

Gisaro clearly emphasizes this aspect of the opposition process. Between the time the first dancer starts to sing and the final compensation is paid, the opposition consists of continually aggravated pain, tension, and violence, with dancers and audience striving against each other to a tremendous pitch of intensity. But the tension of the opposition, though aggravating and painful, is like the stinging nettle applied to a sore arm: the vitalization and energization of living processes.

Looking at Gisaro from this perspective, we can see more clearly the meaning of the particular transformations its symbolism represents from that of the curing sequence. The dancer, like the medium, ultimately provides healing (through paying *su*); but, unlike the medium, he is an exasperating figure, evoking and intensifying the pain while being beautiful and desirable.

Correspondingly, the *aa biʃɔ* do not submit passively to the treatment, as the patient does to the medium, but are aggravated and aroused by it. The tears caused by the ceremony release sorrow, but painfully; the fire revivifies, but in retaliatory violence. Gisaro emphasizes the process of strengthening and vitalization that comes from the tension of oppositions.

We can now make sense of the presence of Gisaro in the journey of the dead. The most striking difference between the journey of the dead and the curing sequence is that the journey of the dead is *not* an opposition scenario (though it retains the ghost of its form). This is, first, because the dead is not really returned visibly from whence he came and, second, because the process of transformation to full social status (as *ane mama*) is not completed until *after* the "return" through the washing in the Sili water and the marriage to the spirit woman.

If the journey of the dead is not an opposition scenario, however, it cannot by itself transform or revitalize anything. In order for the dead to be transformed, there must be an opposition scenario. Hence the presence of Gisaro. The particular vitalizing emphasis of the ceremony is appropriate to the radical treatment required to transform the soul of the dead to full, adult *ane* status. While the transformation is analogous to a cure, the "body" requires more than cleansing and reanimating; it must be entirely regrown. Here Gisaro's vitalizing value reveals its final symbolic analog. While the spirit fiancée plays a mother role to her future husband in her net bag, Gisaro plays the role analogous to homosexual intercourse, which stimulates a boy to attain full manhood. Here the notions of stimulative male energy and the opposition scenario finally come together, symbolically—matching their obvious association in reality. It may be the feeling for this connection, on some level (by people who cannot know it explicitly), that underlies the marked homosexual reference in the way *aa bišɔ* wags tease the dancers before the ceremony.

We are now in a position to sum up the significance of all this for Kaluli experience. From our look at the invisible side of Kaluli reality, it is not surprising that the Kaluli should feel that Gisaro has a death-averting power for the community and perform it or similar ceremonies when they are threatened with epidemic or disaster. In performing Gisaro, people are participating in the same process that reinvigorates their dead, not to mention their social relationships. Few Kaluli actually *know* how Gisaro is related to this rejuvenation process. Indeed, hardly anyone knows the significance of Gisaro in the journey of the dead. Yet, on some level, everyone is aware of it and feels that those who participate in the ceremony become stronger: "You have spirit; you won't be dying quickly!" The medium's description of the invisible Gisaro articulates not what ordinary people know but what is common in feeling to their experience of the ceremony. The curative value of Gisaro that Kaluli feel is not connected with invisible events; rather, the curative value is fundamentally implicit in the symbolic way that they organize and understand their experience. It is a fundamental, though implicit, aspect of the opposition scenario on whatever level of awareness it appears. The Kaluli belief that the key to understanding their own experience lies basically in the invisible side of reality is in this regard quite correct.

Gisaro provides the Kaluli with a continuing tangible link with the invisible, as they remember their dead in the ceremony and sing with them in seance. The invisible dead themselves provide their visible sons with the means (in the *olɔ sæsælɔ*) of continuing the performance.

The ceremony reveals the symbolic, metaphysical significance for Kaluli experience of the fundamental processes of opposition and reciprocity that animate the life of their society. Within its confines, during performance, Kaluli generate and mobilize their strongest qualities and values and intensify their own awareness of themselves as people who think and feel in their particular ways. It is a process of energizing and coming to understand themselves and the world through the very processes that make them both work.

Viewed from a social perspective, the ceremony expresses, not the structural aspects of Kaluli society, but its forms of social process, through which Kaluli social relationships and experience are continually reworked in the course of events. The focus on social process is of a piece with those individualistic values of personal initiative, equality, and vitality that give the Kaluli their particular character and style. It represents an acute and relevant perspective on their own society.

In a society where it is not groups that produce oppositions so much as oppositions that crystallize groups, it is not surprising that social life should be perceived more in terms of the processes that give it shape than in terms of structures that may emerge when those processes take place. It is this perception that is revealed in the Kaluli feeling that the forces of growth and life are generated in oppositions, and it is with this, as a life condition, with all its beauty, exuberance, tragedy, and violence, that they try to come to terms in Gisaro.

Dances and Ceremonies Performed by Bosavi People

Aside from Gisaro, the people of Bosavi perform five other types of dances and ceremonies: Ilib Kuwɔ, Sæbio, Kɔluba, Heyalo, and Iwɔ.

Ilib Kuwɔ

Ilib Kuwɔ is not a full-scale ceremony but a kind of celebratory dance performed in the longhouse during the day by one to four men to project an exciting atmosphere for some significant event. The dancers are costumed as in Heyalo and Kɔluba with characteristic arched-frame headdresses of white cockatoo feathers with palm-leaf streamers (*fasela*), and they wear springing rattles of crayfish claws in their waistbands at the back.

Dancers usually position themselves two at each end of the longhouse facing the interior and bounce back and forth in short hops across the hall from side to side beating hand drums (*ilib*). There is no singing, and the dancers make no effort to coordinate their motion or drumming. As in all Bosavi ceremonies, each performer is withdrawn and does not address or relate to his audience. When a dancer tires, he turns around to face the end of the hall and rests for a while.

Members of a longhouse community may perform Ilib Kuwɔ among themselves to mark a noteworthy occasion such as a successful raid or the preparations to receive a ceremonial party of guests. In the latter case, the dancers customarily move into the houseyard to greet the arrival procession, and the arrivals in turn lead out of the forest with their own Ilib Kuwɔ dancers. The newly arrived dancers then replace those of the hosts in the longhouse to provide the Ilib Kuwɔ entertainment until evening, when a major ceremony may be performed.

Kaluli say that Ilib Kuwɔ originally came up from the southeast side of the mountain at the same time that drums were introduced. Ilib Kuwɔ is now familiar to every longhouse north of the mountain.

Sæbio

Sæbio is also a minor dance, though it occasionally may be performed for a whole night in the absence of another ceremony. It is usually performed from about dusk to ten o'clock at night by the youths and young men of a group visiting another longhouse (for example, as carriers for a government patrol) and seems aimed at catching the attention of the local girls. Alternately, if the occasion for the visit is an important one at which an all-night ceremony is to be performed, people may perform Sæbio in the late afternoon amid the Ilib Kuwɔ dancing until shortly before the other major ceremony is to begin.

In performing Sæbio, the youths stand in two lines facing each other across the head of the hall, wearing no special costume beyond the usual finery of visitors. The singing is led by those at the ends of the lines, who tap the rhythm with ax handles or sticks on the floor, while the others jiggle rapidly up and down in place. The song, which is usually no more than two lines, is passed from one youth to another up and down the two lines in a call-response manner. After about three songs, the youths trot to the center of the hall, where they sing for a while in the same manner. From there they move to the women's end of the hall to sing, then back to the center, and finally return to the head where they may take a short break before forming up again and continuing the performance.

Sæbio songs consist of conventional two-line formulae into

which new words (food names, wealth objects) may be inserted. Place names do not usually appear in Sæbio songs, but without them the performance is not moving.

Kaluli say that Sæbio originated in the area southeast of Bosavi and that only those with connections to clans Wasu and Swabesi know how to do it. It appears, however, that the knowledge of the dance is more widespread among Bosavi people than this.

Kɔluba

Kɔluba is a major all-night ceremony performed at the usual occasions for such things. The performers do not arrive with the rest of the visitors but remain in the forest to prepare for the ceremony. At dark, eighteen to twenty-four young men (costumed as in Ilib Kuwɔ and Heyalo) emerge from the forest in procession three abreast and enter the longhouse. They move with little bouncing steps once up and down the hall singing a procession song. Then all but two dancers sit down in a semicircle along the edges of the sleeping platforms at the head of the hall. The two remaining dancers face each other at the head of the hall and, hopping up and down, tap time with sticks on the floor and sing. At the end of the song, they move with little hopping steps to the middle of the hall, where they sing the song again. Then they proceed in the same way to the women's end, the middle, and back to the head, where they finally sit down and another pair of dancers stands up. After all have danced up and down the hall in this manner, they wind up with a procession around the hall. Then they sit down in the semicircle again and pairs of men dance as before with a new set of songs. Songs are made up for each occasion; they concern place names and evoke sorrow and burning of the dancers.

Kɔluba is said to have originated with clans Wasu and Swabesi to the southeast of the mountain and was still moving westward into the Kaluli area in 1967.

Heyalo

Heyalo (or Feyalo) is a major all-night ceremony. As with Kɔluba, the male performers do not appear until dark, when they emerge in procession from the forest and enter the longhouse. The eighteen to twenty dancers (costumed as in Ilib Kuwɔ or Kɔluba) are joined by five or six women in *sosomaya* regalia. With their backs to the audience, the male dancers sidle up one side of the hall and down the other with a hopping step while singing and beating drums. The women precede and follow the line as it moves around the hall and shout "Aeo! Aeo!" in high-pitched voices. After singing one song several times, which takes about twenty minutes, the dancers all sit down for a five minute break before starting up again with a new song. The songs, which are made up anew for each occasion, mention places in the local territory and evoke weeping in the audience and burning of the dancers.

Heyalo is said to have originated among the westward Bosavi neighbors of the Kaluli, and the origin myth of the ceremony associates it with Lake Campbell. Heyalo is as familiar and widely practiced north of the mountain as Gisaro. It evidently has changed in form since the 1930s, when it was danced without drums, with a different song style, and with male and female dancers alternating in the line around the hall.

Iwɔ

Iwɔ is danced only on the night before pigs are killed, making it the one ceremony in Bosavi that relates to a specific type of event. The performers (both hosts and guests) decorate themselves openly amid the afternoon gathering of people in front of the pigs "so that the pigs will see them and turn out fat." The performance begins after dark when two men burst through the door of the longhouse, shouting and banging axes on the floor in the middle of the hall. They are immediately followed by the dancers, who are arranged in order of height, the tallest first and the shortest last. In Iwɔ, boys from the age of about five to men well into their fifties may dance.

Singing is led by a man (host or guest) who knows the traditional one- or two-line songs. The songs are picked up and repeated by the dancers for about fifteen minutes as they shuffle around the hall in single file. After each song, the dancers rest for a minute until two men burst through the door as before and bang axes on the floor, following which a new song is introduced.

The songs are supposed to be traditional and known only to men who have connections to the southwest of the mountain among the "Aibalisɔ" people (Kokonesi longhouse), who are said to be the originators of the songs. Unless there are a few men present who know the songs, the ceremony cannot be performed. Song lines mention rivers and place names framed in references to pigs. However, the places mentioned are all on "Aibalisɔ" ground unfamiliar to Kaluli and hence are not moving. Iwɔ seems to have been performed among the Bosavi people for at least thirty years.

References

BATESON, GREGORY
1958 *Naven*, 2nd ed. Stanford, Calif.: Stanford University Press.

CHAMPION, IVAN
1938 "The Bamu-Purari Patrol." *Geographical Journal*, 96, no. 4, 243.

ERNST, THOMAS
1970 Personal communication.
1972 "Onabasulu Social Organization." Mimeographed. University of Papua New Guinea.

FRANKLIN, KARL J.
1968 "Languages of the Gulf District: A Preview." In *Pacific Linguistics*. S. H. Wurm, ed. *Papers in New Guinea Linguistics*, no. 8, Series A, Occasional Paper no. 16. Canberra: Australian National University Press.

GLASSE, ROBERT
1968 "The Huli of Papua: A Cognitive Descent System." *Cahiers de l'homme*, Nouvelle Série VIII. The Hague: Mouton Publishers.

HIDES, JACK
1936 *Papuan Wonderland*. London: Blackie & Son Ltd.

KELLY, RAYMOND
1970 Personal communication.

1973 "Etoro Social Structure: A Study in Structural Contradiction." Unpublished Ph.D. dissertation. Department of Anthropology, University of Michigan.

LÉVI-STRAUSS, C.
1966 *The Savage Mind*. Chicago: University of Chicago Press.
1967 "The Story of Asdiwal." In *Structural Study of Myth and Totemism*. Edmund Leach, ed. ASA vol. 5. London: Tavistock Press.
1969 *The Elementary Structures of Kinship*. Boston: Beacon Press.

MITCHELL, CLYDE J. (Ed.)
1969 *Social Networks in Urban Situations*. Manchester, Eng.: Manchester University Press.

RAPPAPORT, ROY
1967 *Pigs for the Ancestors*. New Haven: Yale University Press.

RULE, MURRAY
1964 "Customs, Alphabet and Grammar of the Kaluli People of Bosavi, Papua." Unpublished Manuscript. Lake Kutuba, Papua, New Guinea.

SAHLINS, F. MARSHALL
1966 "On the Sociology of Primitive Exchange." In *The Relevance of Models in Social Anthropology*. Michael Banton, series ed. ASA vol. 1. London: Tavistock Press.

SCHIEFFELIN, EDWARD L.
1975 "Felling the Trees on Top of the Crop." *Oceania*, 46, no. 1 (June).

TURNER, VICTOR
1964 *Schism and Continuity in an African Society*. Manchester, Eng.: Manchester University Press.

WAGNER, ROY
1967 *The Curse of Souw*. Chicago: University of Chicago Press.
1972 *Habu: The Innovation of Meaning in Daribi Religion*. Chicago: University of Chicago Press.

WILLIAMS, F. E.
1940 *Native of Lake Kutuba*. Oceania Monograph no. 6. Sydney: Australian National Research Council.

WURM, S. H.
1971 "The Papuan Linguistic Situation." In *Linguistics in Oceania*. J. D. Bowen et al., eds. *Current Trends in Linguistics*, vol. 8. The Hague: Mouton Publishers.

Index

Page numbers in italic refer to illustrations.

About the Author

Edward Schieffelin received his B.A. in physics and philosophy from Yale University in 1960 and then went to the West Coast to become a carpenter. After two years he entered the University of Chicago, where he received a Ph.D. in anthropology in 1972. Dr. Schieffelin was assistant professor of anthropology at Fordham University from 1970 to 1974 and in 1975 returned to Papua New Guinea under the auspices of the Research Institute for the Study of Man and the Institute for the Study of Human Issues to undertake further research among the Bosavi people.